THE
TWO PERCENT
SOLUTION

THE
TWO PERCENT
SOLUTION

Fixing America's Problems in Ways
Liberals and Conservatives Can Love

MATTHEW MILLER

PUBLICAFFAIRS
New York

Published in the United States by PublicAffairs™,
a member of the Perseus Books Group.

Book design by Jane Raese
Text set in 11-point Hoefler

Library of Congress Cataloging-in-Publication Data
Miller, Matthew, 1961–
The two percent solution : fixing America's problems in ways liberals and
conservatives can love / Matthew Miller.
p. cm.
Includes index.
ISBN 1-58648-158-4
1. United States—Social policy—1993– 2. Health care reform—United States.
3. Living wage movement—United States. 4. Campaign funds—United States.
5. Fiscal policy—United States. I. Title.
HN63.M496 2003
361.1'0973—dc21
2003046867

FIRST EDITION
10 9 8 7 6 5 4 3 2 1

For Jody and Amelia

CONTENTS

PROLOGUE
Here's the Deal

Suppose I told you that for just two cents on the national dollar we could have a country where everyone had health insurance, every full-time worker earned a living wage, every poor child had a great teacher in a fixed-up school, and politicians spent their time with average Americans because they no longer had to grovel to wealthy donors? Suppose I also said we'd largely be using "conservative" means (like tax subsidies and vouchers) to reach these seemingly "liberal" goals—and that when we were done, government would be smaller than it was when Ronald Reagan was president?

If you're like most people, I'd wager that for two cents on the dollar you'd say this sounds like an intriguing deal. But then suppose I explained that "two cents on the dollar" means two percent of our $11 trillion national income (gross domestic product, or GDP), which is $220 billion a year—orders of magnitude beyond the boundaries of Washington debate? If you listen to the "experts" who set the terms of that debate—the politicians, the mainstream press, and the vast associated network of analysts, advocates, and other talking heads—you'd conclude such a plan was impossible. If you listen to common sense, however, finding two cents on the dollar to reach the goals I've mentioned seems almost a snap.

Between our proper intuition that two percent is a small number and the Washington consensus that a $220 billion shift in national priorities and resources is beyond imagining lies a chasm in which nearly every claimed "solution" from our political leaders—indeed much of public debate itself—turns out to be a hoax. Things don't have to be this way.

The Two Percent Solution will do more than simply reframe the national debate about our collective possibilities; it will help us make dramatic inroads on some of the nation's biggest domestic problems in ways that are broadly acceptable, pragmatic, and just. If this sounds audacious, it has to be, because the price of persisting with today's false fixes will soon be too high. Fewer than ten years remain before the baby boomers' retirement will drain away all the cash and political energy to do anything but cope with their colossal health and pension costs. If you think it's hard now to get a serious discussion going about the 42 million Americans who lack health insurance, the 15 million who dwell in poverty despite living in families headed by full-time workers, or the 10 million poor children whose lives are blighted by dysfunctional schools, then starting in 2010 it will be next to impossible. These problems will take federal cash to help fix—cash that is mistakenly viewed as "unaffordably liberal" under existing terms of debate, but that as a practical matter will be hard to direct to these priorities if we haven't gotten serious before 76 million boomers start hitting their rocking chairs.

How unserious are we today? Here's all you need to know: In the last decade our economy has grown by 40 percent, but the problems we're talking about have gotten worse, and serious talk of addressing them has all but vanished. Our shrinking ambition is depressingly measurable. In 1992, for example, the first President George Bush proposed a plan to insure 30 million of the then 35 million uninsured, and Democrats slammed it as "too little, too late." Today the outer limit of the current President Bush's "compassion" is a plan that would insure 6 million of the now 42 million uninsured. Meanwhile, no Democrat who wants to be president today would endorse Richard Nixon's plans from the early 1970s for universal health coverage and a minimum family income: Nixon's package is far too "liberal"! Instead, the two parties debate when and how to eliminate the estate tax, the bulk of whose burden falls on the heirs of only three thousand of the nation's wealthiest families.

What happened to America's political will to solve the problems facing ordinary people? The short answer is simple. Since 1994, when the Clinton health care plan imploded in a fiasco that cost Democrats control of the Congress, Democrats have been too scared to think big again. Republicans, emboldened by this Democratic timidity, have chosen to push harder for their traditional priorities of cutting taxes and regulations. What's been lost in the dysfunctional debate of the last decade is a commitment to two long-standing American ideals: equal opportunity and a minimally decent life for citizens of a wealthy nation.

What American politics urgently needs, therefore, is not a new left, but a new center. Domestic debate needs to be re-centered around a handful of fundamental goals on which all of us can agree, whether we call ourselves Republicans, Democrats, or Independents. Yes, there will always be fights over details. But if we first ask, "What does equal opportunity and a decent life in America mean?" can't we agree that anyone who works full-time should be able to provide for his or her family? That every citizen should have basic health coverage? That special efforts should be made to make sure that poor children have good schools? And that average citizens should have some way to have their voices heard amid the din of big political money?

My aim in this book is to show that these problems have solutions that are affordable, practical, and within reach—solutions that both liberals and conservatives can embrace. Indeed, both sides will have to join hands to solve them because political power is going to remain closely divided for the foreseeable future. It has been nearly a decade since either party has had a sizable majority in either house of Congress, and no presidential candidate since 1988 has been able to win a majority of the popular vote. That leaves only two options: Either we tackle these challenges together, or we go on pretending to solve them while letting them fester until they explode down the road.

The case I'll make on how we can get serious is simple:

We can't solve our biggest problems without money. It's true that money isn't everything. But for the problems we're talking about it's a lot. We can't buy health insurance without money. We can't lure better college graduates to teach in our toughest schools without money. We can't lift workers out of poverty without money. We can't offset the corrosive influence of big political donors without money.

We have the money.   Consider two numbers (22 and 20) and one mystery. Federal spending compared to the overall size of the economy is the best measure of the "size" of government. Under Ronald Reagan and the first George Bush, federal spending averaged 22 percent of GDP. Under Bill Clinton, faster growth combined with spending restraint pulled this figure down to 20 percent of GDP. In ways the press and public still haven't appreciated, the budget was balanced (and then unbalanced again) "downward." Yet today, even after historic spending increases for defense and homeland security, and after making provision for a costly new prescription drug benefit under Medicare, George W. Bush wants to hold federal spending at 20 percent of GDP or less in the coming year because, as he puts it, we've "met our needs." If Bush were to run the government at the size his father's and Ronald Reagan's budgets routinely proposed, the feds would soon have more than $200 billion more to spend each year. The mystery, of course, is why we never hear about the fact that, in overall terms, the rest of government is being downsized this dramatically. The upshot: Two cents on the national dollar can get us a long way toward real answers, and can do so through a government as small as the one we were accustomed to under a conservative Republican icon.

There's a deal to be made.   On health, schools, wages, and more, a series of problem-solving "grand bargains" can be reached that involve the same basic approach. Liberals have to be open to market-friendly approaches to these problems, as opposed to simply expanding traditional government programs. In exchange, conservatives have to be willing to pony up money equal to the size of these problems, rather than offering token sums that let them cynically pretend to have a "plan."

The good news is that such "grand bargains" are entirely possible and make for the kind of innovative solutions that we need. The bad news is that our two major political parties are organized around ideologies and interest groups that systematically ban the expression of commonsense ideas that blend the best of liberal and conservative thinking. The result is a "solutions gap" in public life, which leaves Americans discouraged, cynical, and tuned out. And why shouldn't we be? How else should we respond when it's clear that *neither party has a political strategy that includes solving our biggest domestic problems? And when it's equally clear that both parties are lying to us about the answers that are possible!*

The way to get past the bipartisan make-believe is to look at our problems in a different way. Our leaders usually ask, "How can I address this, or at least seem to address it, in a way that keeps my interest groups and political donors and ideological allies with me?" This is very different from asking, "What's the best way to make serious progress on this problem?"—and then figuring out how to get a majority of people to follow you. The policies you pursue after the first question are pre-sold, because a constituency for the pseudo-answer already exists. The downside, of course, is that you don't solve the problem. Needless to say, we've been trying it this way for years.

If you look at the problem head-on, however, and ask, "What's the best way to really solve this?" the solutions tend to be pragmatic blends of ideas from different camps. Some aspects of these fixes will be favored by liberals; others will be favored by conservatives. If we're serious about results, we have to draw on both. If you don't like the idea of acknowledging what's right in the other side's worldview, I have three words for you: *Get over it.* With the boomers' retirement closing in, we no longer have the luxury of pretending to be serious about these problems. We actually have to *be* serious.

The boomers' retirement will bring an unprecedented fiscal collision that forces us to rethink much of what we ask from government and how we pay for it. The sheer size of this challenge will make it hard to take up new causes unless we've built them into our vision of American society in advance. In this context, getting serious about the uninsured, the working poor, inner-city schools, and rigged elections isn't a job for altruists and do-gooders; it's about self-interest. To get the economic growth we'll need to pay for all those gray boomers, we can't afford to leave a huge swath of the country ill-schooled, ill-paid, or just ill—not to mention closed out of the democratic process altogether. Instead, if we're to sustain America's greatness, this next decade will have to be one of those rare moments in which real answers trump ideology and political jockeying.

Who am I to make this case? Here's the two cents so you'll know the biases I bring. I'm a Democrat who spent several years as a business executive and management consultant before going to Washington on a nonpartisan fellowship in 1991. For a year I worked for the Republican chairman of the Federal Communications Commission, helping modernize old regulations that made no sense. From 1993 to 1995 I served in the White House as a top aide in President Clinton's budget office, working to slay the big deficits Clinton inherited. After leaving government I worked as a journalist for *The New Republic, Time,* and *U.S. News and World Report,* where I spent a great deal of time digging for the facts obscured by political rhetoric. And as a syndicated columnist, radio host, and consultant for the past five years, I've tried to develop and promote this "ideologically androgynous" agenda. I've written this book out of deep frustration with today's politics in the hope that it might give voice to others who feel the same way, and offer both an angle of a vision and a concrete agenda that can change the terms of national debate.

I've explored these ideas in conversations over the last few years with top officials in both parties; with business, labor, and media leaders; with university and foundation presidents; and with policy experts of all stripes. You'll hear many of their voices in the pages ahead—from Bush cabinet members to top Democrats, from the superintendents who run our biggest school districts to the editors who run *The Washington Post* and *The New York Times.* You'll also hear from less well known thinkers whose ideas can point us toward progress. In addition, I'll share the views of average citizens from two focus groups and a national poll I commissioned specifically for this book. From these hundreds of conversations, I'm convinced that a new agenda is possible that blends the best of liberal and conservative approaches in ways that can command broad support. All it will take— that is, apart from the usual impossible hurdles confronting any scheme to move national politics—is a little imagination and an open mind.

Here's how we'll proceed. In Part One of the book we'll get clear on the problem: namely, that we're not serious when it comes to addressing our biggest domestic challenges. We'll tease out how and why we've ended up with today's "tyranny of charades," and why time is running out to change course because of the collision ahead when the boomers retire. Part Two then focuses on the Two Percent Solution itself. We'll first step back and lay a little philosophical groundwork by examining the pervasive role of luck in life, and how taking life's "pre-birth lottery" seriously can bring the consensus we need to make progress. We'll then examine the "grand bargains" we need on health care, poor schools, wages, and campaign finance—with the help of many of the officials who'd have to implement them. We'll explore how to sensibly pay for it all and make sure we can still fix everything else (like Social Security and Medicare) the nation needs to address as well. In the book's final section, we'll look toward a Two Percent Society, examining public opinion, the role of the press, and the ways that the Two Percent mind set can help foster the leadership and the followership we need to turn these ideas into reality.

As I've made the rounds refining these ideas, I've heard a thousand variants of "sounds great, but it'll never happen." The unions will kill it; the politicians won't risk it; business won't buy it; you can't reallocate the money. Given the poverty of today's debate, this skepticism makes perfect sense. But in the broader scheme of things, it's nonsense. Of course getting from here to Two will take work. Compared to what Americans have achieved together before, however, the package this book lays out is literally small change. When a country is just two cents on the dollar away from social justice, there's plenty of grounds for hope.

THE
TWO PERCENT
SOLUTION

PART ONE

The Problem

I

WE'RE NOT SERIOUS

What do we do when neither major party has a political strategy—that is, a strategy for winning power—that involves solving our biggest domestic problems? And when a looming demographic and fiscal collision means the time left to get serious is running out? That's the predicament we face today, and if you haven't been encouraged to think of it in those terms, there's a reason. The illusion of action is Washington's oldest con. Barely a day goes by without a dozen new "plans" being unveiled to Save Something Good (the schools, the Everglades, Social Security) or Stop Something Evil (HMOs, trial lawyers, tobacco makers).

The reality, of course, is different. While the brands of deception vary, and intentions run the gamut from good to malign, the result of these bipartisan shenanigans is the same. Make-believe responses to national problems vie in a competition for votes that has almost nothing to do with solving the problem in question. The media ends up in cahoots with politicians in creating this illusion of meaningful action, both because (1) media norms don't allow reporters to say "this is a charade" even when they know it is (reporters are supposed to be "objective"), and because (2) for reporters to admit they are often tacit conspirators in such hoaxes cuts too close to the bone.

Look around: On the questions we'll be examining—health care, schools, wages, and campaign finance—there are few honest debates to be found. We'll get to how decent, intelligent people end up offering this disappointing gruel, but first it's important to establish that we are fundamentally not serious.

The Great Shrinking Health Care Debate

The most vivid illustration of today's lack of seriousness concerns health coverage, where our ambitions regarding the uninsured have shrunk dramatically in the last decade, even as the country grew wealthier and the problem got worse. To see what I mean, go back for a moment to the 2000 Democratic primary campaign, when Al Gore faced a challenge from Bill Bradley. Bradley, to his credit, offered a serious $50-billion-a-year plan to expand health coverage to just about all of the 40 million uninsured Americans. Gore's plan was to insure only the 10 million or so uninsured children (a cheaper proposition since kids almost never get expensively sick the way older folks do). Gore blasted Bradley's plan as fiscally irresponsible, and the press dutifully cast the debate as a showdown between Bradley's pricey liberal dream and Gore's more modest, centrist approach. But here's what the press never figured out (and what the rest of us therefore didn't get to hear): Bradley's "liberal" plan to cover uninsured Americans was a slightly *cheaper* version of the proposal offered by President George Bush in 1992.

Every so often a fact emerges in politics that, in Copernican fashion, renders the settled view of the cosmos obsolete. So let's mull this for a minute. Both Bradley's plan and the 1992 Bush plan would have made it possible for families to buy private insurance via tax credits and deductions that tapered off as income rises. Both called for insurance market reforms to let folks participate in the larger risk pools that assure reasonable premiums. Bush's plan, adjusted for inflation, offered up to $5100 per year per family, slightly more generous than Bradley's scheme, which offered up to $5000.

Bush Sr. offered his plan after Harris Wofford's surprise health-care-inspired win over Richard Thornburgh in Pennsylvania's special Senate race in 1991. With health care suddenly politically "hot," the White House needed a plan that addressed the problem on more market-friendly terms than Democrats were offering. Yet here's what is so stunning: At a time of $250 billion deficits, Bush put out a $50-billion-a-year plan (three times bigger than what Gore would offer in 2000) only to have Democrats bash it as "too little, too late." Fast forward eight years, and Bradley's plan, offered at a time of equally outsized surpluses, was damned as a liberal fantasy and trashed by Gore's team as evidence of a "reckless spending mentality."

But the ironies deepen. The current President George Bush, who campaigned as a "compassionate conservative," has offered the same kind of tax subsidy plan as his father but in embarrassing miniature—about $9 billion a year over the next ten years, which the White House figures will cover 6 million of the now 42 million uninsured (Bush Sr.'s plan covered 30 million out of 35 million uninsured).

Why have our leaders been content to let the problem worsen as our ability to address it has grown? The unflattering answer is because doing so is both safe and cheap. The rising roll call of today's uninsured is made up of low-income workers with little political voice; in the broad-based recession of the early 1990s, it was middle-class anxieties that got politicians scurrying to respond. Today's policy of rationing health coverage by income also saves money; while the uninsured do get taken care of in emergency rooms, county hospitals, and other sites of last resort, the absence of preventive care, regular checkups, and other services most people take for granted means these citizens consume just half as many health resources as their insured neighbors. We can only fix the problem of the uninsured by spending fresh money on people with little political clout, or by somehow disguising that this is what we're up to.

Any such attempt takes place in the shadow of the Clinton health care fiasco of 1993–1994. The political lesson both parties drew from that meltdown was that efforts to expand coverage must be "incremental." "Step by step" is the approved mantra.

Yet incremental "achievements" since 1994 have been a bust. Senators Edward Kennedy and Nancy Kassebaum passed a bill in 1996 hailed by both parties as a model for future health reform. The measure was supposed to assure continued access to insurance for those who changed or lost their jobs. But since insurers remained free to charge whatever they like in these situations, people quickly found that "access" meant nothing when policies might cost $15,000 a year. Similarly, a $5-billion-a-year plan for the nation's 10 million uninsured kids passed to great fanfare in 1997; aid was targeted with such narrow complexity, however, that even proponents say its impact has been to lower the percentage of poor children who lack coverage only modestly.

Meanwhile, as this trot through recent history suggests, the terms of reference in America's health care debate remain bizarre. Consider: In Great Britain, Margaret Thatcher would have been tossed from office if she'd proposed anything as radically *conservative* as Bill Clinton's health plan—which still would have left several million people uncovered and had the private sector deliver the medicine. This comparison proves the bankruptcy of most ideological labeling in the health care debate, which is used by foes of expanded coverage to divert the media and sink serious attempts to remedy the problem.

The Institute of Medicine estimates that 18,000 people die prematurely each year owing to lack of health coverage, the equivalent of the Vietnam War's death toll every three years. The uninsured get preventable diseases and are avoidably hospitalized more often than the insured, and are vulnerable to devastating financial loss from illness in ways unthinkable in other advanced nations. All this is widely known. While it is encouraging that several Democratic presidential contenders are at last beginning to talk more ambitiously, how can it be that America will enter the 2004 election season having gone a full decade without any serious attempt to address the plight of more than 40 million uninsured citizens?

If we were starting from scratch, after all, no one would urge us to ration vaccinations and checkups for children based on their parents' ability to pay—yet that's been national policy for decades. No villainous HMO would ever deny timely preventive care to its members the way our nation does to millions of its uninsured—yet that is America's officially sanctioned method of cost control. "The politically dominant thought in this country," said Uwe Reinhardt, a health economist at Princeton University, "appears to have been that the deprivation and suffering of several million Americans, albeit regrettable, nevertheless is a price well worth paying for the good economic fortune that our health system bestows on so many, and for the rapid technical progress that a less fettered system can sustain."

Leave No Teacher Crisis Honestly Addressed!

Washington politicians in both parties love to say they're for educational "testing" and "standards" and "accountability," but nearly every state had already adopted such systems before the feds congratulated themselves for adding another bureaucratic layer in the much-touted No Child Left Behind Act of 2001. But the new law largely punted on the teacher crisis in our poorest neighborhoods, which any serious attempt to leave no child behind would make its first priority. Indeed, this is one of the few things on which researchers across the political spectrum agree: Half of the achievement gap facing poor and minority students is due not to poverty or family conditions but to systematic differences in teacher quality. "Fifty years after *Brown v. Board of Education*," Alan Bersin, the superintendent of schools in San Diego, told me, "the maldistribution of quality instruction is the key determinant of underachievement in large urban school systems." Despite lofty pledges, our latest "education president," and the Democrats assailing him, are shooting blanks.

Start with President Bush. His No Child Left Behind Act tells states "thou shalt have a quality teacher in every classroom" by the end of the 2005–2006 school year. But this command can't change the facts of life in poor urban and rural districts. Republicans would ordinarily recognize this as a question of market economics—the supply of good teachers who will work in difficult conditions with challenging children isn't adequate at prevailing salaries. "They may as well have decreed that pigs can fly," Wayne Johnson, who runs California's teachers union, has said. California and other states have tried to wiggle out of this unfunded mandate. Not that they're proud of this, for who wants to admit that they can't scare up enough decent teachers for the kids who need them most? But if forced to comply, and stick only with teachers who pass muster under normal definitions of "qualified," class sizes in the toughest districts could rise to 50 or 60. In the triage environment of urban schools, this route is almost certain to make matters worse.

It's hard to imagine a more demoralizing presidential dodge: Mandate the politically appealing result (and take credit for having addressed the problem) while offering no cash to poor districts to make it a reality. Then, to add insult to injury, make the penalty for noncompliance a cut in existing federal funding, putting the goal even more beyond reach than it is today!

But that spirit captures the symbolic nature of Bush's entire education agenda. Republicans love it because its pseudo seriousness and media appeal neutralizes the traditional advantage Democrats have enjoyed on the schools issue, while its no-cost emphasis on testing and accountability doesn't divert money from the tax cuts they want. The GOP knows that poor districts lack the tax base to do more on their own. Yet they hide behind lofty-sounding commitments to "federalism" and "local control" to justify denying poor schoolchildren federal cash that might make a difference.

Bush's other teacher quality "initiatives" similarly fail the seriousness test. Because of coming retirements and rising enrollments, 2 million teachers must be recruited over the next decade. It's either a crisis or opportunity, depending on how the nation handles it. Laura Bush, a former teacher herself, is a wonderful voice to lead this crusade. By all accounts she brings sincerity and passion to the cause. But the symbolic "agenda" the White House has cooked up for her is laughably unequal to the challenge.

Mrs. Bush first touts "Teach for America," which brings graduates from elite universities into inner-city classrooms for a few years, and turns them into lifelong advocates for schooling. It's a fabulous program. But its scale doesn't begin to deal with the magnitude of the teacher gap. In its first eleven years it recruited a total of 6000 teachers. But America now needs to recruit 6000 teachers every eleven *days*. Program founder Wendy Kopp, who is grateful for the White House's support, doesn't pretend otherwise. "We're not at all the answer to the broader problem," she told me.

Then there's Mrs. Bush's other pet program, "Troops to Teachers," which helps military personnel move to the classroom when they leave the service. Again, it's a great idea, but it delivers only about 650 teachers a year. We need 200,000 a year. Mrs. Bush's big push has been to raise funding for "Troops to Teachers" toward $30 million a year from $3 million. If you're the White House, you boast of the "tenfold increase." If you pull out a calculator, you'll figure out that at today's rate it would take 300 years for the Bush administration to recruit enough veterans to fill the teaching gap we face over the next decade.

The average teacher, despite low pay, spends about $500 a year out of his or her own pocket for classroom supplies. The president's response to this shameful burden: a tax deduction under which some teachers can deduct a portion of the money they've spent for these purposes. Sounds nice at first, but on reflection it's an absurd half-measure. Would Bush offer soldiers a tax deduction for ammunition they had to buy out of their own pockets—or would he insist that they have the equipment and resources to do their jobs right?

Bush might say that when it comes to schooling, money isn't everything, and he'd be right. But how about when it comes to creating incentives for young Americans to enter a teaching profession where the starting salary now averages $30,000 and rises to only $44,000?

Every free-market fan knows that you get what you pay for. When the affluent suburb of Scarsdale, New York, pays teachers with a masters degree and five years of teaching more than $60,000, and New York City pays her counterpart in the 40s, is there really a question about where most of the top talent goes? Given this context, it's hard to see Bush's deeds as being anything but a moral mockery of his words.

Democrats have predictably been willing to spend more money on the teacher challenge, but their "plans," too, have been more symbol than cure. In the last presidential race, for example, both Al Gore and Bill Bradley proposed a mix of college scholarships, loan forgiveness, and bonuses for some people who teach in high-need areas. Gore, to his credit, proposed that federal money be used (for the first time) to give a $5000 raise to many urban teachers. Other Democrats, doubtless inspired by the fact that teacher unions are among their top campaign donors, have weighed in as well. California governor Gray Davis made teaching a focus of his early agenda, offering some bonuses to teachers at high-achieving schools that later budget woes forced him to renege on; Senator Charles Schumer of New York once cobbled together the inevitable "Marshall Plan" (including mentors for new teachers, grants for training, and small federal bonuses for math and science teachers). As the 2004 presidential campaign unfolded, North Carolina senator John Edwards talked about paying college tuition for students who commit to teach in tough schools for five years; Representative Richard Gephardt packaged similar ideas into a call for a "Teacher Corps." Still, none of this has added up to anything that would make, say, a 22-year-old engineering grad swap the $60,000 salary she can earn in a technology firm for $30,000 at the local school. "I don't think $5000 across-the-board increases are going to accomplish much," said Michael Casserly, executive director of the Council of Great City Schools, which represents big urban districts.

Meanwhile, when Democrats attack President Bush for underfunding his plan to leave no child behind, they unintentionally mock their own seriousness. Democrats fault Bush for failing to provide the additional $6 billion for poor schools that he had pledged, as if this figure represented some meaningful assessment of what it would cost to address these schools' challenges. But national k–12 spending is roughly $420 billion; within that amount, teacher compensation comes to roughly $150 billion. Does anyone really think $6 billion, sprinkled (as it would be) among everything from salaries for teacher's aides to capital improvements to teacher training, amounts to a serious attempt to address these schools' problems? While the money would doubtless do some good, honest Democrats have to acknowledge that blasting Bush over this shortfall is more about political symbolism than serious problem-solving.

Just as important, Democrats have been unwilling to challenge union practices that would make spending on schools more effective. Teacher unions have resisted calls for "differential pay," for example, defending instead their traditional "lockstep" pay scale under which salary is determined entirely by the academic degree a teacher has earned and the number of years the teacher has been in the classroom. This compensation scheme ignores the obvious reality that certain teachers—such as science and mathematics graduates—have more lucrative options than those who studied, say, physical education. It also makes no room for rational attempts to link pay in some way to performance or student achievement. In addition, teacher unions make it notoriously difficult and costly to fire bad teachers. The Democrats' unwillingness to urge sensible reforms on one of the party's most powerful interest groups bolsters the conservative case that more money for schools would simply be wasted.

The depressing reality underscored by our teacher woes is that today's high-profile education wars are largely a sideshow. For a decade now, most of the oxygen in the schools debate has been consumed by the standards and accountability movement, and by structural innovations like charter schools and vouchers. These ideas all have merit, but they can't trump a larger truth: If we can't lure hundreds of thousands of talented teachers into the nation's toughest schools, all the "systemic" reforms in the world won't make much difference.

The Living Wage Cul de Sac

In the United States today, 15 million people live in or near poverty despite living in homes headed by full-time workers. Millions more live close to the edge, including countless former welfare recipients who have learned that having a job doesn't mean being able to pay your bills. In response, a growing movement has won the passage of "living wage" ordinances in about 80 communities over the last decade, including Baltimore, Los Angeles, Detroit, and Chicago. These laws typically require government contractors and some other employers to pay workers substantially more than the minimum wage, which is now $5.15 nationally, but higher in states such as California and Massachusetts ($6.75) or Rhode Island and Washington, D.C. ($6.15). Often the "living wage" is set at the level needed to lift a family of four at least to the federal poverty line, which requires about $18,000 a year, or more than $8 an hour. Some cities require health benefits (or a further stipend per hour) to be offered atop this wage.

To judge from the screams of the business lobbies and the breast-beating of living wage advocates, something sweeping is taking place. But here again, the battle is almost entirely symbolic, because none of the ordinances matches the scale of the problem.

At first glance, the "living wage" fight replays many of the *reductio ad absurdum* arguments made famous in the regular minimum wage wars. Bosses shout that if raising the minimum wage from $5.15 to $10.00 an hour plus $2 for health care is good, what is to stop legislators from making it $20, or $50? Labor answers that if a decent wage floor is so intolerable, what is to stop employers from calling for a return to child labor and sweatshops—or, for that matter, slavery?

The problem is that while liberals are right about the injustice facing unskilled workers, they're wrong about the economics of fixing it. As much as well-intended activists dislike hearing this, it is simply not possible to solve the problem on a sustainable basis by mandating that private firms pay wages as high as $10 or $12 an hour for employees who, in economic terms, are "worth" only $6. Imposing such a mandate produces all sorts of perverse consequences. To avoid a doubling of their payroll costs, for example, some restaurants may decide to stop serving lunch, thereby shrinking their business below the minimum sales volume at which many living wage laws apply. They'll make this choice because lunch is less profitable (since less liquor gets sold). As a result, a bunch of workers get fired so the firm stays viable. In addition, such laws naturally lead managers to upgrade their workforce, replacing $6-an-hour staff with $10-an-hour talent. If they have to pay up anyway, employers reason, they may as well hire workers with more skills. In this way a law meant to help the $6 worker ends up costing him his job. Of course, employers make sure local politicians understand these realities, which is why the scope of coverage of living wage laws is always tiny, affecting only a small fraction of an area's workforce. Typically they target those working for government contractors, so that the cost ends up being shifted largely to taxpayers.

The sad truth, then, is that advocates for living wage laws have gotten them on the books by arguing, in effect, that they really don't do much. That's a strange rallying cry for a movement, but proponents feel it's a start. "It puts the arguments and the message out there as a handle to move the debate forward," said Madeline Janis-Aparicio, who headed L.A.'s Living Wage Coalition.

The best estimate is that living wage ordinances cover perhaps 100,000 to 250,000 workers, out of the roughly 25 million full-time workers who are within striking distance of poverty-level wages today. After a decade of the living wage movement, in other words, we're operating entirely at the margins. Unions reply that the movement helps galvanize local organizing efforts, which they say is the real long-term answer; but there's nothing in recent history to suggest that labor is poised to make major inroads outside the public sector.

But at least the left is trying. While liberals settle for baby steps, the right merely sidesteps. Faced with millions of unfortunate people who hold low-wage jobs and can't provide their families with the basics, the conservative slogan (echoed by some on the left) is "training and education." But when asked what this will do in the here and now for the janitors, dishwashers, and home health aides not destined to be retooled into software whizzes, the education caucus falls silent. If we're honest, we have to admit that education and training, while important, could take years, even decades, to make much dent, and then mostly only for tomorrow's workers.

So there is our national "living wage" debate: a showdown between the inadequate and the ineffectual. Shouldn't there be a better way?

Campaign Finance Reform — Much Ado About Little

The McCain–Feingold bill, which ended large, unregulated "soft money" contributions to the national political parties, became a cause celebre in 2002, partly because of the stature of its cosponsor, Senator John McCain, and partly because *The New York Times* editorial page made the bill the centerpiece of a crusade. Like so many other make-believe fixes in Washington, however, the measure acquired such symbolic power as "reform" that it seems subversive merely to utter the fact that it won't do anything to get money out of politics.

Yet as even many McCain–Feingold champions told me, the influence of special interests in politics will never be offset without a major role for public financing of campaigns. Even before the new law passed, lobbyists and legislators breezily announced their strategies for evading its spirit. A ban on soft money for the national parties has not stemmed the flow of political cash, but merely diverted it into other modes of giving (to state parties and issue campaigns, for example) that pass legal muster. "Parties Create Ways To Avoid Soft Money Ban," shouted a *New York Times* headline in October 2002, as if this were a surprise. "I've said from the beginning that this was exactly what was going to happen," said then Republican Party chairman Marc Racicot, calling the idea that "this reform was going to change things" a "pipe dream." As the ongoing battle over the new law's constitutionality proves, it's become another festival for lawyers, as is invariably the case with byzantine rules that defy human nature.

Some proponents of McCain–Feingold insist that the new law is a step forward nonetheless, because it stops members of Congress from directly extorting vast gobs of soft money, a transaction felt to be particularly corrupting (though even this solicitation ban may be interpreted to mean pols can "suggest" a donation so long as they don't "solicit" it!). But for most reformers, the case that McCain–Feingold made any difference involves well-meaning rationalization. As their logic runs, we can't propose measures (like public financing of campaigns) that would solve the problem because they wouldn't pass, so let's propose something that is passable in hopes that it can create momentum for further changes down the line. Don't get me wrong: I'm usually in favor of taking half a loaf where necessary—but in this case it's not clear that we got anything more than crumbs out of this transaction. The trouble, meanwhile, is that enormous amounts of emotional and political energy were invested in passing McCain–Feingold, creating a national hoopla over its "importance." Although it can't begin to solve the problem, proponents feel forced in various ways to pretend that it does. Eventually the public will realize that little has changed, and cynicism about Washington's false claims will deepen.

Don't take my word for it. Take the word of Ellen Miller (no relation to me), who is one of the leading campaign reform activists of this generation, having served as executive director of the Center for

Responsive Politics and Public Campaign. In the summer of 2002, after McCain–Feingold passed, Miller wrote an article in *The American Prospect* titled "The Road To Nowhere." Her heretical view: Three decades of reform effort have come to little. Monied interests have more power than ever in Washington and in state capitals. And this may get worse, she predicted, after McCain–Feingold.

Part of the reason for the McCain–Feingold bandwagon, she told me, is that the foundations who were major funders of campaign reform groups "put pressure on them to stop fighting and get behind a single reform." "It was purely a symbolic victory," Miller said. "The reform groups needed a reform passed so badly for political reasons that they were willing to accept anything."

———

We've looked in this chapter at the phony fixes being peddled on the issues at the heart of the Two Percent agenda. But these charades are ubiquitous. And their cumulative message is depressing. Our aspirations for public problem-solving seem to shrink even as national wealth grows and problems worsen. Make-believe answers corrosively dominate public debate. Yes, there has always been flimflam in politics, but today's "solutions gap" has not always been the rule. Countless public policies in the past have been reasonably scaled to their goals; think of the GI Bill; Medicare; the interstate highway system; regulations for food, worker safety, and the environment; the lowering of marginal tax rates under Ronald Reagan. Solutions are always provisional, of course—complex social problems are never in any ultimate sense "solved"—but history shows that major progress is plainly possible. Yet today, especially when money is involved, the scams seem chronic. The curious reality nowadays is that our leaders almost never propose ideas that, if enacted, would make major progress on the problem they purport to address.

Which leads to a simple question: Why?

2

WHY WE'RE NOT SERIOUS

As we've seen, from schools to health care, from wages to campaign finance, when we scratch both parties' "bold plans," we find far less than meets the eye. But why? Why do our leaders offer symbolic proposals to signal that they "care" about an issue, or to show whose "side" they're on, rather than ideas that might actually fix things? Why do the boundaries of debate exclude options that are equal to the magnitude of our problems?

Five main forces mesh to produce today's dysfunctional debate. These include the paralysis that parity in the electorate inspires; the logic and habits of mind that shape what policies Democrats and Republicans offer; the way the national press sees its role vis-à-vis these party agendas; and the way campaigns are funded. Together these forces have produced a "debate" so remote from real answers and so infected with double-talk that citizens turn away in disgust.

The Paralysis of Parity

The defining feature of American politics in recent years has been the remarkable parity between the parties. You can't get closer than the presidential tie in 2000; and even the hype over the Republican win in the 2002 midterm elections masked the fact that we continue to have narrow majorities in Congress. At the congressional level this divide has been further entrenched by the redistricting done after the 2000 census, as both parties conspired to redraw the lines to make Democratic districts more reliably Democratic and Republican districts more reliably Republican. It's not as if they had far to go: The number of competitive congressional races was already down to a few dozen seats out of 435.

Yet periods of closely divided power are unusual in America. Our system of government has generally favored the creation of effective majorities. Think of FDR and the New Deal coalition, which lasted from the 1930s until it gave way in the late 1960s under the strains of Vietnam and the backlash against civil rights. Ronald Reagan's huge electoral victories ushered in a period of conservative power from 1980 to 1992. Most analysts view eras of closely divided power as periods in which one system of effective majority has broken down and the next system of effective majority has not yet come into being. In this view, the 1990s were transitional: Reagan's majority broke down, but Bill Clinton couldn't get the Democrats to the promised land. Today the struggle continues.

In eras featuring a dominant ideology, like Lyndon Johnson's or Ronald Reagan's, there's an obvious mandate for ambition. By contrast, political professionals say, in eras of parity voters don't tend to think as big—nor are they invited to do so by politicians, who fear pushing beyond whatever fragile consensus may exist. If voters seem more focused on their families than on the wider world, politicians oblige them by talking about nursing home standards, or pension security, or prescription drug coverage. "We're not talking about the 'big fix,'" said Bill Carrick, a political consultant advising Richard Gephardt's presidential campaign. "We're talking about tiny little fixes that are directly relevant to people. That makes it more difficult for people on either the right or the left to have 'big picture' agendas."

At the presidential and statewide levels, today's parity also breeds a maniacal focus on "swing" voters, that narrow universe of uncommitted citizens who (once we move past safely gerrymandered congressional seats) determine American elections. Democrats know they'll get union members and minorities and most women; Republicans know they can count on gun owners and religious conservatives and small businessmen. But those groups, and their brethren in each party's coalition, leave things deadlocked. The people left over decide who wins. Campaigns therefore obsess over them: Who are they? How can we move them? What can we say that will attract them to our candidacy?

"In the last thirty days of a campaign you're fighting for the same voters," said Bob Kerrey, the former Nebraska senator who is now president of New School University in New York:

> Largely undecided, non-ideological suburban white folks who are concerned about crime and Social Security. These are people with incomes over $50,000 a year. *In a political campaign it's too risky to lead them. And so what you do is you pretend to lead while basically you're trying to follow their opinions.* . . . The stakes of a mistake are huge. You can see it in this last [presidential] race. You're down to a single electoral vote. It makes a difference in who is president and who is not. (emphasis added)

The result is a risk-averse game of inches, driven by the calculation that the right tactic—a dash of tax cut pandering here or Social Security demagoguery there—can lure the two or three points to put a candidate over the top. Such small-bore maneuvering not only fails to inspire voters; it's also inhospitable to serious policy ideas. And the "mandates" emerging from such contests are trivial. For Democrats, the upside is winning a few seats and then enacting sideshows like the "patients' bill of rights" (which already exists in some form in over forty states) on more Democratic terms. For Republicans, it means winning the power to do such things as impose slightly tougher work requirements on those moving from welfare to work (while not doing anything to help low-wage workers support their families).

When elections come in this era of parity, two strategies are at work simultaneously, strategies whose contradictions help reinforce the primacy of symbolic appeals and policy orthodoxy. At the presidential (and statewide) level, we see candidates like Bill Clinton and George W. Bush governing and campaigning in ways that are consciously centrist, seeking to assemble broad coalitions, and distancing themselves from their base's most alienating traits. This is why Clinton felt compelled to prove he was no Jesse Jackson in 1992 by "dissing" Jackson's unsavory ally, Sister Souljah; it explains why George W. Bush in 2000 stressed his "compassion," making a contrast to the personality of former Speaker of the House Newt Gingrich, and in 2002 denounced Trent Lott after the Mississippi senator waxed nostalgic about Strom Thurmond's segregationist presidential race in 1948.

But in the congressional trenches each party's base remains king. Candidates focus on which "hot buttons" to push or "red meat" to throw to bring the faithful to the polls. These groups tend to have strict ideological litmus tests. Any attempts to blend liberal and conservative ideas can run afoul of these demands. "Those are pretty hardcore constituencies when it comes to these issues," said Leon Panetta, the former eight-term congressman from California who served as White House chief of staff under Bill Clinton. "That basically limits each party's flexibility to be a little more imaginative about how you solve these problems."

Democratic Timidity and Confusion

If parity gives American politics its overarching "game of inches" quality, the Democrats have special fears and reflexes that drive them to deeper levels of timidity and confusion. They start with the psychic scar of the Clinton health care fiasco of 1993–1994. Most Americans don't realize how devastated the Democrats were by the experience, which cost the party control of the Congress for the first time in forty years, and taught a searing lesson about the risks of trying to lead public opinion, rather than following or accompanying it. David Gergen, who served in White House posts under presidents Nixon, Ford, Reagan, and Clinton, called it "a terrible psychological blow," adding, "They've never found themselves since." "They're traumatized like a young child," agreed Bill Bradley, the former New Jersey senator. "They're traumatized so that they're unwilling to go back into that room where that bad thing happened."

Some Democratic professionals sense that the statute of limitations on this political disaster may have run its course. "The conventional wisdom usually dictates too long in the wrong way," said Frank Greer, a longtime Democratic consultant. As Democrats tiptoe toward bigger steps in 2004, the immense cost of the Clinton health plan has come into view: a lost decade for any attempt to think ambitiously, and not only on health care, but on virtually every question of national policy.

This timidity has been reinforced by the increasing importance of suburban voters to the Democrats, a key constituency as the party shed its Great Society image as the champion of poor minorities, offering little to mainstream America. Given how poorly Democrats do with white men in particular, the role of suburban women to Democratic victories today cannot be overstated. Suburban women gravitate toward the Democrats because they like the party's focus on education, health care, and the environment. They share the Democrats' acceptance of modern gender roles, and find conservative cultural intolerance off-putting. But suburban women also believe in fiscal prudence. "People who focus on that [suburban] growth in the coalition tend not to be very bold about what government should do," said Stanley Greenberg, a Democratic pollster. Since upscale suburban districts account for most of the congressional seats Democrats have picked up since 1994, "fiscal responsibility" is a value (and an image) Democrats need to take seriously. The phrase itself appears in virtually every paragraph uttered by presidential aspirants Joseph Lieberman, John Edwards, Howard Dean, John Kerry, and Richard Gephardt. Before the 2001 tax cuts brought back deficits, "fiscal responsibility" explained why many top Democrats oddly boasted of plans to pay down the national debt before spending fresh sums on schools or health care.

The irony is that the Democrats deserve to be considered rock-solid on fiscal prudence, because they recently delivered the most fiscally responsible era in memory. Bill Clinton inherited record budget deficits and bequeathed record surpluses. He took over a government that spent 22 percent of GDP under presidents Reagan and Bush, and left office with spending at 18.5 percent of GDP, averaging 20 percent during his two terms. What more could suburban women want? Yet the Democrats can't seem to get credit for these accomplishments, or to shake lingering doubts that they're plotting to sneak off and go on a spending spree. To be sure, endless Republican attacks feed this stereotype, which the GOP desperately wants to keep in voters' minds. But it's also true that the case for how well Democrats managed things can seem complicated. The shift from deficits to surpluses on their watch was understandable—though it took time before voters believed it had actually happened in the late 1990s, and that success was swiftly undermined by a Bush tax cut passed with Democratic help. But the size-of-government argument has seemed too arcane to stress in political debate.

"I don't think we've figured out how to explain to the American people that there are two numbers when you're trying to figure out the size of government," said Bob Kerrey. "One is a numerator and one is a denominator." The denominator is the size of the economy; the numerator is government spending. Republicans rail about the numerator because it always goes up. But that number isn't meaningful without being compared to the size of the economy. When Democrats fail to frame the issue this way (and fail to persuade the press of the merits of doing likewise), they miss the chance to talk about spending that can boost the economy even as it furthers traditional Democratic social goals. In his 1992 campaign Clinton brilliantly shorthanded this case for "investment" as opposed to mere "spending." But this emphasis was lost when Clinton had to focus on taming the deficit upon taking office, and it was hard to hear during the later travails of his presidency. Besides, as Kerrey told me, if you're a politician, "it's difficult to use the two words 'numerator' and 'denominator' and get a round of applause."

In addition, Democrats have split into two incoherent and suspicious camps with mirror-image philosophies that complicate any attempt to regroup. Broadly speaking, "Old" Democrats have traditionally liberal (if prudently disguised) spending ambitions but loathe market-friendly approaches to public problems. "New" Democrats have market-friendly instincts but are afraid to put up money equal to the size of today's problems. It's important to understand each camp's worldview and its brief against the other.

In their hearts, Old Democrats—think Ted Kennedy or the late Senator Paul Wellstone—view the "fiscal responsibility" and "balanced budget" themes as political necessities with scant policy merit. When upset they go further and accuse New Democrats of a de facto conspiracy with the right to put liberal goals in a straitjacket. First the New Democrats made a fetish of deficit reduction in Clinton's early days, they charge, scrapping the big public investments in health, infrastructure, and education on which he campaigned. Then, after their balanced budget dreams came true—an effort that consumed most of Clinton's presidency—the New Democrats handed off fat surpluses to Bush to use for tax cuts for his rich pals. New Democratic positioning may win statewide and national elections, they concede, but the New Democrats have lost their souls.

Old Democrats see market-friendly ideas—like using tax credits to extend health coverage, or bigger tests of vouchers in urban school districts—as deeply suspect. They feel you haven't guaranteed anybody anything unless government has done so itself, because private firms are too self-interested to protect the public interest. Old Democrats also have political reasons to prefer direct government fixes over diffuse solutions involving multiple actors. "That may be good policy," Old Democrats say to New, "but how do we as a party get credit for something that isn't seen as a nice packaged benefit with a ribbon around it that we've given to the fortunate taxpayer."

New Democrats, whose numbers include nearly every current presidential aspirant, think Old Democrats are fuzzy-headed on economics. Yes, balanced budgets in the 1990s may have been smart politics, they say, but they were also needed to lower interest rates, increase national savings and investment, and thus boost productivity and growth, relationships they feel the economically illiterate Old Democrats don't appreciate. Instead, Old Democrats wrongly act as if economic growth "just happens" and treat politics mostly as a way to transfer resources to America's have-nots. The reality, say the New Democrats, is that unless the economic "pie" keeps growing through rational policies, the nation can't afford to pursue social justice.

New Democrats also realize that harnessing market forces for public purposes can be the most effective policy, as well as the only way to get bipartisan support. But New Democrats are generally petrified of ideas that require serious spending, and so their ideas are rightly criticized for being token or symbolic. A prime example was the much-hyped but puny $200 million school-to-work initiative early in the Clinton administration, which, as one Old Democrat quipped, "ended up helping dozens if not hundreds of people and then got killed." Yet New Democrats say they're doing the best they can in a world where spending is politically risky because voters already think their money is being wasted. New Democrats vow not to give the GOP any rope to hang them with.

Democratic timidity largely comes down to this fear. "They're convinced people wouldn't buy what we believe the country really needs," said Bill Bradley. "So we have to say what we want them to hear—that we're with them," but without offering policies equal to their problems. "Then we'll try in the margins to help people who really need the help." This pattern of what Bradley calls "the big rhetoric and the little mouse" was a winning formula for Clinton after 1994—or, more precisely, a sufficient formula for political survival. Bush has copied the technique on domestic policy. "That's cynicism," Bradley concluded. "And that's infected the political process. Somebody's got to break out of this straitjacket, and put the Democrats' values into an agenda, and put the price on it, and confront the country with the fundamental choice between short-term ledger and long-term well-being." This yearning runs deep among Democrats. "This incremental bullshit is not going to get us where we've got to go," said Jim McDermott, a seven-term congressman from Seattle.

The trouble is that Bradley tried to break out of the straitjacket in the 2000 primaries, and he was neatly diced up and disposed of by Al Gore. Bradley's campaign represented the first road test of a potential synthesis of Old and New Democratic thinking. As we've seen, his plan for universal health coverage, using tax credits along with insurance market reforms, was similar to the scheme offered by George H. W. Bush in 1992. Bradley called for big money to reach this and other goals, including the elimination of child poverty. His message mixing ambitious liberal rhetoric and market-friendly means drew the support of New Democrats Bob Kerrey and Daniel Patrick Moynihan as well as traditional liberals Paul Wellstone and Jim McDermott.

Yet Bradley faced nearly impossible odds. As a sitting vice president, Gore was the presumptive nominee in the eyes of the Democratic establishment and enjoyed enormous built-in advantages. Gore also decided that the most effective way to take Bradley out was to swing the New Democratic "fiscal responsibility" club. One Democratic presidential contender in 2004, who would not speak for attribution, assessed the contest this way:

> Bradley left himself open. Bradley had a pretty good basic approach [on health care] and didn't know how to defend it well enough. . . . Bradley had grabbed the ground with universal. Gore was put in the position of "me too" and he didn't want to be a "me too." He didn't know how to afford it so he took the ground of "I'm going to be the fiscally responsible one, I'm going to be conservative and responsible because we're the people who balanced the budget." . . . And so he could responsibly say, "How are you going to pay for it?" and make it look like it's too big. That's essentially what happened.

Did Bradley's experience prove that thinking big while offering "ideologically androgynous" solutions is a loser? Or was Bradley's circumstance unique, meaning that a new candidate in a wide-open field could carry and defend such an agenda and unite the party? Much depends on how the party's presidential aspirants answer this question.

The final forces shaping Democrats' behavior are their profound phobias about taxes and defense. The tax story is simple. In 1984, the Democratic presidential nominee Walter Mondale stated that he would raise taxes to rein in the deficit. His reward for being a "truth teller" was to lose forty-nine states in the general election. The Democrats know they're perceived as too eager to reach into voters' pockets. For this reason, whenever Democrats oppose Republican tax cuts that favor the rich, they invariably roll out tax cuts for "working families," so that they can't be accused of being "against tax cuts," especially by a president with the megaphone that comes with the White House.

On defense, Democrats feel they're on equally treacherous terrain. President Bush has proposed the largest defense increase in history, which would lift Pentagon spending from the $300 billion he inherited to $470 billion over the next few years. This would make the defense budget more than 50 percent higher, after adjusting for inflation, than it was on average during the Cold War. Many top Democrats privately think the sums Bush has proposed are insane and represent a cynical strategy to use September 11 to crowd out domestic spending. But the key word here is "privately."

I asked Senator Evan Bayh of Indiana if it was possible for a Democrat who wants to be president to challenge Bush's defense budget. Bayh, a former governor, isn't running in 2004, but is likely to be on the Democrats' short list for vice president. Bayh said it was obviously impossible for someone to be elected president who was deemed weak on national security. "So your question is," Bayh continued, "can you be perceived as being strong on national security and defense while still arguing about the amount of money that we're spending on it?"

> It's difficult and let me explain why. A lot of research has gone into these things. The public basically doesn't know who to believe. They see the spin and the counter spin and the general trust in public figures is pretty low-level anyway. So they fall back on their preexisting notions about what the two parties stand for. Intuitively, they tend to trust Democrats more on issues of health care, Social Security and education. . . . On the Republican side, the issues that work for them are taxes and national security. . . . Because of those preexisting notions about the two parties, Democrats have an added burden to bear on issues like national security.

Candidates like Republican senator John McCain, with impressive records of service and sacrifice, have obvious standing on defense and can therefore be critical of Pentagon policies. The classic example of such a leader was President Dwight D. Eisenhower, the original scourge of the military–industrial complex. "The problem is that there are very few Democrats who can speak with that kind of credibility on defense issues," Bayh said, "and so they're all running for cover." This fear is even more potent in the wake of 9/11, when the Democrats' broader vision gap on national security strategy has left them vulnerable in ways that squabbles over defense spending would only compound.

If a Democrat did feel bold enough to challenge Bush's defense budget, his political consultants would bar the door. We have a hard enough time getting white men to vote for us as it is, they'd say. Now you want to look soft on terror? The press wouldn't focus on the substance anyway. "The press will say, how could this moron do this?" said Carter Eskew, a Democratic consultant. "There will be a bunch of analysis stories that say, 'Bold Move or Suicide?' They'll talk to people like me who will say, 'because candidate X has now come out with an innovative plan to reform the military that's at odds with Bush, he's going to be dogged by that and he's not going to be able to talk about prescription drugs or health policy or education and all the areas where Democrats enjoy an advantage.'"

"There are these rules in politics," Eskew added, "one of which is you don't try and have a debate on the other guy's turf." Even Howard Dean, the former Vermont governor and presidential candidate who has said breezily from day one that we should totally repeal Bush's tax cut, thinks taking on the defense budget is nuts. "From a tactical point of view," Dean told me, "why would you want to quibble on defense?"

But here's the problem. If you've been keeping score as we've catalogued the party's inhibitions, you'll see that the Democrats have painted themselves into a corner. They can't spend. They can't tax. They can't take on defense even if Bush's plan is excessive. As a result, even if the Democrats win, they can't do anything, except offer the kind of symbolic appeals and make-believe fixes we've discussed. Democratic policy "strategy" comes down to dreams of snookering Bush himself into saying his tax cut was too big by arguing that his tax cut threatens our military buildup. If you're a Democrat, sometimes the fog is so thick you can't even see the myopia.

In the end, the party has been reduced to what Lawrence Summers, the former Clinton treasury secretary who now serves as president of Harvard University, called a "reactionary liberal strategy." "Democrats like arguing that the Republicans will take it away," Summers said, "rather than arguing that we will do 'x,' because they've found that to be a better and a more convincing strategy." As a matter of politics it's easy to see why. As a matter of public problem-solving, though, where does that leave them? As Churchill said after Dunkirk, "Wars are not won by retreats."

Republican Indifference: Hypocrisy, Principle — Or Deep Psychic Angst?

If the Democrats are trapped by fear, something more mysterious is at work with the Republicans. F. Scott Fitzgerald wrote that "the test of a first-rate intelligence is the ability to hold two opposed ideas in the mind at the same time, and still retain the ability to function," but no one ever suggested Fitzgerald should run the country. Yet the contradiction I kept bumping up against in conversations with George W. Bush's cabinet, top Republican officials, and other conservative thinkers and activists left me stumped. Most of them insisted they were as concerned with equal opportunity and the problems of disadvantaged Americans as were Democrats, and resented the way their party was caricatured as heartless or indifferent. When I listened to them, in the offices of men like Mitch Daniels, the first director of Bush's Office of Management and Budget, or then-Treasury Secretary Paul O'Neill, they seemed sincere. But I had to tell them that I couldn't square their avowed concerns with Republican budget priorities, unless they honestly believed that we could address the problems facing the uninsured, disadvantaged children and the working poor without new federal money. This, after all, was the result of Bush's tax cuts, defense hikes, and deficits (along with the reality that neither party, rhetoric aside, is prepared to reallocate much of the rest of federal spending). And here's the surprise: It turns out when you frame it this way, and press them on it, most Republicans (not all, but most) do not in fact believe these problems require no new money.

So what's going on when they say they're concerned about these problems? I see six possibilities:

1. They don't really mean it.   This is the Pure Hypocrisy theory and it's what many Democrats believe. "They have no interest whatsoever," said Howard Dean. "They're just going to put out whatever rhetoric they have to in order to try to fool the American people into thinking that they care." Doubtless this applies to some subset of Republicans—just as it's doubtless true that some Democrats who swear "the era of big government is over" have nothing like that sentiment in their hearts. There's no way to put a percentage on it, but I don't think this is as big an explanation as Democrats presume. Undistilled hypocrisy is rare, as compared with grayer shades of moral and intellectual confusion, which we'll get to.

2. They mean it but these aren't their voters.   This is the Raw Politics theory, and it makes a lot of sense. Whatever noble thoughts may lurk in the Republican heart, these issues and these voters are not what get them elected. "Conservatives haven't really thought the problem through because their own political interests are not served," said Bill Bradley. "Their attitude toward this subject politically comes from showing enough leg to convince the independents they would like to attract that they're not neanderthal." The late Daniel Patrick Moynihan summed up the Republican mind here: "Those folks never vote for us and we have our priorities for the money."

I suggested to Vin Weber, an influential Republican lobbyist who represented Minnesota in the House from 1980 to 1992, that it's hard to square conservative claims to care about such issues as the uninsured with their actual proposals. "I don't know if there's a good answer to that," Weber said, "other than to say it's a priority but not all priorities are equal." He explained the dynamics.

I see from your [Democratic] party a prescription drug benefit mainly benefiting middle class seniors, and when Republicans are put on the defense on that issue—as they always are in every election—what are they supposed to do? They come back and say, if we're going to have to compromise on our small government–fiscally conservative principles in the health care area, it looks like we're going to have to do it here because this is where we're going to get nailed in the next election if we don't. At the end of that discussion you say, "and then what about the uninsured?" We say, well, they're not Republicans, it doesn't seem to be a cutting political issue against us. Do we care? Yeah. But politics trumps that conviction.

3. They mean it but government can't make things better.   Much of this sentiment is the "money's not the answer" mantra. "We've spent $5 trillion on these people since the 1960s," went the conservative rallying cry during the debate over welfare reform in the mid-1990s, "and they're still on the dole!" Now, welfare did need to be reformed, but conservative outrage here has always been highly selective. After all, via the mortgage interest deduction, we've spent a trillion dollars since World War II subsidizing a house-buying spree for nonpoor Americans, and *those* people are still on the dole, too. What's more, Republicans seemed to feel money was precisely the answer when they enacted a generous living wage for corporate farmers in 2002 while refusing to consider the same for millions of struggling workers.

The better conservative position here is a healthy skepticism about the efficacy of government action, since many programs have had spiraling costs and unintended consequences. Whenever government gets involved, conservatives say, it tends to fossilize that form of social provision, inhibiting needed innovation (the fact that Medicare doesn't cover prescription drugs is a prime example). These critiques are fair. But conservatives apply them too broadly. In areas like health care, moreover, the government is already, with Republican assent, both regulating and spending hundreds of billions of dollars a year, so it's not as if some virginal threshold choice of "government versus no government" is on the table. Finally, the conservative critique should apply equally to the defense bureaucracy, a fact the GOP routinely (and conveniently) overlooks. If we're serious and not just scoring political points, the real question in every case is how to use government to achieve the public purposes we want while trying to minimize the potential downsides of government involvement.

Honest conservatives know this, yet to preserve their "government ain't the answer" bumper sticker, they perform intellectual somersaults. Consider this specimen from President Bush in February 2002, in a speech describing his tax credit for health coverage (which, as we'll see in Chapter 5, would be a good idea if Bush's version of it wasn't so cheap):

> We'll work with our nation's governors to create purchasing groups to negotiate with insurers for the people who use the health credit. In other words, people who don't have insurance must be given incentives [that is, a subsidy] to purchase insurance; the states can help them pool in order to get decent coverage; but *it's not a government program.* (emphasis added)

Sorry, Mr. President, but giving federal subsidies to poorer folks and regulating the insurance market to assure them affordable rates *is* a government program—just a different kind of one.

Some conservative skepticism of government seems flinty or downright harsh. To my surprise, Representative Christopher Shays of Connecticut, a moderate Republican, embodied this view. When I raised the idea of a bigger wage subsidy for the working poor, Shays said, "To me, the solution to poverty, it's working 80 hours a week, it's working your butt off, it's saving money and it's having that kind of initiative." No one can argue with that: It's how millions of immigrants have pursued the American dream. But what about the millions of Americans who already work 80 hours a week but aren't skilled enough ever to earn wages that lift them from poverty? What should they do about health coverage, or clothes for the kids? Don't these workers have as strong a claim on our help as, say, wealthy farmers?

4. They mean it, but it's crazy to spend more money without reforming the system.   This is an important argument, but it shouldn't end the discussion. First, you can agree on the need for systemic reform (as I do) and also believe that money can help bribe the interest groups involved to get it. In addition, insisting on reform before adding fresh cash is a position that's easy to take when you're not affected by the wait. "Look, kid," this approach basically tells poor inner-city and rural students, "I know you've got lousy teachers every year, and it's a disgrace your building is falling apart, and that you've got no libraries or textbooks or computers, but we've really got to get the incentives right before we can tackle all that."

Nor (again) do conservatives apply their principles consistently. Studies show, for example, that in many functions that could be privatized—like housing, payroll processing, travel and inventory management—the Pentagon wastes up to $30 billion a year compared to more efficient private sector practices. Why would an administration full of former CEOs throw so much fresh cash into a structure that Donald Rumsfeld would be the first to acknowledge is outdated and inefficient? Follow the logic: When it comes to providing new cash injections for America's most troubled schools, the White House says it's wrong to pour good money after bad; the system must first be reformed. But even before September 11, Bush & Company happily threw vaster pots of money at the unreformed Pentagon without hypocrisy or inconsistency because . . . well, because.

5. They mean it and over the long run things take care of themselves.   This is the argument for the genius of capitalism, and Milton Friedman is its most cogent advocate. "Everything starts out as a luxury for the rich and ends up as a necessity for the poor," Friedman told me. "That's true with television, that's true with electricity. You need to have somebody who's willing to support it. Who buys the first television set at $2,000 apiece or something? It's got to be the rich people. But that provides the capital which enables you to develop."

This pattern of capitalism, Friedman argued, has produced higher living standards for more people than any rival form of social organization. Friedman is undeniably right over the long run, a fact that liberals need to acknowledge. But this long-run truth can be corrosive. The conviction that the invisible hand will make poor folks better off in the next century lets conservatives off the moral hook today. It condones a weirdly principled indifference to the fate of blameless people who are suffering *now.* And this indifference is based on what we'll see is a false premise: that every attempt to improve the lot of today's disadvantaged will impede the capitalist engines that generate growth and innovation over time. Heavy-handed socialism would; market-friendly methods won't.

"The way we can salve our conscience," says David Gergen of his fellow Republicans, "is by assuming that a healthy, robust economy brings people out of poverty." But growth is clearly not enough. After adjusting for inflation, the U.S. economy has doubled in size since 1980, yet the problems we're discussing have gotten worse. How long does the right think we should wait for growth to help the least among us?

6. They mean it, but they don't act on it—and deep down this really bothers them.   Here's where it gets interesting: In fact, this last option in many ways incorporates the rest. In 1957 a psychologist named Leon Festinger published a book called *A Theory of Cognitive Dissonance.* Festinger posited a simple theory to explain certain aspects of human motivation. An individual strives for consistency within himself, Festinger said. His opinions and attitudes tend to exist in clusters that are internally consistent. Similarly, people seek consistency between what they know or believe and what they do. A person who believes college is a good thing will urge his children to go to college; a person who thinks he will be punished for some crime will not commit it, or at least try not to be caught if he does. All this is plain enough; what catches our attention, Festinger said, are the exceptions to such consistency. A person knows smoking is bad for him yet keeps smoking; people commit crimes even though they are likely to be caught. Festinger argued that *such inconsistencies are rarely accepted psychologically as inconsistencies by the persons involved.* Instead, they attempt to rationalize things in ways that render them consistent. The smoker who keeps smoking even knowing it's bad for his health, for example, may also feel that (a) he enjoys it so much it's worth it, (b) his lucky genes mean the chances of his getting cancer are less than experts say, (c) you can't live life and avoid every possible risk, or (d) if he quit he'd gain so much weight it would be worse for his health. So continuing to smoke remains consistent with his ideas about smoking.

But people can't always explain away such inconsistencies. When they can't, and an inconsistency persists, Festinger said, people experience psychological discomfort. His elegant hypothesis (which has inspired decades of research and made "cognitive dissonance" a staple of contemporary culture) follows:

1. The existence of dissonance, being psychologically uncomfortable, will motivate the person to try to reduce the dissonance and achieve consonance.
2. When dissonance is present, in addition to trying to reduce it, the person will actively avoid situations and information which would likely increase the dissonance and seek out situations and information that reduce it.

What does this have to do with Republicans? A fair-sized chunk of the Republican establishment, I'm convinced, is coping with a serious case of cognitive dissonance. As a result, a fair amount of conservative intellectual activity is devoted to reducing this dissonance. Operating in a cocoon of like-minded souls, the right has developed a series of pseudo facts and incomplete arguments *that they sincerely believe* in order to protect themselves from the discomfort that would come from honestly facing the contradiction between a moral self-image that includes concern for the disadvantaged and budget plans that reveal this concern to be a fraud. I know this sounds condescending, so let me be the first to say that most of us couldn't get through the day without a little dissonance avoidance. Democrats, including me, suffer from their own brand of this affliction (we'll take up a prime example in a moment). But on the issues we're discussing, the GOP's dissonance is striking, and a barrier to progress. Since the alternative is to conclude that many Republicans are hypocrites, I prefer to view them as victims of psychic distress—with apologies in advance, of course, to conservatives who I know deplore this modern tendency to medicalize character flaws.

What persuaded me that this phenomenon was central to Republican behavior was the way certain selective "facts" popped up (or didn't pop up) in my dealings with top conservative thinkers and institutions. The Heritage Foundation, for example, publishes a detailed chartbook on federal spending that slices and dices spending in several dozen ways that show the line of "big government" constantly rising. Yet it omits the one relevant macro measure—spending as a share of GDP—that shows the size of government shrinking in the last decade.

Or take Ed Gillespie, an influential lobbyist and strategist who recently became chairman of the Republican National Committee. I met with Gillespie in his Washington office and laid out the Two Percent Solution concept. "My first instinctive reaction is that two percent on the dollar sounds attractive," Gillespie said, "except that we're already taking 40 percent on the dollar of national income for government purposes, so it's really 42 percent. As a conservative I back away from the notion that 2 percent is nominal. Two percent on top of what's already being taken is significant."

If government were in fact taking 40 percent of national income, Gillespie would be right; this might give one pause. But it's not. As we've discussed, federal spending and taxation is a little under 20 percent of national income today. When you toss in states and localities, overall receipts are 28 percent of GDP. Two percent on top of that—even assuming we were financing it all through taxes, which we won't be—doesn't seem nearly as big a deal. (The average among the major industrial democracies is 44 percent.)

Or consider John Cogan, an economist at the Hoover Institution who helped write President Bush's 2000 campaign economic plan, who articulated another of the right's common concerns about more spending for the uninsured or the working poor:

> You end up in a world where we've divided the population—half the population pays, and the other half of the population receives from the tax system. If you exempt a large segment of the middle class from taxation and in fact you provide them with government grants, put them in effect on the dole (although that's a harsh term to use), you might say, "Hold on a second. Maybe this isn't such a good policy." . . . If you ask most Americans: Do you think it's proper that the bottom half of the population from $50,000 and below should be receiving grants from the government and the top half should be paying for those, they'd say no.

Bruce Josten, the top lobbyist at the U.S. Chamber of Commerce, the powerful Washington business group, expanded on the point. "Five percent of the population pays over 50 percent of the income taxes collected by the federal government," he said. "You're getting to the point where there are more people on this side of the seesaw not paying any income taxes, and the burden is simultaneously increasing on the smaller and smaller portion of the population."

If what Cogan and Josten laid out were the full picture, it would indeed be cause for alarm—how can we have so few Americans pulling the cart and so many riding in it? But the instinctive way conservatives have come to reason and argue about the federal tax burden is misleading, incomplete—and yes, dissonance avoiding. Here's why.

Table 2.1   A Nation of Freeloaders, as Seen by the Right . . .

Who's Paying Taxes in 2001

Percentiles	Percent of Income Tax
Top 1%	36%
Top 5%	57%
Top 10%	68%
Top 20%	83%
Bottom 80%	17%

. . . But Look at the Full Picture and—Presto!—
We Have a Modestly Progressive Tax System

Who's Paying Taxes in 2001

Percentiles	Percent of Income	Percent of Income Tax	Percent of Total Federal Taxes
Top 1%	17%	36%	23%
Top 5%	31%	57%	40%
Top 10%	42%	68%	52%
Top 20%	59%	83%	69%
Bottom 80%	41%	17%	31%

Source: U.S. Congress Joint Committee on Taxation

The top portion of Table 2.1 shows the tax world as perceived by conservatives, a view espoused most prominently by the *Wall Street Journal*'s influential editorial page. As it reveals, the top 5 percent of taxpayers do indeed pay 57 percent of federal income taxes; the top

1 percent pay 36 percent all by themselves; while the bottom 80 percent pay a trifling 17 percent. If this table is all you carry in your head (and all that the people you spend time with carry in their heads), then it's obvious that Ayn Rand was right: We're a nation of freeloaders who enjoy the blessings of liberty thanks to a handful of generous giants.

But wait! The bottom half of Table 2.1 paints in the remainder of what any fair-minded person should acknowledge is the fuller picture. Two columns are added. First, the percentage of total income each slice of the taxpaying public earns. Next, the percentage of *total* federal taxes, not just income taxes, that are paid. The conservative worldview inexplicably ignores payroll taxes (as well as excise taxes), which take their biggest bite, proportionally, from lower-income Americans. Yet as Table 2.2 shows, while the income tax accounts for 49 percent of federal revenue, the payroll tax accounts for 37 percent (up from 16 percent in 1960). If you count the portion of the payroll tax paid by employers (which economists agree effectively comes out of workers' wages), four in five workers pay more in payroll taxes than in income taxes. When you add these necessary facts to the conservative analysis, America doesn't look like an Ayn Rand novel after all.

Table 2.2 Federal Revenues by Source

	Percent of Total Revenue	
Types of Revenue	*1960*	*2003*
Income tax	44%	49%
Payroll tax	16%	37%
Corporate tax	23%	10%
Excise taxes and other	17%	4%

Source: Office of Management and Budget

Consider: The top 1 percent of America's taxpayers earn 17 percent of the income and pay 23 percent of federal taxes; the top 5 percent earn 31 percent of the income and pay 40 percent of the taxes; the bottom 80 percent of the earners make 41 percent of the income and pay 31 percent of the taxes. In other words, in aggregate, we have a modestly progressive federal tax system.

So: Why do conservatives stress only part of the picture? Most of the explanation, in my humble armchair Freudian opinion, is dissonance avoidance. But to be fair, part of the reason is that Democrats have spooked the GOP into shying away from talking about payroll taxes. This takes a little explanation—and gives us a chance to examine some Democratic dissonance to boot.

Every time the White House updates budget projections showing that Social Security's surplus (that is, the excess of payroll taxes over current Social Security checks) is being used to reduce the deficit in the rest of the budget, Democrats pounce. "Ah ha!" they cry. "That means you're dipping into the Social Security surpluses to fund evil schemes like missile defense." The Senate Democratic leader, Tom Daschle, rushes to remind citizens that the payroll taxes that fund Social Security and Medicare—those "FICA" deductions from everyone's paycheck—are sacred. "To use them for any other purpose," Daschle once said, alarmed that any civilized person would entertain such depravity, "is a deceit, a shell game, that we just can't afford."

There are two things to note about Daschle's statement. The first is that for two decades Daschle and the Democrats (joined by the Republicans) voted merrily each year to use Social Security and Medicare surpluses for other purposes in precisely the "shell game" that now draws Daschle's dudgeon. But Daschle's statement is worse than hypocritical; it's ineffective. While Democrats think this "don't touch the Social Security surplus" drumbeat is a political winner, it cuts them off from a stronger line of attack that is truer to progressive values.

Here's the reason. Democrats want to: (1) slam the GOP for using payroll taxes for any purpose other than Social Security, and also (2) slam the GOP for unfairly excluding low-wage workers who pay payroll taxes (but not income taxes) from all their big tax cuts.

Slam number 2 is a serious charge that goes to the heart of the difference between the parties. As we've seen, four in five Americans now pay more in payroll taxes than in income taxes. Ignoring these workers while giving big breaks to the wealthiest 1 percent represents trickle-down economics at its most brazen.

But because Democrats also push bogus slam number 1, the Republicans have a plausible response to slam number 2. "We couldn't cut payroll taxes," Republicans reply every time they're confronted with the matter, "or even monkey around with payroll tax rebates of some kind, because Democrats would say we were undermining Social Security, for which everyone knows payroll tax financing is sacred."

You see the dilemma. The answer is for the Democrats to lead us beyond the outdated fiction that payroll taxes are sacrosanct and urge us to view public finance instead as one big "cigar box"—like those "mom and pop" storekeepers of old, who took cash into the cigar box behind the counter and then spent it as they saw fit, without some mystical regard to what "earmarked revenue stream" the money came from.

Simple as it sounds, taking the position that taxes are taxes and spending is spending would be a radical departure. But not so radical as our leaders let on. Behind closed doors, both parties admit that Social Security will require huge bailouts from general tax revenue after the baby boomers retire. So payroll tax purity is living on borrowed time anyway. Much of Medicare, meanwhile, is already paid for by the general fund.

And with the payroll tax having quietly soared from 2 percent to 37 percent of federal taxes since World War II, it's high time to reframe the issue to permit a discussion of its crazy burdens. This is a debate Democrats could lead to great effect if they weren't torn between the substantive desire to ease payroll taxes and the demagogic convenience of etching them in stone.

The good news in all this is that where there is dissonance, there is hope, because it means that people with consciences are suppressing or avoiding certain aspects of reality that if acknowledged would tend to undermine their self-image. I'm not saying true-blue conservatives will happily submit to my brand of "fact-based" reeducation anytime soon. But I don't think its unreasonable to think a critical mass of centrist Republicans can be coaxed into weighing new ideas—especially if Democrats, as a sign of good faith and intellectual honesty, are willing to reexamine their own antique thinking at the same time.

The Media: It's the Stenography, Not the Ideology

Let's review where we are when it comes to getting serious about such problems as the uninsured, urban schools, or the working poor. Democrats, thanks to the shadow of Clintoncare, fiscally prudent suburbs, internally incoherent camps, and fears about defense and taxes, are timid and confused. Republicans, owing to some blend of principle, politics, and psychology, are largely indifferent. How do our most influential media outlets then contribute to our unseriousness? By faithfully reflecting and choosing not to challenge the boundaries of debate set by the two major parties.

Many people would say this is exactly what the press should be doing, especially in its news pages as opposed to its editorial pages. But when it comes to public problem-solving, this means the usual carping about the media misses the point. Conservatives say the mainstream media is liberal, and they're right. But that's not what's interesting. The interesting question is this: If the media is so liberal, why has America's political center of gravity shifted so dramatically to the right in the last two decades? The answer is that *the news coverage of influential national media outlets is shaped more by stenography than by ideology.*

Some journalists will object to the word "stenography," but I mean it to be descriptive, not critical. "News" is largely defined as what public officials say and do. The poles of debate on major issues are thus set by the mainstream Republican position (today set by the Bush administration) and the mainstream Democratic position. The national press faithfully reflects these two poles, and the 50-yard line in American politics is between them.

To illustrate, look at what's happened in the last decade or so. Before 1994 "the left" was more to the left, with Democrats talking about such things as universal health coverage, and with the right opposed. After the Clinton heath fiasco and the Republican ascent in Congress, the left moved rightward for all the reasons we've discussed. The right, emboldened, moved further to the right—aggressively calling for bigger cuts in marginal tax rates, the elimination of the estate tax, et cetera. And so as the official poles of debate shifted, so did the political center of gravity, even though all of these events were filtered by the "liberal" media.

While stenography as a news value may seem preferable to a situation in which top national news outlets pursue their own untethered agendas, it also brings a clear downside: In times when neither party is serious about addressing major problems, stenography assures that public debate remains impoverished. Stenography gave us a 1988 presidential campaign, for example, without a peep about the burgeoning savings-and-loan crisis. Since both parties were knee deep in blame, neither wanted to discuss it. Without candidates bringing it up, the national media didn't pursue the story either. Yet George H. W. Bush (to his credit) made it his first priority upon taking office—and so the biggest financial meltdown in U.S. history hit the front pages and national consciousness like a bolt from the blue. Stenography explains why Ross Perot had to show up with his charts to get any meaningful discussion of the budget deficit in the 1992 campaign. In 1996, thanks to the quixotic candidacy of the magazine heir Steve Forbes, stenography subjected us to more than anyone should have had to hear about the "flat tax." In 2000, when no candidates or sitting officials ran with it, stenography meant that former senators Gary Hart and Warren Rudman couldn't get much play for their prescient commission report that stressed how vulnerable the country was to major terrorist attacks.

To be sure, smaller print outlets—from *The Nation* and *The American Prospect* on the left to *The Weekly Standard* and *National Review* on the right—challenge the official debate every week, as do online "bloggers" of all stripes. The rise of conservative voices on talk radio and cable television has also had some impact on the tilt and tenor of public life. But these outlets have very little influence on what is considered to be "news" compared to the judgments made by the editors and producers of *The New York Times, The Washington Post,* and the major television networks—and these top outlets do not generally feel it is their proper role to challenge the official boundaries of discussion. The famously "adversarial" nature of the press is manifest mostly in the pursuit of scandal or wrongdoing, not in questioning the major parties' definition of the nation's chief challenges and their potential solutions. Indeed, editors come in for grief when they are seen as departing from this norm—as conservative critics charged the *Times* did under former executive editor, Howell Raines, in 2002, with the paper's alleged hyping of opposition to an invasion of Iraq.

"We tend to be and, probably should be, guided by what public officials . . . are debating," said Walter Isaacson, a former president of CNN and editor of *Time* magazine.

"News gathering is essentially a reactive process. It's not an initiative process," said Bill Keller, the *New York Times* veteran who was recently named the paper's executive editor.

"It's largely driven by the candidates," said NBC's Washington bureau chief, Tim Russert, of campaign coverage in particular.

Len Downie, executive editor of *The Washington Post,* told me that the *Post* certainly doesn't conceive of its general news coverage as being confined to what is said or identified by the parties. On health care, for example, the *Post* has published exhaustive looks at the problems facing managed care, troubled hospitals, and more. But Downie said that when it comes to solutions, there may be a difference. "You're talking about whether or not the coverage that we do of the proposals to do something about it are limited to the framework of what the two parties have proposed, and I guess that's possible," he said.

> I would stipulate that it's a weakness of the media in terms of solution-searching. It's not in the natural course of news coverage to be searching out solutions, absent the "Outlook" section [the *Post*'s expanded Sunday opinion section] where we invite people of all kinds to write provocative suggestions and arguments. . . . And in the editorial and op-ed page. But in terms of [news] coverage, I guess I would say it's difficult for us to find ways to go and search out innovative potential solutions as opposed to reporting on those things that are advanced by people in power and commissions and other people that have credentials and the means to reach the media.

This stenography means that as liberal timidity has reigned, and conservatives have felt emboldened, debate has shifted almost imperceptibly to the right. "What's been interesting over the last fifteen to twenty years is the degree to which the conservatives have come together and really moved the 50-yard line," said David Gergen. Jeff Greenfield, a senior political analyst at CNN, expanded on this assessment:

> One of the reasons the debate has shifted as far as it has to the right is because many people who once had a very strong belief in government-

directed economic policy have given it up. . . . *The media are not going to create a debate,* and this is where it goes to the right, if nobody outside the media is making the argument. (emphasis added)

Their rare crusades aside, then, the editors running influential outlets like *The New York Times* and *The Washington Post* do not see their job as systematically setting some broad public agenda, even though they're aware that on many individual issues they end up defining that agenda as a by-product of "just putting out the paper," particularly via stories they choose to place on page one. "I don't set out each day to create a national agenda," said Gerald Boyd, then managing editor of *The New York Times* when we spoke in 2002. "It's important to me that we're relevant to our readers." "I don't think that if you sat in on page one meetings over the course of six months," said Steve Coll, managing editor of *The Washington Post,* "you would hear any discussion about, 'we ought to do this because we want to put it on the map.'"

In other words, if Democrats are too cowed to push more ambitious domestic goals, the "liberal" press isn't going to do it on their behalf. "You have to see the media as chronicling the public square," the *Post*'s Coll said. "When nobody shows up in the public square to talk about what you would wish them to talk about, is the person standing in the back with an open notebook the structural cause of that?" The national press, despite its power and occasional hobbyhorses, sees its role as "witnessing," as serving up a "daily diary of debate," as offering "a platform for independent inquiry and investigation"—but *not* as setting the terms of public discussion.

There's a related reality to press coverage when it comes to campaigns: If candidates do put forward ambitious ideas, the top news outlets generally aren't equipped or inclined to assess them. "Asking the political press in the middle of a political campaign to judge the public policy implications of an idea or proposal is very, very difficult," said Jeff Greenfield. "For one thing it requires you to have the time to check it out and look at it. . . . And it gets so caught up in the welter of 'What's the latest hourly poll out of Iowa?' and 'What's the new ad that's running?'" Political professionals assume the press is unwilling or unable to explain where truth lies on public policy when they plot campaign strategy. "They're all about process, and not about policy at all," said Ed Gillespie, the Republican party chairman. "The daily press doesn't really have much time to evaluate whether or not the proposals are any good or what they mean," said Carter Eskew, an adviser to Al Gore during the 2000 presidential campaign.

> They just report about what's going on. [For that reason,] in the case of Gore–Bradley, when Bradley released his health care plan, we were able to dismantle it. As a Gore partisan I will tell you that I think his health care plan was in fact really bad, but did it get a fair hearing? I don't know. I'm not sure that it did.

"The press has succumbed to the 'he said, she said,' form of journalism," added former Clinton chief of staff John Podesta, recalling the 2000 race.

> So Bush says, "x"; Gore says "y." You decide. But people don't have any capacity to decide. And I think they feel—the mainstream press—like it's putting their thumb on the scale too much to say. . . . They [the press] either said they're both full of it or they say we're not going to decide who's full of it, but they never come down hard one way or the other that one guy's numbers are based on sand and the other guy's may be fudging it a little bit but they make more sense. It becomes very difficult for the public to make informed and intelligent choices. How do you make a decision about that? They both say they're balancing the budget. They both say they're not going to spend Social Security. One guy says we're going to cut taxes. The other guy says he's going to cut taxes but in a sort of different way. One guy's going to spend a little bit more on one thing or another, but there's no crystallization that these are two very different paths that are going to lead to very different social outcomes. . . . The press is pretty terrible at explaining those paths.

Note the depressing cycle we've sketched. First, our leaders generally feel it's too risky to lead in campaigns. Next, many in the press feel you can't really look to them during campaigns to make sense of what rival policy agendas might mean for the country. So you can be forgiven for asking—*then what are campaigns for?* The honest answer, which flies in the face of your sixth-grade civics class, is that campaigns are a dueling series of pseudo events, misleading arguments, and symbols managed by candidates in order to gain power by attracting the support of 50 percent-plus-one of those citizens who bother to vote. Just as the standard disclaimer at the front of novels informs us that "any resemblance to persons living or dead is coincidental," so do political campaigns deserve the disclaimer, "ANY EDIFICATION YOU MAY RECEIVE ON THE COLLECTIVE CHOICES FACING THE NATION IS PURELY ACCIDENTAL." Sometimes it happens. It's not the main mission. Can we (and the press) change that in ways that might help us solve our problems?

It's a good question. But we're getting ahead of ourselves. For now the important point is that stenography journalism mirrors the boundaries of official debate. Even though the press is largely liberal, if official debate has moved to the right, that's where the national debate will be. Although conservatives often have legitimate gripes about one outlet's skewed page one story or another's liberal spin on a poll, they shouldn't whine. When stenography trumps ideology, so long as conservatives keep the left cowed, they win.

The Money Skew

If the press mirrors official debate, political money warps it. "The boundaries of debate are controlled by the amount of money that is put into the political system by the controlling interests," Senator John Kerry of Massachusetts told me. Every issue has these organized, well-funded groups. In health care, for example, it's the doctors, the hospitals, the insurance companies, the HMOs. "Can you challenge those boundaries?" Kerry asked. "The answer is yes. . . . But you want to challenge them intelligently by figuring out what the fears are and the tendrils of the resistance that is motivating that money, and seeing if you can harness that energy in a constructive way."

Kerry's take represents the thoughtful politician's aim in dealing with the ubiquitous campaign cash that can boost a candidate's odds or spell defeat. We don't need to belabor the truism that money is power in politics. For our purposes it's merely worth recalling the four main ways that money skews public debate. The money chase (1) puts sensible policy options off-limits; (2) turns politicians' attention to wealthier Americans and business interests; (3) allows politicians to shake down business for campaign cash; and (4) discourages promising candidates from running for office.

Take policy options first. Smart liberals know that giving trial lawyers unfettered license to sue HMOs isn't really the way to improve health care. Campaign fundraising habits, however, drive Democrats to push bad policy here (allowing endless suits in a "patient's bill of rights," for example) to keep the plaintiffs' bar happy, just as Republicans wrongly sanctioned the looting of California taxpayers by their Texas-based energy pals. The list seems endless. Democrats didn't want to give President Bush more flexibility in hiring and firing employees in the new homeland security department because public employee unions made a stink. Republicans won't tolerate sensible gun reforms because of the National Rifle Association's fear of the slippery slope. Democrats who want to be president have to forswear vouchers to appease the teacher unions, or recant whatever youthful flirtation they may have had with the idea (as did Joseph Lieberman in 2000). Republicans write entire laws to please pharmaceutical companies, who want to be sure Medicare's inclusion of prescription drug coverage leaves their pricing practices unchallenged. The accounting industry pressed both parties for a decade to kill reforms that might have helped forestall such meltdowns as Enron and Worldcom. Republican funders demand tax relief that limits the party's willingness to do more for the disadvantaged.

Beyond the explicit way the money chase takes options off the agenda is the subtler way the process alters the perspective of politicians—particularly of Democrats, once viewed as champions of the underdog. "It drains people's time and energy from being able to focus on these issues," Bill Bradley said, "and fills it up with catering to the rich."

My theory is politicians complain about raising money, but the really good ones are usually not themselves independently wealthy. By raising money they associate with a whole new class of people and they like it. They personalize their political bank account, and it comes in their subconscious to be their own personal bank account. They've raised $10 million. Here's this guy they're with on a family yacht. There's a certain comparability there. So you get locked into all of this . . . in order to raise the money from which you derive your deep self-esteem. That is the most corrupting aspect of this process.

"The amount of money that you have to raise in order to go on television corrupts the decisionmaking process in politics," said Bob Kerrey, who ran the Democratic Senate Campaign Committee in the late 1990s. I asked what he meant. "I'm not going to ask somebody for money who gets a minimum wage," Kerrey said.

So I ask somebody who is college educated whose income is over $250,000 a year—and then I have to say things like, "Why don't you get rid of the estate tax, why don't you lower the capital gains tax, why don't you make our tax system less progressive, blah-blah-blah." Same thing on corporations. There's nothing wrong with being presented with the corporate agenda of General Electric or General Motors, but you do have to understand it's unlikely that General Motors or General Electric are going to come and say, the problem is you're not spending enough on our workers. You're just not likely to get that agenda.

Then there's the corporate shakedown. The usual assumption about the evil of political money is that lawmakers are in effect being bribed to vote the way they vote. It doesn't work that way. "The more serious problem," said Norman Ornstein of the American Enterprise Institute, "is people in positions of influence in government shaking down donors, using the power of the state to engage in a protection racket." It happens on issue after issue; politicians make clear to the relevant industry groups that there's a certain ante to be heard. Usually the financial interests on either side of big commercial legislation—think banking or telecommunications or insurance—then fight themselves to a stalemate. Policy ends up being calculated to make sure legislators can keep the contributions coming the next time around. Membership on the committees that handle such legislation is viewed as a career boon because of the outsized fundraising prospects they offer.

Finally, at every level, the "money primary" determines which candidates will be heard at all. The most striking illustration came in the 2000 Republican presidential race, when in theory the field should have been wide open. A number of well-known and accomplished Republicans started down the road, including Elizabeth Dole, Lamar Alexander, John McCain, and Dan Quayle, as well as candidates such as Gary Bauer, John Kasich, John Ashcroft, and Pat Buchanan, whose appeals were narrower but still credible to important segments of GOP voters. By July 1999, seven months before the first primary vote in New Hampshire, George W. Bush had already raised $36.3 million, compared with $4.1 million for McCain, $3 million each for Dole and Quayle, and $2.2 million for Alexander. The big-name Republicans started dropping out left and right. By the time New Hampshire voted, McCain was the only serious rival left. Bush by that point had raised $72 million to McCain's $21 million. Then McCain, in a surprise, won New Hampshire by 10 points. But even a spike in the Arizona senator's fundraising afterward couldn't help him compete with the Bush financial juggernaut, which soon sank him.

The Tyranny of Charades

The upshot of the forces we've discussed—electoral parity, Democratic timidity, Republican indifference, media stenography, and the warping effect of campaign cash—is a debased political culture in which potential answers to our major domestic problems cannot find expression. Even if some factors shaping our leaders' calculations seem understandable in isolation, when you add them up we're left trapped in an elaborate charade. Since our leaders can't or won't talk about what it would take to make serious progress on health or schools or wages or campaign reform, they pretend they're serious as a way of communicating their good intentions and letting us know which "side" they're on. Every player in the system knows this is what is taking place, but no one lets on. The press knows it, too, but feels obliged to report it straight. Public life becomes a complex and mystifying con—not a search for solutions, but the pretense of a search for solutions as a means of jockeying for power.

Not only is this tyranny of charades corrosive for the political people caught up in it, it also subjects citizens to an endless stream of orchestrated hoaxes that sours them on public discussion altogether. The tools of modern political campaigns are deployed on behalf of every feud. Generally these "tools" involve spreading a fair amount of half-truths expensively across the nation in the hope they will stick and shape policy outcomes. Pharmaceutical lobbies, for example, fund ads featuring gray-haired actors who fret that Democratic plans to add prescription drugs to Medicare could kill biomedical research—a fear on which no struggling real-life senior has ever uttered a peep. Democrats scream that schools will be gutted by Republican budgets, a mathematical impossibility when federal spending accounts for barely 7 percent of overall education funding. The stakes in most debates are never this dramatic, but today's mode of argument requires a pledge of apocalypse, or paradise, now. The theory of politicians and consultants who shape these showdowns is that you have to be shrill to "break through the clutter." A subtler variant of this rationale is that with attention spans tiny and media time costly, advocates have no choice but to oversimplify in ways that signal their side's "values." Doubtless there is truth to this. But the cost in credibility is high. The ubiquity of preposterous claims helps explain why so many people tune out of public life.

If the landscape is littered with perversions of truth and logic that poison our political culture, a few core scams need to be repeatedly underlined on each side for their special toxicity. Take conservatives first. The cardinal Republican sin is the party's ceaseless drumbeat for deeper tax cuts—when Republican leaders know full well that the baby boomers' retirement can't be funded with today's expected revenues, that further long-term tax cuts only deepen that hole, and that marginal federal tax rates in today's range are simply not an impediment to robust growth (as the 1990s proved). Republicans cry that money is never the answer to social problems—though what else they expect poor workers to use to buy health care, or poor school districts to use to attract better teachers, remains a mystery. Republicans shout that government does little but waste money. Yet they know that *just seven programs make up 75 percent of federal spending: Social Security, Medicare, Medicaid, military pensions, civil service pensions, defense, and interest on the debt.* That's "big government." Republicans aren't trying to cut a dime of it. And that's before you toss in everything from NASA to the national parks to the National Institutes of Health, not to mention the FBI, the border patrol, student loans, and farm subsidies—all things Republicans support, and that take up a goodly portion of the quarter on the federal dollar that's left. Finally, Republicans pretend that only the private sector creates wealth—when they know that government investments in infrastructure, research and development, and education create the conditions that make wealth creation possible.

Democrats harbor their own deceptions. Liberals insist that only government can be trusted to provide services directly—when it's perfectly possible (and often preferable) for government to fund a service's availability without delivering the service itself. Liberals act as if mandates on business are costless ways to get desired social results—when such mandates impose costs and unintended consequences that nearly always end up borne by employees or consumers. Worst of all, Democrats are addicted to Social Security and Medicare demagoguery, assailing the GOP for plans to "privatize" America's most successful social programs. Yet on Social Security, for example, the most any GOP plan (usually offered in tandem with New Democrats) seeks to do is give workers a chance to put 2 percent of today's 12 percent Social Security payroll tax into accounts they control. There are pros and cons to such a scheme, but leaving Grandma eating cat food in the street isn't among them.

The clash of philosophies behind this bipartisan dissembling is profound, but the real stakes are different than the rhetorical smoke screen. This is best illustrated by the perennial war over "class warfare." Every time Republicans propose a big tax cut, a Washington ritual unfolds. Democrats produce a table showing to what extent Americans at various income levels stand to benefit. People earning a million a year stand to receive, say, $50,000 in tax relief; people making around $40,000 get five bucks a week. "How can Republicans push another big tax cut for their rich pals?" Democrats scream. "Class warfare!" the Republicans shout back.

Let's put aside labels for a moment and cut to the underlying question that explains this divide but that is never explicitly asked: *Is the distribution of income produced by the free market presumptively moral?*

People who say "yes" tend to believe there's a necessary connection between accepting markets as the best means of organizing economic life and accepting the results that markets produce as making moral sense. To see things differently, they argue, would be to deny that there is any moral bias in favor of markets in the first place—so why would we organize economic life around a free exchange among free people? On this view, market outcomes reward virtues and qualities that it is right to reward—such as work, responsibility, thrift, innovation, and risk-taking. You can reject markets, they say, but you can't accept them (as most Americans do) and then deny that their distributional results have some claim to being considered presumptively fair.

People who say "no" start from a different premise. Markets are a human construct, they say, with an infrastructure of property law, contract law, central banking, and myriad other mechanisms devised by the mind of man to serve human purposes and social goals. They also note that the distribution of income in free markets is affected dramatically by factors beyond the virtues cited above—such as a person's inherited brains, health, talents, wealth, and looks. These are things for which people can't take credit or be blamed. Given how heavily these factors influence the distribution of income and wealth, they argue, it makes no sense to think that market outcomes could be presumptively moral.

Now step back into the contemporary tax debate. If you're a "markets are presumptively moral" type, you're almost certainly in favor of President Bush's tax cuts. Government would simply be giving people their own money back, or "not taxing it twice." Opposition to such simple justice must be motivated by envy or resentment—that is, by "class warfare."

If you don't think markets are presumptively moral, you probably oppose Bush's tax plans. But when Warren Buffett, William Gates Sr., Peter Peterson, or Robert Rubin—all of whom would benefit hugely from President Bush's tax cuts—oppose them, it's not because they hate, resent, or envy "the rich." Rather, they oppose them because they don't think tax cuts mostly benefiting those already well-off should be a national priority.

The stakes are clearest on GOP calls to end the estate tax. It's easy to amend today's rules to make sure family farms, firms, and reasonable-sized bequests can be passed on. But is it right to eliminate the estate tax entirely for the few thousand extremely wealthy heirs who bear its brunt?

The answer depends on what you think politics should be about. It's easy to feel, as former Bush economic adviser Lawrence Lindsey told me, that when you've been taxed once when you earned the money, and again after you saved it, then seeing the feds swarm in for one last bite after you're dead takes matters too far. But that shouldn't end the debate. The more reasonable view sees politics as an endless series of moral trade-offs. The issue isn't some platonic ideal of tax policy. It's about asking, given where we are as a nation today, what the next set of public priorities ought to be. Over the last two decades the best-off Americans have thrived immeasurably. We should thus compare a $30 billion annual rebate for a handful of heirs (rising to $60 billion after 2011) with what that same sum could do for, say, America's 42 million uninsured, or poor children without preschool opportunities. In that context, making sure that a billionaire's kids will be able to divvy up the full billion, rather than have to scrape by with only $500 million or so, hardly seems pressing.

Conservatives feel otherwise. Their unstated premise is that there is indeed something presumptively moral—and therefore beyond legitimate question—about the distribution of income produced by the free market. It's a view that many (mostly well-off) people implicitly hold, though it's not clear that many have been asked to question the premise. As a matter of political strategy, the right's "class warfare" salvo is an attempt to delegitimize such a discussion and rule out policy trade-offs that explicitly weigh America's unmet social needs versus the moral status and claims of those seeking further tax relief.

Bob Shrum, the veteran Democratic consultant advising John Kerry's presidential campaign, knows as much. "I always take that class war critique," he told me, "as a desire on their part not to have us make that argument."

If Republicans want to delegitimize all talk of the distribution of income in public policy, Democrats want to scare people into embracing the succor that only a benevolent government can provide. As a result, both parties keep pressing on us a cartoon choice between "free markets" and "government" that insults our intelligence, when the question is always about striking the proper balance.

The curious thing is that each side in this standoff feels aggrieved, convinced that the other plays ruthlessly in ways they wouldn't stoop to match and weren't cut out for anyway. Republicans still nurse wounds from the 1987 destruction of the conservative Supreme Court nominee Robert Bork, an unforgivable liberal crime in their eyes. For Democrats—well, what more do you need to know, they cry, than the fact that the GOP went so far as to impeach a president for lying about sex! Clinton himself told a Democratic senate retreat in 2002 that if Al Gore had been in the White House after September 11, Tom Delay would have been on the floor of the House of Representatives every day marking off a giant calendar that said, "Day 256 that the failed Gore administration, despite the biggest military budget in the world's history, has failed to capture Osama bin Laden." "We're just not like them," Clinton told his colleagues, intimating that Democrats operated on a higher road. Conservatives shed similarly virtuous tears. Meanwhile, the frequent socializing across party lines that thirty years ago helped foster the empathy and friendship that made bipartisan cooperation easier has largely vanished. In its place is the deadly litigiousness of modern Washington, where small fortunes in legal fees are regularly borne by officials under dubious investigation from political rivals, a state of affairs that breeds new levels of bitterness that are hard to transcend or forget.

It's not always clear how we should judge our leaders amid this maddening mess. It's easy, on the one hand, to be outraged. "Look at the hypocrisy of the whole situation," Tom Donahue, the president of the U.S. Chamber of Commerce, told me. "Everybody is going to protect Social Security, everybody is going to protect the elderly, everybody's going to get health care, everybody's going to get get get, and they're all lying right through their teeth because . . . nobody is ready to step up and put a bill [for all this] on the table." On the other hand, what can individual officials do to turn a tide of disingenuousness that existed long before they took up their place on the public stage? This isn't to let them off easy, only to wrestle with what angle of vision seems fair. What should we have thought (to choose one among endless such examples) when Bill Clinton said he would subsidize the wages of mothers leaving welfare to encourage employers to hire them, but then offered a tiny fraction of the funding needed to give 4 million ill-equipped welfare moms a shot at permanent work? Should we have applauded the president for making a nod in the right direction? Or damned him for falling so far short of what was needed while pretending to deliver?

This tension between the incremental step that is achievable and bolder calls to alter the boundaries of what is possible is an enduring schism in public life. Our founding fathers designed a government of diffused powers whose natural tendency is gridlock. Politics has always to some extent involved choosing the caricature of reality that most closely approximates our values. But our predicament today is different and troubling in two ways.

First, our two major political parties are organized around ideologies and interest groups that systematically ban commonsense, well-funded policies that blend liberal and conservative ideas. Suppose, for example, you look at the uninsured and think money is the answer ("liberal"), but you also think government should basically give people who need it the money to buy private coverage themselves ("conservative")? What's your ideology? Suppose you see tens of thousands of low-paid, unqualified teachers in urban and rural classrooms and think money must be part of the answer ("liberal")—but you also think salary hikes should focus on the best teachers or those hardest to keep in the field ("conservative")? Which party do you join? Suppose, like most sensible souls, you think some rules and regulations are needed in this world ("liberal"), but not so much as to stifle innovation and growth ("conservative")? If you're drawn to any of these notions, you're simply too subtle a thinker for what the political establishment says can be safely processed or communicated, or for what well-funded interest groups will allow their hired hands to embrace. But then what? What do we do if most of us would, in fact, find such commonsense ideas appealing, and these ideas have the potential to move us forward, but our leaders won't talk about them for the reasons we've catalogued?

Many thoughtful politicians and officials privately believe there's little hope of changing today's tyranny of charades short of a galvanizing social explosion. The other possibility, they say, is that the American people become so frustrated that they "kick the bastards out" and start electing people willing to challenge the status quo. No one thinks either of these scenarios is likely anytime soon. Which brings us to the second way today's national dilemma is different: Time is not on our side.

3

THE CLOCK IS TICKING

In a bland office in downtown Los Angeles, a fortyish Filipino man blinks at his computer and hits "Enter." Dressed in a sports shirt and jeans, with an earpiece running to the portable radio at his side, Fred (not his real name) looks weirdly frozen from the neck up; below, however, his fingers race across the keys. His office is in the bowels of National Heritage Insurance Company, one of the major processors of Medicare claims in California, a few blocks from the Staples Center, where the Democratic Party convened in 2000 and announced its intent to spend a fresh $700 billion on the health program that serves 40 million seniors. That will mean more work for people like Fred. Fred's job is to correct some of the 29 million claims NHIC gets from doctors each year that have been imperfectly scanned into the system. He edits four claims per minute during his eight-hour shift, each review involving a mind-numbing sprint through a set of screens and prompts. Framed posters spur Fred and his colleagues to "Teamwork" and "Achievement" as the quotidian alchemy through which doctor bills turn into government checks proceeds. The room is hushed save for Fred's clackety-clack on the keys, but if you close your eyes, you hear the tapping rise from other clerks nearby, then blend with the echo from hundreds more on higher floors, until the mad rhythm of finger against keyboard surges in a frightening crescendo worthy of George Orwell, or at least Rod Serling.

This is the sound of your government at the dawn of the twenty-first century. If Eliot Ness was the G-man for the 1930s, and Neil Armstrong the emblem of the 1960s, then "Fred," and thousands like him, embody the millennial American state. Each year they process roughly 900 million Medicare claims and 500 million Social Security checks and goodness only knows how many other payments. Call it government by ATM—you walk up, hit the buttons, and the cash to which you're entitled pops out. Ask not what you can do for your country; ask what claims your country can process for you.

With little public understanding and no official objection, the "ATM-ization" of government has advanced dramatically over the last generation. In 1960, when Social Security was in its youth, and Medicare didn't exist, 70 percent of federal spending went for so-called "discretionary" items subject to yearly congressional review—things like roads, bridges, fighter planes, and FBI agents. Today the ratios have reversed: 70 percent of federal monies go instead for "mandatory" spending, transfer payments made automatically, via entitlement programs like Social Security, Medicare, and Medicaid, to citizens (mostly seniors) we've said are entitled to them.

Federal Reserve Board chairman Alan Greenspan likes to observe that the modern economy is "lighter" than it used to be, weighing less per dollar of gross domestic product, as software has become more essential than steel. It's the same with "new" government: Highways, dams, and research laboratories have lost their primacy as cold cash—for pensions, doctors, and hospitals—has taken over.

To date, of course, the results have been impressive: Social Security has nearly eradicated elderly poverty; Medicare has lifted the fear of medical bankruptcy from old age. But as the federal ATM gobbles up the budget, the costs are becoming clear. Bill Clinton came to office in 1992 pledging big spending boosts for infrastructure, education, and research and development. Yet such public investments, which dropped from 2.6 percent of GDP two decades ago to 1.9 percent by 1992, actually fell to 1.7 percent on Clinton's watch. George W. Bush has shown little interest in reversing the slide. The results aren't hard to detect: Has anyone seen many rail beds, national parks, or inner-city schools lately that *don't* look run down?

This lost decade of public investment could turn into a lost generation, because the government ATM is on the verge of an epic expansion. Once 76 million baby boomers begin to retire starting less than a decade from now, the costs of the big health and retirement programs will explode. The mere one in six federal dollars not devoted today to such "entitlements" or to the Pentagon is slated to shrivel further, slipping from a level that is already lower relative to the size of the economy than at any time since bean counters started tracking such things in 1962. Yet these functions are what most Americans tend to think of as "government": border cops, college loans, cancer researchers, air traffic controllers, the inspectors who make sure the food on the shelves won't poison us, the construction crews who expand highways increasingly gripped by gridlock.

The reality dawning as we look over the horizon is that virtually all of government spending has been pre-committed to the seniors-only ATM, leaving future voters effectively disenfranchised. This can't be acceptable. We need to tackle the challenges that accompany the aging of America now to avoid a showdown later. But it's equally urgent that we address our unfinished agenda for health care, schools, and the working poor, because if we don't make political and fiscal room for these concerns today, the boomer age wave will make it hard to carve out places for them down the road. Daunting as the aging challenge seems, there are sensible ways to address these questions, especially if we start sooner rather than later.

Since the fiscal collision ahead involves unpleasant choices, Washington has preferred to ignore it. Yet demography here really is destiny. Before this decade is out, the ATM juggernaut should therefore inspire the next great overhaul of American political philosophy. "We don't want to have a government that is consumed only with passing out money," said John Kasich, a Republican who chaired the House Budget Committee before leaving Congress in 2001, "and where all the discretionary programs, whether it's the National Institutes of Health or higher education, basically get eliminated. That's not an acceptable proposition."

It is, however, the current long-term plan.

Because elected officials tend to think in cycles of two, four, or six years, few have wrapped their minds around what happens when the boomers retire. That's scary, because aging boomers will reshape every corner of public life. A few facts suffice to paint the picture:

More retirees, fewer workers.   In 1960, there were five taxpaying workers for every retiree drawing benefits. Now there are three. By 2040 this will shrink toward nearly two. Seen another way, between 1990 and 2010, the workforce will have grown by 32 million, while the number of people on Social Security will have grown by 13 million. Between 2010 and 2030 this pattern reverses: The workforce will grow by 13 million, while the number of Social Security recipients will grow by 31 million.

Health and pension costs will soar.   Between 2000 and 2020, the combined costs of Social Security, Medicare, and Medicaid are slated to rise by 3.7 percent of GDP, from 7.6 percent to 11.3 percent. In today's dollars, that's like adding roughly $400 billion a year to a federal budget of $2.2 trillion. Then, in the decade that follows, from 2020 to 2030, the three programs are scheduled, without reforms, to rise *another* 2.5 percent of GDP.

The system is unsustainable.   In 2018, Social Security will start paying out more in benefits each year than the system collects via payroll taxes. Social Security will thus add to the overall budget deficit each year, rather than help reduce it, as it does today. These deficits will quickly rise. On our current path, moreover, if tax and spending policies are not reformed, five entitlement programs—Social Security, Medicare, Medicaid, military pensions, and civil service pensions—will take up all available revenue by 2030, leaving not a penny for anything else.

The nation has not prepared.   If government accounted for future benefit commitments as businesses must, these programs would show $25 trillion in unfunded liabilities. That means $25 trillion in promised benefits for which no money has been set aside. The pledge to honor them amounts to a promise to raise taxes on our children. If payroll taxes were raised to meet these costs, they would have to roughly double to 32 percent in 2030, an unthinkable and economically devastating burden. This won't happen, of course: Its obvious insanity means that long before then we'll have to rethink how these benefits are designed and financed.

These problems will be considerably worse in other advanced nations. The same forces are at work, only more so: People are living longer, having fewer children, and enjoying the benefits of costly new health technologies. As a result, publicly funded pension and health costs in other wealthy nations are set to rise from 9 percent of GDP today toward 16 percent by 2030. By 2030 the developed world will gain nearly 100 million elders, while the number of working-age adults will shrink by 34 million. Many advanced countries will experience serious population declines: Japan, for example, will shrink from 126 million in 1998 to 105 million by 2020; Italy from 57 million to 41 million; Spain from 39 million to 30 million.

The social and economic implications are profound. As the blue-ribbon Commission on Global Aging of the Center for Strategic and International Studies found, shrinking populations will mean labor shortages in every industrial country, as well as smaller product markets in Europe and Japan. This could slow economic growth in the developed world at the very moment the baby boomers are retiring expensively. Such trends raise the prospect of deficit spending on a scale that could consume all world savings (as advanced nations borrow abroad to fund retiree benefits), and thus skew global investment patterns.

In one sense, to be sure, these are good problems to have: We're living longer, and, thanks to medical innovations, enjoying a quality of life into old age that was once unthinkable. But if the United States is better positioned than some others, we're still in a situation that is not financially sustainable. It's not that the situation isn't solvable—it plainly is. But there are no easy answers: We'll have to raise taxes, trim projected benefits, or some combination. Beyond these inevitable realities, our overriding goal should be to boost economic growth. The bigger we can make the overall pie out of which the boomers' golden years will be funded, the better off we'll be.

One hopeful note is that the politics of these issues are slowly changing. Social Security has traditionally been known as "the third rail" of American politics—as in "touch it and you die." But George W. Bush campaigned in 2000 explicitly on the need to reform Social Security, and in 2002, Republicans Elizabeth Dole of North Carolina, Lindsey Graham of South Carolina, and John Sununu of New Hampshire won Senate seats despite fierce Social Security attacks from their Democratic rivals. Still, by any absolute standard the debate remains deeply dishonest. Social Security demagoguery remains the Democrats' political club of choice. Republicans, even when laudably talking about the need for reform, deceive voters about the enormous costs of transitioning to their preferred system of partial private accounts. Meanwhile, no one is talking seriously about how to address the problems of long-term health costs, which will make Social Security's woes look tiny by comparison.

Complicating our politicians' aversion to unpleasant choices is the outsized political power of senior citizens. The AARP is already the 800-pound gorilla of American politics. It will become even more formidable as its ranks swell from today's 35 million members toward 50 million over the next decade. This organized lobbying clout is matched by seniors' disproportionate electoral influence. Roughly 68 percent of seniors vote in presidential elections, compared to 30 percent of voters aged 18–24 and 40 percent of those aged 25–34. In midterm elections the senior presence is even more lopsided: 60 percent of seniors vote in off-year contests, versus 12 percent of those aged 18–24 and 24 percent of voters aged 25–34. If you wonder why adding prescription drugs to Medicare is among the few subjects our leaders debate seriously, the answer is in these numbers. And even the numbers can't capture the full texture of senior activism. Senator Ron Wyden of Oregon told me that not long ago, after CNN aired a report about a new medical device, Oregon seniors were ringing the phone off the hook in his office two hours later demanding that the new device be covered by Medicare.

The cumulative impact of these trends is an irony that liberals in particular need to appreciate. Before long, when it comes to funding unmet social needs, the enemy of the left will not be the heirs of Newt Gingrich; it will be Medicare. Every extra dollar spent on Medicare—especially every dollar that is unnecessary for quality health care—will be a dollar that can't be spent on a poor child. This is the true threat of government-by-ATM. Cries that the coming explosion of health and pension programs would saddle workers with tax hikes that sink their standard of living became popular a few years ago, along with the inevitable backlash against such "whining" by the post-boomers in "Generation X." But the real risks are subtler. While few experts would deny that the boomers' golden years will place a burden on the young, most also say that economic growth will leave incomes higher than they are today. The richest nation on earth can plainly afford the baby boom's retirement. The thornier question is this: Will America be wise enough to do so while leaving room for government to spend money on anything else that middle-aged and younger voters believe is needed? If taxpayers seem tuned out now, wait until they wake up in 2015 to find they have no say in naming their government's priorities.

The prospect that elderly entitlements will crowd out all other public purposes makes the next decade crucial for gaining consensus on how to meet these challenges. Unfortunately, we've suffered from a national blind spot. The exclusive terms of reference when the boomers' retirement is discussed is, "How do we get Social Security and Medicare ready?" This question is obviously important. But it's equally important to acknowledge that there is little time before the crunch hits to address priorities *outside* of health care and pensions for seniors—and to figure out how to make attention to those matters sustainable as well. Yet with eyes on near-term battles, there's either complacency or denial about these long-term challenges. Liberals prefer to pray: The dire forecasts somehow won't be borne out, they tell themselves, and if they are, we'll raise taxes (and/or deficits) high enough to fund the welfare state we need. Conservatives are glad to gloat: The ATM is set to grind down activist government in ways that a thousand Ronald Reagan speeches never could.

The strains and adjustments are harder for the side of the debate that wants government to play an affirmative role. The best example may be the left's torment over the notion of "means-testing," or targeting government programs toward those in need. If programs don't need to be universal, we could plainly save lots of money for other purposes, savings that will be more important than ever in the coming crunch. And with over $200 billion a year in federal benefits going to Americans with incomes over $50,000, such targeting seems a fit with Democratic principles of equity.

Yet "means-testing" faces fierce opposition from most liberals. Their argument runs as follows. First, we already means-test programs to some extent, both through progressive benefit formulas (like Social Security's) and by treating most benefits as taxable income. Looking ahead, they say, the universal nature of programs like Social Security and Medicare, into which everyone pays and knows they'll get out what they're supposed to, is precisely what assures their political viability. Alter this by explicitly scaling back benefits for well-off Americans and you'll stigmatize these programs as "welfare." Wealthier Americans will decide there's nothing in it for them, and will vote to opt out of the system. Before long, the whole notion of social insurance, and the transfers to needier citizens that take place within it, will erode. "Bribing" better off citizens to maintain their support, the argument goes, is a reasonable price to pay for the social good these programs bring.

This political logic affects countless spending issues. In schools, for example, "Title I" money for poor children is sprinkled liberally to districts that aren't poor, making a mockery of the law's aims, but honoring a political imperative to maintain broad congressional support. Or consider the recent rage to shrink class sizes in early grades. Research shows that smaller class sizes deliver measurable learning benefits only in the poorest communities. But politics requires lower class sizes to be offered to all communities, ballooning by billions the costs of such efforts and assuring that most of the cash has little impact. Worse, such moves have had perverse unintended consequences, creating so many new teaching slots in suburbs that top urban teachers have found it easier to escape (leaving the neediest children in worse straits). This is the tragic result of our political system's inability to target resources to need. I'm not saying that this is easy to alter, but as these examples show, few changes in our political culture would accomplish as much.

Such trade-offs, already difficult, will soon have higher stakes. The fiscal collision starting a decade hence will confront every advanced nation with a fateful choice. The slower growth rates and higher public spending that come with older populations will threaten some government safety nets with collapse. Though the dimensions of the challenge will depend on each nation's demographics and the generosity of their programs, all will face a classic problem of political economy. When increased efficiency in market economies creates "losers" amid plenty, there's a case for a strong safety net that redistributes a portion of the economy's overall gains to ease the misfortune of those left behind (and those unable to work). Such safety nets are critical to maintaining a political consensus for the free trade and technological advances that in the long run benefit us all. But, as we've seen, targeted subsidies to an economy's "losers" tend to be politically fragile. Keeping robust safety nets universal, however, will be vastly more expensive with an older population than it is today, potentially requiring taxes and regulations so burdensome they cripple economic growth. How does a society committed to growth with equity strike the right balance? Is there a way to create a consensus for a lower tax model (thus gaining the benefits of growth and efficiency) without leaving the unskilled and unlucky to fend for themselves?

For Americans not content with either liberal denial or conservative indifference, this will be the defining question of political economy for the next generation. If you think there's a limit to how high taxes can and should be raised, but you also want government to serve worthy purposes beyond the ATM scenario, then the macro challenge of public life is to negotiate a new balance between old age entitlements and nonelderly priorities.

This coming showdown between our traditional commitments and their rising costs will force a rethinking of how government works. This is the opportunity. Resolving this tension in ways that honor progressive values will require the commonsense synthesis of liberal and conservative thinking that our politics has heretofore resisted. In the 1980s and 1990s we heard a lot about the need to move "beyond left and right," which was articulated by groups such as the Democratic Leadership Council and championed so successfully by Bill Clinton that it swept the Western democracies. This effort, called the "Third Way" by its proponents, redefined the political center. Yet because of the deficits Clinton inherited, the Republican Congress that his health care fiasco wrought, and his second-term scandals, Clinton was never able to translate his rhetoric into a more fundamental reshaping of government's major functions. Thanks as well to the left's reluctance to call for more spending, the Third Way has been implemented more via symbolic efforts than by deeper reforms. This has sufficed for the last decade because, indispensably, the Third Way offered a potent language for repositioning the left and winning elections—an effort so successful that George W. Bush adopted its playbook. We are all, at least rhetorically, Third Way-ers now.

Yet a new moment is upon us. Though few leaders today realize it, the inexorable math of federal spending leaves farsighted patriots— liberals who see what the coming crunch means for the causes they cherish, and conservatives who are "compassionate" in deed as well as name—little choice but to finish the ideological renovation that Clinton began and that Bush has rhetorically endorsed. The goal is to marry market-based flexibility with serious commitments to equal opportunity and a minimally decent life. The means will entail some version of a fully funded Third Way, a set of well-funded policies that harness market forces for public purposes. The alternative is to see traditional American concerns for the disadvantaged crushed in the fiscal stampede of all-powerful seniors.

The stakes are high. Today, the United States' economy remains an advertisement for the superiority of modestly regulated capitalism; yet if we don't prepare now to hold our social fabric together once crunch time comes, other nations may recoil at our social havoc and turn to less welcome alternatives. For the sake of our national community, as well as for the model of civilized freedom we offer the world, the choices we make—or fail to make—in the next decade matter profoundly.

Clearly we could use a little luck to see us through. And it turns out that the very idea of Luck—and an appreciation of what luck's dominion in human affairs ought to mean for public policy—holds the beginning of the answer.

PART TWO

The Two Percent Solution

4

TAKING LUCK
SERIOUSLY

Let's recap our story so far. We're not serious about fixing our biggest domestic problems. Both political parties offer make-believe answers on everything from health to schools to wages to campaigns. There are reasons that explain this state of affairs. Parity between the political parties breeds an unambitious "game of inches." Democrats fear being cast as "tax and spend" and "weak on defense." Republicans display a complex yet enduring indifference to the disadvantaged, at least when it comes to solutions longer on cash than "compassion." The national press sees its role as mirroring (and not challenging) the boundaries of debate offered by the two parties. Campaigns are financed in ways that put certain policies and candidates out of bounds. The result is that American public life amounts to a tyranny of charades, in which symbolic appeals are ubiquitous, voters tune out, and a "solutions gap" reigns. At the same time, the boomers' costly retirement is closing in, meaning the time left to address major unmet social needs is short. We're poised for a collision between traditional commitments, these unmet needs, and stark new fiscal realities for which we haven't begun to prepare, a collision whose inexorable math will force us to rethink and renegotiate our nation's social contract.

Now then: If this is where we are, where should we go? Since we're destined to have to revisit our social contract in any event, we may as well organize the effort around some first principles. Ordinarily this would mean an appeal to such notions as liberty, equality, and justice, but I want to work toward these ideas via something that's more of a phenomenon than a principle, a phenomenon that's not sufficiently appreciated in day-to-day political discourse: luck. My proposition is that if we took luck seriously we'd be on our way to the commonsense consensus needed to make progress on our fixable injustices.

Since this is sure to strike some readers as an unusual claim, let's start by being clear on what I mean by "luck." For our purposes, luck is the shorthand that describes those things that shape our lives that are entirely outside our control. We're talking mostly about the pre-birth lottery, those aspects of a person's existence dictated by the womb from which he or she happens to emerge: a person's inherited genes, race, wealth, looks, brains, and talents; the values and character of the family in which a person grows up; the education that comes (or doesn't come) in this package. There are certain social norms this notion of luck encompasses as well; if you're born black in America, for example, you'll likely face obstacles that white children don't. All of these factors are outside our control. We can't take credit or be blamed for them. What we make of the hand we're dealt in life is another matter, but our aim for now is to focus on the reach of this initial luck.

To be clear, then, we are not talking about luck in the sense of serendipity, of being in the right place at the right time or vice versa—though this brand of luck, and the way man lives at its mercy, has captured the literary and philosophical imagination from the dawn of time. The Greeks worshipped the goddess Fortuna. Niccolò Machiavelli, in *The Prince,* written in 1513, assigned half of what happens in this world to the mysterious power of Fortuna, with her force tamed only in part by prudent action and planning. Then there's the matter of how we all got here. "You find yourself in this world only through an infinity of accidents," wrote Blaise Pascal, the seventeenth-century French mathematician and philosopher. "Your birth is due to a marriage, or rather a series of marriages of those who have gone before you. But those marriages were often the result of a chance meeting, or words uttered at random, of a hundred unforeseen and unintended occurrences."

Pervasive as life's general randomness is, we'll focus here on what luck, in the pre-birth lottery sense I've stressed, should mean for public policy. Its ubiquity has prompted a fierce debate between rival visions of what luck should mean for justice. Is it feasible or desirable to take steps to redress bad luck, and if so, how far should (and can) society go? The problem with luck from the point of view of justice is that it severs any link between fate and desert—between what actually happens to people and what they seem to "deserve." This disconnect can never be eliminated entirely: that's what a world with luck involves. But the question of whether and how society should respond to luck's influence has been a bedrock dividing line both in the moral outlooks of individuals and in rival political philosophies. Conservatives, worried that an honest admission of luck's role would sanction radical, economy-killing egalitarianism, have always ended up downplaying or ignoring luck. Liberals, while deeply concerned with luck, have typically been unwilling to craft efforts to ease the burden of bad luck in ways that preserve the best of capitalist innovation and the virtues of individual responsibility.

My argument is that a more serious regard for luck's dominion can be integrated into modern capitalism, and that it can command broad consensus if the debate is framed first around this fundamental question, before we translate such concerns into specific (and invariably controversial) choices about taxing and spending. Try too hard to wipe out the inequities spawned by luck and you banish luck's social benefits and go the road of communism. Harness a healthy and balanced awe for luck, however, and you expand the bounds of empathy in ways that make universal health coverage and great schools for poor children a national imperative. What we're led to, I'll argue, is the agenda missing from public debate today, an agenda built around passionate commitments to equal opportunity and to a minimally decent life, achieved in ways that harness market forces for public purposes. This is what our Two Percent Solution will be about. And the path to consensus on it begins when our leaders, and each of us as citizens, agree to take luck seriously.

Friedman's Blind Spot

The relevance of framing the challenge this way can be illustrated by contrasting the role luck plays in the political economy of two of the twentieth century's most influential thinkers: the economist Milton Friedman and the philosopher John Rawls.

Milton Friedman was born in 1912 and grew up in Rahway, New Jersey, the son of Hungarian Jewish immigrants. His mother ran a small dry goods store; his father engaged in what Friedman called "a succession of mostly unsuccessful 'jobbing' ventures." In the biographical sketch he supplied upon receiving the Nobel Prize in economics in 1976, Friedman said that his family's income "was small and highly uncertain; financial crisis was a constant companion." His father died while Milton was a senior in high school, leaving his mother and sisters to support the family. Friedman went to Rutgers University on a partial scholarship, planning to major in mathematics and become an actuary. But after failing several actuarial exams, he grew increasingly interested in economics. Friedman found a mentor in Arthur Burns, who was teaching at Rutgers while getting his doctorate at Columbia. (Burns would later serve as chairman of the Federal Reserve Board under Richard Nixon.) Burns helped him get a scholarship to do graduate work at the University of Chicago, and Friedman was on his way. While he earned his Nobel for technical achievements in consumption analysis, monetary history and theory, and stabilization policy, Friedman's popular writings established him as one of the twentieth century's most formidable apostles of liberty and free-market economics.

Luck, and its implications for political economy and ethics, was on Friedman's mind from early in his career. In 1953 Friedman published a paper titled "Chance, Choice and the Distribution of Income," in the *Journal of Political Economy*. In nearly impenetrable mathematical logic, Friedman set out to show something that seemed relatively straightforward: that inequality of income comes not merely from chance, but also from the choices, tastes, and preferences of individuals. People who have a taste for working less, for example, and for spending more time basking in the sun, earn less. They therefore contribute to inequality of income by choice. Friedman stressed his conclusion:

One cannot rule out the possibility that a large part of the existing inequality of wealth can be regarded as produced by men to satisfy their
tastes and preferences . . . the link between differences in natural endowment or inherited wealth and the realized distribution of income is
less direct and simple than is generally supposed . . . [this analysis] has
implications for normative judgments about the distribution of income
and the arrangements producing it—inequalities resulting from delib-
erate decisions . . . clearly raise very different normative issues than do
inequalities imposed on individuals from the outside.

Friedman wanted very much to prove—and mathematically, at that!—
that luck isn't as important in human affairs as we instinctively presume. Why was he at pains to do this? Friedman doesn't say so
explicitly, but his anxiety seems plain: If luck *is* as important as we in-
tuit, then that means we probably *ought* to do more as a society to redress the burden of bad luck. For a lover of freedom and free markets,
to concede that premise is tantamount to letting all hell break loose.

Yet luck nags at Friedman: His popular books take up the matter as
well. Every time he nears the heart of what luck might signify, however, Friedman uncharacteristically dances around it or serves up non
sequiturs. When one of the towering minds of our time has trouble
dealing straight up with a concept, it's revealing.

Take *Capitalism and Freedom,* Friedman's now-classic 1962 collection
of essays, which has sold more than 500,000 copies and inspired several generations of conservatives. Though it's heresy for a liberal to
say so, it's a wonderful book, filled with Friedman's principled reasoning, frequent insights, and impressive refusal to bend to fashion or
pragmatism. Friedman would rather be right than see some halfway
reform enacted; he insisted on the value of laying out a purer vision to
guide what might one day become politically possible. That the world
has moved a long way toward his philosophy over the last forty years
(witness the Reagan and Thatcher "revolutions" he helped spawn, or
how ideas like school vouchers and Social Security privatization are
part of mainstream debate) shows the power of his persistence.

Friedman arrives at luck in his chapter on the distribution of income. Much of the inequality of income we see, he says, reflects what

he calls "equalizing differences" (for example, the fact that dangerous work is paid more) or "the satisfaction of men's tastes," a nod to his 1953 paper. Yet "a large part reflects initial differences in endowment, both of human capacities and of property," he writes. This is the part that is luck. "This is the part that raises the really difficult ethical issues," Friedman says.

But his treatment of them is unsatisfying. First, Friedman notes that many people urge a distinction between inequalities in personal endowments and in property, and between inherited wealth and acquired wealth. "Inequality resulting from differences in personal capacities, or from differences in wealth accumulated by the individual in question, are considered appropriate," he says, "or at least not so clearly inappropriate as differences resulting from inherited wealth." This distinction is untenable, he says. "Is there any greater ethical justification for the high returns to the individual who inherits from his parents a peculiar voice for which there is a great demand than for the high returns to the individual who inherits property?"

Consider, Friedman says by way of illustration, three different ways a well-off parent might assist his child. He might finance his training in a lucrative profession; set him up in business; or set up a trust fund. Each of these methods will produce higher income for the child than he otherwise would enjoy. The first would come from "human capacities," the second from profits, the third from inherited wealth. Friedman asks, "Is there any basis for distinguishing among these categories of receipts on ethical grounds?"

Perhaps not, but the fact that these situations don't seem ethically distinguishable brings us to the cusp of the deeper question of how society should respond to *all* those instances where luck yields big winners and losers. Yet Friedman stops short of this, and turns instead to other examples "to illustrate the fundamental difficulty," by which he seems to mean the difficulty of dealing with a messy thing like luck at all, especially if it means infringing on freedom. Three friends and you are walking on the street, Friedman says, and you find a $20 bill on the pavement. It would be generous of you to divide it with them or at least "blow them to a drink." But suppose you don't? Would the other three be justified, Friedman asks, in joining forces and compelling you to share the $20 equally with them? Friedman thinks most of us would say no. The analogy to redistributive taxation is clear.

> Can we justify being judges in our own case, deciding on our own when we are entitled to use force to extract what we regard as our due from others? Or what we regard as not their due? *Most differences of status or position or wealth can be regarded as the product of chance at a far enough remove.* (emphasis added)

In this moment Friedman is getting to the heart of things. The role of luck, Friedman acknowledges, is indeed pervasive. But in the next breath, Friedman dances away again.

> Despite the lip service that we all pay to "merit" as compared to "chance," we are generally much readier to accept inequalities arising from chance than those clearly attributable to merit. The college professor whose colleague wins a sweepstake will envy him but is unlikely to bear him any malice or to feel unjustly treated. Let the colleague receive a trivial raise that makes his salary higher than the professor's own, and the professor is far more likely to feel aggrieved. After all, the goddess of chance, as of justice, is blind. The salary raise was a deliberate judgment of relative merit.

And there Friedman leaves the matter. But so what? The fact that we may be more inclined to tolerate chance-based wealth or income differences when a lottery is voluntarily entered into has nothing to do with luck-based disparities that result from a pre-birth lottery for which no one signs up. Friedman returns often to this notion of a voluntary game of chance (and the inequality that results) to illustrate the virtues of a system under which people make their own decisions and bear the consequences. It's a system, he argues, that gave the Henry Fords and the Thomas Edisons the incentive to transform society for the better, as well as the ability to attract the capital that financed risky, ambitious ventures that ultimately served us all. All this is true—but it sidesteps the question of whether there are acceptable ways to respond to the *involuntary* aspects of luck's pervasiveness without undermining these strengths of capitalism. Friedman, in other words, doesn't know quite what to do with luck. He knows it's everywhere; he knows it has to be reckoned with; but he doesn't want to think about it if it means limiting freedom, especially the freedom of lucky people to benefit fully from their own luck.

Free to Choose, the 1980 bestseller popularizing his ideas that Friedman coauthored with his wife, Rose, who is also an economist, exhibits the same intriguing blind spot. "Life is not fair," the Friedmans write at one point. "It is tempting to believe that government can rectify what nature has spawned. But it is also important to recognize how much we benefit from the very unfairness we deplore."

> There's nothing fair about Marlene Dietrich's having been born with beautiful legs that we all want to look at; or about Muhammad Ali's having been born with the skill that made him a great fighter. But on the other side, millions of people who have enjoyed looking at Marlene Dietrich's legs or watching one of Muhammad Ali's fights have benefited from nature's unfairness in producing a Marlene Dietrich and a Muhammad Ali. . . . It is certainly not fair that Muhammad Ali should be able to earn millions of dollars in one night. But wouldn't it have been even more unfair to the people who enjoyed watching him if, in the pursuit of some abstract ideal of equality, Muhammad Ali had not been permitted to earn more for one night's fight—or for each day spent in preparing for a fight—than the lowest man on the totem pole could get for a day's unskilled work on the docks?

But of course no one is proposing this kind of leveling. Even liberals like sports and legs. The only subversive question a liberal might ask is what marginal tax rate it is appropriate for the luckiest to bear as part of a national effort to fund certain minimal commitments for those who are less fortunate.

As these examples highlight, the recurring flaw in Friedman's logic is to suggest that the fairness concerns raised by luck can be accommodated only by an incentive-deadening "equality of outcome" that would kill capitalism's virtues and set us, as the economist Friedrich Hayek famously put it, on "the road to serfdom." This is a false choice. Still, liberals shouldn't judge Friedman harshly. His repeated invocation of the specter of "socialists" and "egalitarians" has an antique ring today, but it was perfectly justified when Friedman developed his philosophy. Friedman began his crusade in an era when communism was deemed a viable model by many on the left, at a time when top marginal income tax rates were set at insanely high and incentive-killing levels of 70 to 90 percent. Passionate opposition was necessary. If his ability to take luck seriously was a casualty, it was because the ghosts Friedman and others saw were real, and opening the door to limits on liberty that honored the role of luck doubtless seemed a third-order luxury amid a more fundamental clash of ideas and regimes.

From today's perspective, however, Friedman and his intellectual heirs ignore ways to remedy some of what "nature has spawned" without killing capitalism's incentives. This pinched vision is not new; John Maynard Keynes recognized it as far back as 1926: "Devotees of capitalism are often unduly conservative," Keynes wrote, "and reject reforms in its technique, which might really strengthen and preserve it, for fear that they may prove to be first steps away from Capitalism itself." Friedman, along with Ayn Rand and Hayek, remains among the first heady influences a young conservative imbibes. Given this fact, and how impoverished our debate is today, it's a pity Friedman hasn't been updated by like-minded thinkers who came of age well after a taste for communism and 70 percent marginal tax rates had been excised from the American left's lexicon. Friedman's voice helped win those seminal battles on behalf of liberty and economic rationality. But when it comes to luck, today he's swinging at a straw man.

Lucky Jack Rawls

While communism's economic failures and monstrous cruelties eventually consigned it to history's dustbin, an important nail in its intellectual coffin came from the work of a philosopher named John Rawls. Before Rawls, who died in 2002 at the age of 81, Marxism had always served as the (inadequate) foil to the classical economic liberalism propounded by the Milton Friedmans of the world (in a confusing turn of language, this has come to be known as "conservative" economic thinking in the United States). Classical liberals cherished the freedom of individuals to maximize their opportunities, however those opportunities happened to have been showered on them. Marxists replied, how can you stress freedom when there's a fundamental structure of society that generates social classes that unjustly constrain people's entire lives? One group talked about class justice and the other talked about individual freedom.

Rawls came along and split the difference. The happenstance of being born in Scarsdale or the South Bronx creates starkly different life expectations, Rawls stressed, a circumstance for which the individual deserves neither credit nor blame. Rawls and his heirs said we have an obligation to make this basic structure of society as just as it can be, an obligation that must be met before we can fairly give individual liberty full reign. At the 30,000-foot level of political philosophy, Rawls thus represents a "Third Way" between Marx and Friedman that invisibly underpins the Third Way evolving even now in practical politics.

Just as Friedman's rise from humble beginnings surely helps explain his individualism, Rawls' background seemed suited to the philosophy he came to espouse. John Rawls was born in Baltimore in 1921. His father was a successful tax lawyer; his mother a feminist and president of the local League of Women Voters. When "Jack," as he was known to everyone, was seven and then nine years old, two of his younger brothers died, of diphtheria and pneumonia, after contracting the diseases from Jack. These deaths were a tremendous blow. Rawls' mother thought they triggered his stammer, which remained a serious though gradually receding handicap for him after that time. Thomas Hogge, a former student and close friend of Rawls who teaches philosophy at Columbia University, believed Rawls' childhood experiences deepened "his lifelong feeling of having been terribly lucky. He had survived the diseases that killed two of his brothers and enjoyed great undeserved privileges of affluence and education."

Rawls was educated mostly at private schools, summered at the family home in Maine, and later went off to Princeton. He served in

World War II as an infantryman in the Pacific (and emerged, luckily, without a scratch). After receiving his doctorate in philosophy at Princeton, and teaching at Cornell and the Massachusetts Institute of Technology, Rawls was invited to join Harvard's faculty in 1961. There his major professional preoccupation—How is it possible for a social order to be just?—found its expression in *A Theory of Justice,* a book he spent a decade writing.

On the road to publication, Rawls again got lucky. He spent the 1969–1970 academic year at Stanford's Center for Advanced Study to finish the book. These were the days before word processors, and so his secretary typed and amended the version of the book he'd arrived with from Cambridge. One day in April, student radicals bombed the offices where he worked. Rawls had left his single copy of the current version on his desk there; the only other copy was the version he'd arrived with eight months earlier. The center's director woke Rawls at 6 A.M. with news of the explosions, telling Rawls, "You have been wiped out." Eight months of irretrievable labor seemed lost. But fortune had smiled on Rawls; his office had not been burnt, it turned out, only flooded. His manuscript was soaked but legible. He dried it out and plodded on.

A Theory of Justice was published in 1971. The book was immediately recognized in the profession and by the serious press as a landmark. It has sold a quarter million copies in English, has been translated into two dozen languages, and is widely credited with being the most important work of political philosophy of our time. It spawned a cottage industry of subsequent commentary and analysis that continues three decades later, and has influenced reform-minded leaders across the globe.

It's impossible to do full justice here to the book's 500 densely reasoned pages, but the kernel at the heart of Rawls' thinking is simple and compelling. The way to create the rules for a just society, Rawls argues, is to first imagine everyone in an "original position" behind a pre-birth "veil of ignorance," where no one knows what their own traits will be—whether they will be rich or poor, beautiful or plain, smart or less so, talented or not, healthy or unwell. Then you'd see what kind of social order people would agree in advance was fair if they couldn't know what place they themselves were destined to occupy in it.

Rawls uses this thought experiment to focus our thinking on the central role he sees luck playing in life. There's the pre-birth lottery that hands out brains, beauty, talent, and inherited wealth. There's a post-birth lottery that (via family) bequeaths values and schooling. "The institutions of society favor certain starting places over others," Rawls writes. "These are especially deep inequalities. Not only are they pervasive, but they affect men's initial chances in life; yet they cannot possibly be justified by an appeal to the notions of merit or desert."

Rawls argues that in this original position people would agree on two basic principles to structure society. The first would be equality in the assignment of basic rights and duties. The second would be to arrange social and economic inequalities so that "they are both (a) to the greatest benefit of the least advantaged, and (b) attached to offices and positions open to all under conditions of fair equality of opportunity."

Rawls' first principle is straightforward, but it is the second—what Rawls dubs the "difference principle"—that for our purposes is so interesting. Rawls is saying that the vast inequalities of wealth and position we observe stem primarily from advantages for which people can't take credit; this is his idea that "no one deserves his starting place." Behind a pre-birth veil of ignorance, therefore, Rawls suggests that we would agree these inequalities are just only if they most benefit those who end up not winning the pre-birth lottery, and if the top spots in life are open to everyone in a system where we've made a serious effort to equalize opportunity.

These two principles seem to be a fair basis on which those better endowed, or more fortunate in their social position, neither of which we can be said to deserve, could expect the willing cooperation of others when some workable scheme is a necessary condition of the welfare of all. Once we decide to look to a conception of justice that prevents the use of the accidents of natural endowment and the contingencies of social circumstance as counters in a quest for political and economic advantage, we are led to these principles. They express the result of leaving aside those aspects of the social world that seem arbitrary from a moral point of view.

"Injustice," Rawls adds, "is simply inequalities that are not to the benefit of all."

This is vague, of course, and Rawls spends hundreds of pages teasing out the implications. Most pertinent for our discussion is the fact that Rawls says there are several ways to structure society that honor his principles, one of which (though Rawls doesn't identify it this way) represents Milton Friedman's ideal. As we've seen, Friedman argues that the free-market capitalism he champions will over time deliver the greatest good for the greatest number; he also argues that the advances secured by entrepreneurial capitalism have most helped the least advantaged, as Rawls requires. Thanks to the technological advances made possible by free enterprise, after all, today's American poor—with indoor plumbing, cable TV, and potable water, among other things—live better than royalty lived a century or two ago. Friedman also calls for careers "open to talent" (that is, not marred by discrimination), so that those who begin life humbly, as Friedman did himself, are able to rise as far as their ability and effort can carry them. In Friedman's view, the distribution of wealth, income, authority, and responsibility that results from a free-market system open to talent is, by definition, just.

Rawls considers this position, and disagrees. But importantly (and unlike some advocates on the left), Rawls understands economics, and so his critique comes from the vantage point of honoring Friedman's best arguments. At one point, for example, Rawls notes that "better prospects [for entrepreneurs and others with advantages] act as incentives so that the economic process is more efficient, innovation proceeds at a faster pace, and so on." Friedman couldn't have asked for more. But efficiency, to Rawls, is not enough.

Let us suppose that we know from economic theory that under the standard assumptions defining a competitive market economy, income and wealth will be distributed in an efficient way, and that the particular efficient distribution which results in any period of time is determined by the initial distribution of assets, that is, by the initial distribution of income and wealth, and of natural talents and abilities. With each initial distribution, a definite efficient outcome is arrived at. *Thus it turns out that if we are to accept the outcome as just, and not merely as efficient, we must accept the basis upon which over time the initial distribution of assets is determined.* (emphasis added)

But there's the rub, says Rawls. The existing distribution "is the cumulative effect of prior distributions of natural assets—that is, natural talents and abilities—as these have been developed or left unrealized, and their use favored or disfavored over time by social circumstances and such chance contingencies as accident and good fortune." In other words, Friedman's approach is insufficient because it still lets power and wealth be determined disproportionately by "the natural lottery," an outcome that remains "morally arbitrary." A society that lets its poor but brainy Milton Friedmans rise to their place in an aristocracy of talent may have done well, according to Rawls— but if that society hasn't also made serious efforts to give opportunities to those who didn't come into the world with outsized brains, it hasn't done enough. Put in terms we've been using, only a system that *takes luck seriously,* and therefore strives to equalize opportunity, can hope to be both just and efficient.

As Rawls puts it, "the natural distribution [of advantages] is neither just nor unjust; nor is it unjust that persons are born into society at some particular position. These are simply natural facts. What is just and unjust is the way that institutions deal with these facts." For Rawls, the question of initial advantages extends beyond native endowments to character. "That we deserve the superior character that enables us to make the effort to cultivate our ability is also problematic," he writes, "for such character depends in good part upon fortunate family and social circumstances in early life for which we can claim no credit." "Undeserved inequalities call for redress," Rawls concludes, "and since inequalities of [inherited] wealth and natural endowment are undeserved, these inequalities are to be somehow compensated for . . . to provide genuine equality of opportunity."

What does that "compensation" amount to in practice? It's a fairly short agenda. To Rawls, fair equality of opportunity primarily means that "the government tries to insure equal chances of education and culture for persons similarly endowed and motivated, either by subsidizing private schools or by establishing a public school system." He also says government should guarantee a "social minimum," his phrase for a decent floor of existence for society's less lucky. Beyond these specific measures, Rawls' just society is imbued with a genuine commitment to equal opportunity, but *not* to such old-time left-wing fetishes as equal incomes, or equal "outcomes." As we'll discuss presently, Milton Friedman would be largely comfortable with these notions, but they are not nearly as central to his sense of what makes for the best society, given his fear that government efforts in this regard lead us down a dangerous path. In other words, Friedman doesn't take luck as seriously as Rawls; or, more precisely, Friedman's less-than-fully-articulated concern for luck's role in life is trumped by his passionate concern for the limits on freedom that an attempt to address luck's role might entail.

For Rawls and his intellectual heirs, the better balance, and bottom line, is clear: In "justice as fairness" (Rawls' shorthand for his approach), "men agree to avail themselves of the accidents of nature and social circumstances only when doing so is for the common benefit." "We Rawlsian liberals," says Yale law professor Bruce Ackerman, "think that we have a special responsibility to arrange the starting points of American citizens in a way worthy of their claim to equality, but we don't have a responsibility to save them from their mistakes as grownups." "The idea," says the philosopher Martha Nussbaum, another pupil of Rawls who teaches at the University of Chicago, "is to set some limits on the power of luck to deform human lives."

———

Rawls' emphasis on luck has posed a special challenge to conservatives, who at some level, as evidenced by Friedman's struggle, recognize the concept as their Achilles heel. In a conference room in his Washington office, commanding a beautiful view of the White House, I asked the conservative commentator William Bennett about luck. Which is a bigger factor in determining where people end up, I asked him: luck (by which I meant the pre-birth lottery) or personal initiative and character? If you had to say that one or the other accounts more for where a person ends up in life, where would you come down?

The normally voluble Bennett fell quiet. His lower lip pushed forward, pensively.

"Genes are part of the first?" he asked.

"Yes."

"Parents are part of the first?"

"Yes."

"The first," he said. That is, luck.

"Why?" I asked. "How would you articulate that?"

"I'll do it backwards for you," he said. "I used to think family and genes and where you were placed were destiny. Having visited the schools [as secretary of education under President Reagan], I'm convinced that it's not, that you can change people's lives and people can change their own lives. But it's hard. It's a little extreme to say that you can grow up to be a happy healthy person living in safety in Lebanon. You can do it—but it's hard. Those things matter hugely. They don't matter completely. But they matter hugely."

What should that imply for public policy? I asked.

"First, a clear recognition of it," Bennett said. "And then no lying about it, being very straightforward about it." Then, he said, it means we have to focus on mediating institutions—family, churches, and schools—that can create opportunities for people to "exercise autonomy and make a difference in their own lives. A lot of people aren't there because they're in crappy families, crappy schools, crappy neighborhoods." Bennett cited the Marine Corps as proof of the hopeful "plasticity" of human nature, of the potential for institutions to alter luckless lives for the better. These kids from the inner city come back from boot camp after eleven weeks and they're *transformed,* Bennett said—with new values, a new spirit, a new future.

Bill Bennett, meet John Rawls, I thought. Despite philosophical differences, a conservative like Bennett is stressing *how to design public institutions to ameliorate some of the burdens of bad luck.* The Marines might be just one example. Schools are obviously another. It's a glimpse of common ground. I began to wonder, if William Bennett had this reaction, perhaps Milton Friedman might be open to dealing with luck more directly.

I met with Friedman in his lovely San Francisco apartment, which boasts a 270-degree wraparound view of the city. He and Rose have lived there for twenty years, since Friedman retired from the University of Chicago and became a fellow at the Hoover Institution at Stanford. Friedman looked professorial in a blue sweater, white shirt, and beige slacks. He welcomed me into a study that had an academic's clutter. Boxes were scattered on the floor, alongside a computer. A globe that apparently lit up lay unplugged on the carpet. We talked a bit about the Two Percent Solution concept. Then I asked Friedman what role he thought luck played in determining one's place in life.

"I think that luck plays an enormous role," he told me. "My wife and I entitled our memoirs, *Two Lucky People.* Luck is enormously important. Society may want to do something about luck. Indeed the whole argument for egalitarianism is to do something about luck. About saying, well, it's not people's fault that a person is born blind, it's pure chance. Why should he suffer. That's a valid sentiment." Friedman brought up his early article where he tried to think some of this through. He chuckled at the thought. It must have been sixty years ago, he said. (It was fifty, but who's counting?)

How old are you today? I asked.

"Eighty-nine," he said. "To use that phrase, I'm lucky. My genes are bad. My father died at the age of 49; my mother died at the age of 70. I had three older sisters all of whom died at ages below 70, so I'm very lucky, indeed."

So what are the implications of luck for public policy? I asked. What are the proper objectives given the role of luck in life?

"You've asked a very hard question," he said. "I don't know that I have the simple answer to it." In part, he added, because it's not clear that what we think of as luck really isn't something else. "I feel," he said, "and you do, too, I'm sure, that what some people attribute to luck is not really luck. That people who are envious of others, you know, 'that lucky bastard,' when the truth of the matter is that fellow had more ability or he worked harder or he did something more. So that not all differences are attributable to luck."

I told Friedman I saw his point, but that I was on a different side of the line. I felt I'd been extremely blessed by the pre-birth lottery, I said. I was born with a decent brain, in a well-off, loving family, and was given a great education. I've tried to take that luck and build on it, I said. "But if you asked me what's the biggest difference between me and someone who's down there," I said, pointing to the street out his window, "I would say it was luck."

"No," he jumped in. "A lot of it is but it's not all luck. Because people who grow up in poverty . . . I didn't have your advantages. I came from a family that would never have been above the poverty line. . . . But if you look at the people who are born much worse off than I was, some of them do come out of it and make it."

"I know it's not all luck," I agreed, but I pointed out that the contours of this conversation suggest that there's an interesting question about the degree to which a person thinks luck as opposed to personal initiative and character accounts for where he ends up.

"That's right," Friedman said. "*But that's luck, too.*" Was Friedman saying that character was ultimately a matter of luck—as John Rawls maintained? "See, the question is, what you're really talking about, is determinism versus free will."

Now *this* was getting interesting.

"I'm not a determinist," I said.

"But how can you avoid being one? In a sense we are determinists. In a sense we are and in another sense we can't let ourselves be. But you can't really justify free will."

Milton Friedman, the author of *Free to Choose,* isn't sure about free will? I glanced at my tape recorder to make sure it was working.

I said, "I guess I feel there's a certain amount of luck and things that put you in a certain position and you're taking that and building on it—"

"But what gives you the characteristics that leads you to take that—?"

"You're right," I said, "because you can keep going back."

"You can keep going back," he agreed. "There's no first cause. Nobody has ever solved the argument of determinism versus free will. And you and I aren't going to do so either."

"So do you believe it's just an open question?"

"No, I believe, well . . ." He paused. "I believe that there's free will but I'm not sure. We're just not smart enough to be able to comprehend all of the infinite little steps that brought us here."

Well! I felt I had learned something. This awareness of luck's role—even if he wouldn't have put it quite this way as a younger man—is what led Friedman, to the extent he was willing to trade off liberty for equality at all, to stress equal opportunity via education and careers open to talent. Friedman also told me that this concern for luck inspired his call for a decent minimum to be provided to the disadvantaged, not unlike Rawls' call for the same. Friedman's preference was that this minimum be provided by charity, which he believed would have been up to the job had government not usurped and over time deadened this private virtue. But as a practical matter, given that government was going to be involved, his second preference was for government to provide this minimum via a "negative income tax." This meant, in essence, cash grants for the poor, as opposed to the series of earmarked programs we now see for food, housing, transportation, and the like. Friedman pioneered this notion in the 1950s. Daniel Patrick Moynihan pushed it unsuccessfully as the Family Assistance Plan when he served as Richard Nixon's domestic policy advisor. George McGovern, in his losing 1972 presidential campaign, called his version of it a "Demogrant." In the late 1970s it was enacted as the earned income tax credit (EITC), which today devotes some $35 billion a year to supplement the wages of low-income workers. This idea also provides the basis for part of the Two Percent Solution.

———

What do these ruminations on luck mean for public policy? What's needed is a synthesis of Rawls' call to take luck seriously with Friedman's desire to keep private markets free enough to deliver their miracle of growth. This synthesis would involve fierce commitments to equal opportunity and to a minimally decent life in a wealthy nation like ours. It would honor liberal notions of the duty we have to partially ameliorate bad luck, as well as conservative objections against forcing society into administrative knots or economic nonsense. Its hybrid policies would harness market forces for public purposes, backed by resources equal to the magnitude of the problems. This agenda has never been tried in America. As we've seen, Bill Clinton had the rhetoric right, and George W. Bush has largely mimicked it, but the conventional pieties of American politics have always ruled out any real-world application.

This synthesis, properly conceived and marketed, can move us past today's tyranny of charades to a debate over fundamental questions of political economy that America now answers only by accident. What level of income redistribution is legitimate and for what purposes? How does this fit with overall levels of taxation and a government role that will promote and not damage economic growth? Some leaders know this is the grown-up debate that's been missing. "If we want to have a conversation about equities, then we ought to have a complete conversation," former Bush treasury secretary Paul O'Neill told me.

> It should not be about health care. It shouldn't be about education. It should be a broader conversation about how much resources should be provided from those who have something to those who have less or nothing. That's the clean conversation. . . . It's about purchasing power for the things one needs to lead a decent and civil life. That's the question.

Some on the right don't want to put the question this way, because it legitimizes the idea of redistribution, which they prefer to discredit. Other conservatives think the aim of wedding what they deride as "European-style" security with American-style market flexibility is a pipe dream—but how would they know, if this American hybrid, at far smaller levels of government, hasn't been tried? Many on the traditional left resist the question because when framed this way, it seems clear that cash transfers are better than myriad bureaucratic programs for the poor. Some corporate interests chafe as well, because they know no broadly debated notion of sensible redistribution will save a place for business subsidies won through campaign donations.

But if some powerful interests won't like it, voters are plainly open to fresh ways to ease some of the burdens of bad luck, as we'll see in Chapter 12. And the remarkable thing is that Friedman and Rawls have already gone far to negotiate the contours of common ground: "Suppose one accepts, as I do, this line of reasoning as justifying governmental action to alleviate poverty; to set, as it were, a floor under the standard of life of every person in the community," Friedman has written. *"There remain the questions, how much, and how."* On "how," we know Friedman feels some kind of cash supplement is the most efficient and least bureaucratic and paternal route. And as for how much? "I see no way of deciding how much," Friedman says, "except in terms of the amount of taxes we—by which I mean the great bulk of us— are willing to impose on ourselves for the purpose." In other words, it's for the political process to decide.

Rawls is very close here. He also insists on what he calls a decent "social minimum." But when it comes to "how much," Rawls, the economically literate liberal, has a framework in mind for determining it. Rawls says to set the minimum by not taxing past the point where economic efficiency is interfered with in a way that leaves the least advantaged worse off (that is, don't kill the golden goose); or by setting taxes so high that it undermines the savings and investment we need to generate in order to hand society off in good condition to the next generation. As to "how," Rawls explicitly discusses Friedman's cash-based approach in favorable terms, saying it "more systematically" addresses the matter than separate programs for food, shelter, and the like. As a practical matter, of course, Rawls' "how much" formulation comes down to a political choice as well. But it's easy to imagine Rawls agreeing with Friedman that old-style 70 percent marginal tax rates are very harmful.

Look where we are. There is a consensus among icons of left and right on the need for equal opportunity and a decent minimum, and no principled way to determine the levels of spending and taxation appropriate to achieve these goals except via politics, bearing in mind

Rawls' sensible economic constraints. My point is that *the answer to "how much" cannot be considered intolerable if we do it today at levels roughly equal to the Reagan administration's level of spending—22 percent of GDP.* Both liberals and conservatives know that spending will have to rise down the road to accommodate the boomers' retirement. Investing now in fixing these lingering injustices will bring millions of people into the economic mainstream, citizens whose productivity will be essential to pay for all those gray boomers. "It ought to be the lowest you can be consistent with a just society," said Mitch Daniels, President Bush's first budget director, of government spending. I agree. That's a standard that can get us where we need to go. The fight, naturally, comes over what one means by "just." That's precisely the debate we need and it should take place in those terms.

But the debate is never framed this cleanly. Instead, it proceeds issue by issue. Cut welfare! Prescription drugs now! Death to the death tax! Win or lose, these battles are isolated from any broader framework defining the common good. Yes, there will always be disputes over how best to realize these goals. But if we ask, in the spirit of taking luck seriously, what does equal opportunity and a decent minimum in America mean, can't we agree that full-time work should enable a family to live a decent life? That every citizen should have basic health coverage? That serious efforts should be made to make sure schools for poor children are good? And that average citizens should have some way to have their voices heard amidst the din of big political money?

The road to justice leads through luck, and it's a road conservatives and liberals can walk together. It's a way of remembering that social justice is a form of enlightened self-interest, for so long as we leave tens of millions of the unlucky unhelped, our economy will not grow as fast, our crime rates will be higher, our collective potential will suffer in ways that ultimately harm us all. When we can have more justice and more economic growth, what are we waiting for?

Over the last few years I've searched for an ambitious yet pragmatic agenda in this spirit, engaging in conversation on health, schools, wages, and campaign reform with politicians, interest groups, press leaders, policy thinkers, and average citizens. In the chapters ahead we'll examine, piece by piece, the Two Percent Solution that is the result of that search. We'll also see how to sensibly pay for it. In the book's final section, we'll then discuss how the public, the press, and our politicians can help us get there—and how a Two Percent Society can help us sustain America's greatness. Like the change in the national conversation we've been discussing, one prerequisite is the creation of demagoguery-free zones in which liberals and conservatives can talk to each other about ways to reconcile their competing values. As we'll see when we start with health care, when you get thoughtful politicians away from the TV cameras and the pollsters, that's not as impossible as it seems.

5

UNIVERSAL COVERAGE,
AMERICAN STYLE

T he moment Jim McCrery walked into Jim McDermott's office,
near the capitol, I felt relief. At least the meeting was going to
happen. For two weeks we had been planning this session, yet every
day I'd half expected one or both of them to call the whole thing off
as unnecessary and strange. Why, after all, would a Republican and a
Democrat on the health subcommittee of the powerful House Ways
and Means Committee want to sit down for a session resembling a
"negotiation" with an outsider? Politicians don't generally volunteer
for encounters they can't control. And, as I had learned while making
the rounds of Washington's health policy gurus, getting a liberal and a
conservative to discuss a pragmatic way to push toward universal coverage can get complicated.

But not more complicated than life can get for the 42 million
Americans who lack coverage. More than four in five uninsured
Americans work year-round, or live in families headed by such workers. These waitresses, taxi drivers, and retail clerks earn too much to
be eligible for Medicaid, but too little to buy coverage in the notoriously high-priced market for individual policies (or to afford their
share of the premium if their employer offers coverage). They get
preventable diseases and avoidably hospitalized more often than the
insured, and are vulnerable to bankruptcy from illness in ways un-

thinkable in other rich countries. To be sure, some people go without insurance only briefly, and a few who can afford it go without by choice (mainly young people in their twenties who feel certain they'll live forever). But, as one House leader wrote to his colleagues not long ago, "The hard fact is this: the percentage of the population going without insurance involuntarily is growing year after year, in good times and bad. This is clearly a structural problem we ignore at our peril." The writer? The conservative Republican Richard Armey of Texas, then the House Majority Leader.

My hope, after several dozen conversations with senators, congressmen, interest groups, and assorted health analysts, was to see if I could get a conservative and a liberal to agree on the rough contours of what I think of as "The Bradley–Bush Sr. Health plan." As you'll recall from Chapter 1, this approach offers tax subsidies to folks who need help to buy insurance from competing private health plans. This is basically the scheme the first President Bush offered in 1992 and that his son, in embarrassing miniature, offers today. It's the same general idea that Bill Bradley proposed in the 2000 Democratic primaries, and that policy gurus from shops as diverse as the conservative Heritage Foundation and the centrist Democratic Leadership Council have been refining for a decade. Although tax subsidies are not a perfect tool (many experts say the poorest Americans, for example, will still need direct programs and well-funded local clinics), and plenty of details remain to be thrashed out, this scheme offers the most realistic way to get both parties to join in a push to right this enduring wrong.

It was an easy decision to seek out a duo in the House rather than the Senate, since debates in "the people's chamber" are marked by the stark partisanship that any consensus would have to transcend. If you can make a deal there, you should be able to make one anywhere. After making some inquiries, I turned to Democrat Jim McDermott of Seattle and Jim McCrery, a Republican from Shreveport, Louisiana. McDermott, 66, went to Congress in 1988 after fifteen years in the Washington state legislature. A psychiatrist by training, he is the long-time leader in Congress of those who support having the government take over the role of health insurers, an approach commonly known as the "single-payer" plan. In a nod to pragmatism since the GOP sweep of 1994, however, McDermott has backed off advocating the pure version of this approach, under which the government doles out cash to state and local health authorities that cover everyone, and private insurance essentially doesn't exist (this is the case in Canada). He even cosponsored a GOP bill backing modest health tax credits in 1997.

McCrery, according to several prominent GOP policy analysts, is the man to watch on health care in the Republican Party. Like McDermott, he was elected to Congress in 1988, and he has studied the issue intensively in recent years, arguing (along with Bill Frist, the Senate Majority Leader) that smart politics and sound policy require Republicans to shed their traditional view that health is not "their" issue.

McDermott scored 85 percent "liberal" and McCrery 83 percent "conservative" on rankings compiled by *National Journal*. They voted opposite ways on ten of twelve key votes tracked by that magazine in a recent Congress. Personally, too, as I couldn't help noticing while they chatted in McDermott's office, they're a study in contrasts. McDermott is a big man with a hearty laugh, whose boisterous energy seems better suited to the stump than to the Freudian couch. McCrery, 54, is slender and soft-spoken. I had to ask him to speak up for my tape recorder.

Staffers for both men had been pressing me for days for a write-up of the plan I'd said I would offer as a point of departure for our talk. In the end, however, I decided that putting anything in writing was too risky; it would be combed by staff for unacceptable terms and could easily become the pretext for cancellation. Now, while a photographer posed McDermott and McCrery in unnaturally close positions to commemorate the occasion, the two men, who plainly like each other, cracked uneasy jokes about what they've gotten themselves into. Finally they sat down—McDermott to the left, of course, and McCrery on the right—on a standard-issue government couch, beneath a wall of photos that included Mahatma Gandhi, and a younger, dark-haired McDermott with Ted Kennedy. McDermott, smiling, said he appreciated his colleague's gesture of agreeing to meet in the office of the minority party. The tension soon eased and they took off their jackets; in the event, they put off meetings and skipped a vote to extend an hour of planned conversation to nearly two.

"What We're Gonna Give Everybody"

We began. I sketched out an approach that my interviews had suggested could gather broad support. The basic idea would be to offer a tax credit usable for the purchase of a health insurance policy (and to pay the amount of the credit directly to those too poor to owe income taxes). The subsidy would be generous enough to buy a decent "Chevrolet" from among competing private health plans. Individuals would have access to some form of insurance pool to assure affordable group rates. It might be phased in to establish a system parallel to today's employer-based coverage—offered first, perhaps, to those not covered by either a government plan (such as Medicaid) or a company. The idea would be to avoid giving employers an incentive to drop current coverage in the near future. Over time, however, it could move the nation away from a system centered on coverage offered by employers to one where individuals received subsidies and were responsible for—and perhaps mandated to buy—their own coverage in the private market.

Obviously, a hundred difficult details are glossed over in this sketch, I said, but could something like this be the beginning of a deal?

McDermott spoke first. "In order to get us off dead center," he said, "we've got to try something in the middle here and see if it'll work. I'm so frustrated by having spent thirty years watching it get worse that I'm willing to try practically anything to get us moving."

"Jim's not going to get what he wants [that is, a single-payer system] anytime soon," said McCrery. "I or some right-wing person is not going to get an unfettered market, which is the individuals fending for themselves. So if we want to solve the problem we've got to come up with something that's kind of a combination. I think that's possible along the tax subsidy lines. If we don't do anything, if we just keep going like we're going, eventually I think we'll end up with single-payer, we'll end up with the government controlling just about everything in health care."

This was an argument McCrery had made to me earlier: that today's tendency to put a patch here and then a band-aid there, typified by the push for an HMO patient "bill of rights," leads inexorably toward heavy-handed federal solutions. "That might take forty years or fifty years," he continued, "but we're going that way now. So I'm willing to accept a lot more government intervention in the market than I normally would to create a system that will have some vestige of the market left in it."

We turned to the key components of a potential health deal, starting with benefits. If a tax subsidy is used, McCrery said, "there would be the element of different levels of health care for different people. Somebody who is wealthier is probably going to buy a policy that would be richer in benefits than the basic benefit package that I would pay 100 percent for from the government. That would enable the market to continue to be more innovative than under a single-payer system."

It's the classic conservative argument, as we've seen: Beneficial innovations always begin as luxuries for the wealthy. Think of automobiles, telephones, or airplanes: First come the breakthroughs funded by the rich, later their dissemination to the masses.

McDermott seemed unconvinced. "But if you and I both need to have doctor visits and all this stuff, right up to the level of a bone marrow transplant at $120,000 a crack," he asked, "why wouldn't you guarantee that to everybody in the United States? What would you leave above the line that you would say that people who are wealthier can get for themselves?"

"The catastrophic examples are not the kinds of things I'm talking about," McCrery replied. "I'm talking about variances in bells and whistles in insurance policies—if you want a private room, if you want extra [nursing] help in the room, all those things that people could purchase if they wanted to. The basic plan that would be provided by the government to low-income folks would not have all those."

McDermott wasn't satisfied. "One of the big difficulties will be us agreeing on a basic package."

"But having said that," McCrery added, "I don't think it's impossible."

"No, it's not impossible," McDermott agreed.

McCrery, as Bill Bradley had proposed in his 2000 campaign, suggested the federal employee health plan as a model. It doesn't define benefits down to every test and procedure, but assures general areas of coverage, such as major medical and surgical. This way there's no stifling of the extraordinary innovation now sweeping health care delivery, whose future shape can't be foreseen. Go too far in defining things rigidly, the Republicans argue, and you end up with inanities like Medicare, which unaccountably still fails to cover prescription drugs thirty-eight years after the program's inception.

"Ultimately," McDermott said, "there has to be a come-to-Jesus meeting someplace where that package is defined: This is health insurance for the country. This is what we're gonna give everybody."

I asked McDermott why defining a detailed benefit package is so crucial to liberals, when there's no government-defined package in the employer-based system under which 170 million Americans now get their coverage. What's more, as Bill Thomas, the Republican chairman of Ways and Means, argued, any honest observer has to concede that a move to what Democrats deride as "two-tier" care would be a vast improvement over the five- or six-tier care we have today, which runs the gamut from princely to truly pauperish. And as Dick Armey told me, there are precedents for leaving the actual benefit undefined: With food stamps, Uncle Sam provides the wherewithal but doesn't tell poor folks what to eat; the mortgage interest deduction helps millions without any need for the government to tell people what kind of house to buy. The impulse to mandate this benefit and that procedure helps drive costs higher, making it harder for those in the cold today to afford a basic package. Why not simply make the health subsidy generous enough and let folks pick among competing offerings?

McDermott responded that it's hardly an advertisement for the system of different employers' plans we have today in which one person may be covered for, say, certain cancer treatments whereas another cancer patient is exposed to financial ruin. In any major reform such inconsistencies should be rationalized in favor of some common notion of what every citizen ought to have. It will also be a fight, McDermott believes, to make any tax subsidy rich enough to buy a decent package, since many Republicans essentially want a cheap tax-style voucher they can ratchet down over time to limit costs.

Yet both men think that the differences here can be bridged. Several experts suggested using the standard benefit package that members of Congress get—something that's hard for them to vote against, and hard for foes to scare the public into thinking is "inadequate." The occupant of the Oval Office, McCrery said, needs to "lock us in a room with his people and say, okay, let's come up with a benefit plan that Jim McDermott, Jim McCrery, and the president can support." McDermott agreed. "If you locked the door and said we don't get any lunch until we come up with a benefit package," he said, "we would have one and be out of here."

"It Would Fundamentally Alter the Insurance Business"

I asked the congressmen to turn to another central issue: If individuals are subsidized to buy coverage from private plans, how do we protect people who have predictably high medical costs from shouldering the full burden of their care? Everyone agrees that access to reasonably priced insurance for these unlucky souls should be a priority. How to go about it is another matter. Chip Kahn, then the head of the powerful Health Insurance Association of America, the industry's lobbying group, told me that insurers want a separate "high-risk" insurance pool funded by broad-based taxation to handle these folks (as happens now in some states). Liberals say such ghetto-like funds invariably assure lousy care, and prove that greedy insurers only want healthy customers who don't actually need the insurance. Pete Stark, the senior Democrat on the health subcommittee, had a whole lecture on this theme: "Let's cut the crap," a longtime aide told me he has said, and just redline. "You tell me, Mr. Insurer, which healthy folks you want to make money off of, and which sick folks you want the government to take, and we'll cut out all the make-believe."

McDermott was warming to a similar rant when McCrery interrupted him. "I wouldn't have a high-risk pool," he said. "I'd just do community rating."

"Community rating" means that everyone pays the same premium, regardless of age, sex, or medical history. This is, of course, the liberal dream. Rates for decent policies in the individual market can easily top an unaffordable $10,000 a year for people with a history of health problems. Community rating, though controversial in theory, is actually widespread today. Employees of large companies enjoy it on a de facto basis, as health risks are spread among thousands of workers. It's the chief virtue of today's otherwise anomalous employer-based system, in which the United States, alone among advanced nations, looks to employers to manage most health coverage.

Our employer-based system was a federally engineered accident. Wage freezes during the Second World War left fringe benefits as the chief way that big firms competed for employees. Health care as a job-related perk became common. The government then established a large tax subsidy to ratify this arrangement. Every big company is essentially a socialized health republic, in which the young subsidize the old, and the healthy subsidize the sick—all of whom pay the same premiums for the same plans.

Reorganizing the individual insurance market to make such pooling work would be more complicated. If insurers were forced to offer the same rate to all comers, young workers would pay far more than they would under policies that recognized their relatively low actual health costs. In large companies young workers opt into such a system because their bosses pick up most of the tab. For this to work in an individual market, the incentive must somehow be replicated—or else coercion must be involved.

What cannot be done is to let young, healthy workers opt out, or the insurance pool will face a classic actuarial disaster. If younger workers decline coverage, the average health costs of those remaining in the pool will be higher, and premiums will rise. But higher premiums will prompt more young, healthy workers to drop coverage. The vicious cycle will continue until premiums are sky-high and only the sickest are insured, at exorbitant rates.

This is essentially what happened in New York in 1993, when the state forced insurers to apply community rating to their individual policies. Well-meaning officials hoped to extend affordable coverage to everyone; instead, they generated a new glut of uninsured. The lessons of Insurance 101 are clear: Community rating in an individual insurance market requires either a mandate that everyone buy insurance or a subsidy generous enough to keep younger and healthier people in the pool (or both).

McCrery said he was for both the mandate and the generous subsidy—at least for people of lower income. That a conservative on the health subcommittee of Ways and Means backs these ideas is stunning. McCrery is one of few in his party at present who take this view. He is also one of the few Republicans who have studied the issue so closely.

"What brought you to community rating?" I asked him.

"I looked at it nine ways to Sunday," he explained, "and I don't think there's any other way to do it. I mean, that's not true, there is another way to do it, but I think the simplest way to do it is just to have community rating. Yes, you can have a high-risk pool with people moving from under the red line to above the red line, but why fool with all that? It's complicated, it's troublesome, it distorts the market. Why not just have community rating and then let insurance companies compete on the basis of value."

"Covering everybody," McDermott said.

McCrery nodded. "They'd have to take all comers, but they would compete on the basis of service, economies of scale, efficiencies that they could muster to provide better prices, all those kinds of things. They could still be in the business, they'd just have to compete on those bases and not on getting lucky"—that is, picking healthier people to insure.

I turned to McDermott. "You like that?" I asked. His eyes opened wide.

"Yeah," he said. "I don't want to say anything to mess it up." Both men laughed.

The top insurance lobbyist insists that community rating is a nonstarter, I pointed out. Is there anything legitimate in his opposition?

"Depends on what you mean by legitimate," McCrery said. "To them it's legitimate. Because, I mean, much of their business now—"

"They don't have the problems that Jim and I face, which include equity in the society," McDermott injected. "They have a different mandate. I mean, a corporation takes in as much money as they can, pays as little out so that they have it to give to their stockholders. It's not good or bad, it's just what they are." He looked at his colleague. "That's not what you and I are. He represents all 600,000 in his district, and I represent all 600,000 in my district. . . . I can't say, well, I represent 440,000 and the other 160,000 are not my concern. I don't have that option."

"It would fundamentally alter the insurance business," McCrery said.

It would—by bringing it back to the way it was, in a sense. Community rating was the way health insurance worked, even in the individual market, until the 1960s. Before then insurers didn't have the data to segment people in sophisticated ways according to health risks. Just as important, health costs were a fraction of what they are today, meaning customers didn't have much to gain by shopping for cheaper plans, and unlucky insurers burnt by a few high-cost illnesses weren't left reeling. But costs and premiums have soared famously for decades now. The data and technology needed to identify and price policies for lower-risk customers became available. It didn't take long for entrepreneurs to realize they could target younger, healthier people with lower rates, sweep up a ton of customers, and make a bundle. The fragmentation of the insurance market—with its emphasis on "cherry picking" the best risks—began in earnest.

"The Human Genome Project is going to have impact on this whole process unlike anything we can really imagine at this point," McDermott said. "Because if I'm an insurance company and I get a drop of your blood and I can do your genetics and I find you have these and these and these proclivities, I'll insure you for everything but those. What is insurance at that point?"

"The game is over at that point," McCrery agreed.

I told them I had asked the insurance association about this and they assured me that insurers would never use genetic information this way. The two legislators exploded in thigh-slapping laughter.

"No comment," McDermott finally managed to say.

Is it reasonable to think that community rating could succeed politically? I asked McCrery. Sure, he said—group insurers already operate under such a system in big companies. I then asked, But what about the individual marketplace?

"Well, I may have to settle for less [than its purest form]," McCrery said. "I've talked with insurance companies about this. They tell me that as long as they can underwrite based on age and gender [but not health status], they have no problem, they can make it work."

Cecil Bykerk, executive vice president and chief actuary of Mutual of Omaha, one of the largest insurers in the individual marketplace, later told me the same thing. Mutual looks at people's health status only when they sign up, he explained: Once they're in the pool, Mutual doesn't go back and adjust their rates for subsequent health developments (as auto insurers do after accidents). As it turns out, prudent pricing can be based largely on age and sex. (This is true, of course, so long as everyone buys insurance as insurance, and doesn't buy in only when he or she becomes sick; as the famous example has it, buying insurance only when the house is on fire defeats the risk-pooling concept altogether.)

At a minimum, then, McCrery's approach would remove any detailed assessment of health risk from the underwriting process, making it impossible to demand unaffordable premiums from sick Americans or to leave them uninsured. McCrery added that if insurers could go this far they could go all the way and offer the same rates to everyone, period. He would use a reinsurance fund to compensate unlucky insurers that ended up with an undue share of high-cost cases. McCrery conceded that his scheme would make health insurance look more like a regulated utility, and would put today's entrepreneurial "cherry pickers" out of business. But better that government guarantee access to insurance at equitable prices, he reasons, than that government involve itself directly with the delivery of health care, or in drug prices, doctor fees, and more—as it is sure to do, he thinks, if the present system continues to erode until voters ask liberals to fix things their way.

"If we want to save the private health care system," McCrery told me in a separate conversation, "Republicans are going to have to accept some things that normally would be contrary to our basic philosophy."

"I Want to Hear About Equity"

I asked McCrery and McDermott if business would support the reform they were discussing. If eventually offered to everyone, a sufficiently ample tax subsidy would encourage companies to drop the coverage they now offer and let the government pick up the tab. Over a period of years, this might spell the end of employer-based coverage as we know it. Would that be a bad thing? I mentioned that I've never understood why employers didn't want this $300 billion expense off their payrolls anyway.

"Most do, I think," said McCrery.

"You think so?" McDermott asked. He was not so sure.

"Uh-huh," McCrery said. "Most would want to get that off their backs, particularly small employers. Some big companies would, too. I've talked to a number of big employers and many of them are very interested in converting to an individual-based system."

The fear that an HMO "bill of rights" might make employers liable for deaths or injuries in which their health plans were implicated has accelerated this thinking. CEOs wonder why they should be on the hook for misjudgments they can't control and that don't even involve their main business. They reason they would be better off giving each employee a lump sum to buy his or her own policy. Though experts say that a tax credit approach would encourage such changes, this aspect of it is highly controversial; even most advocates of a shift to an individual-based system think prudence requires a decade or more for the transition. Indeed, when a Xerox executive mentioned the idea a few years back, labor unions denounced it. Yet McCrery thinks the shift can and should happen relatively quickly.

"My impression is different than Jim's on this issue," McDermott said, "because I have a feeling that it's almost a religious issue of being unwilling to concede that the government will take care of it. Companies figure that ultimately they will have to pay for it. They worry they'll spend more than they're actually spending now."

"That's a legitimate fear," McCrery said, "but if we construct a package which can allay those fears, I think they'll be fine—and I think we can. I don't envision putting the burden of financing this on the backs of employers."

"I see the employer community as two distinct groups," McDermott said, "those who provide and those who don't. And the 'those who don'ts' are the really sticky ones to deal with." When he was promoting the single-payer idea, McDermott recalled, it was "a real dilemma to say to them, we're going to actually put a plan out there and you're going to have to ante up 'X' amount in new taxes to fund it."

"I don't think we have to do that," McCrery said. He explained that each company could "cash out" its employees—that is, take the amount it was spending on health benefits and distribute it as wages to workers on an equal per-employee basis. This uniform wage hike would fit with McCrery's community rating requirement, enabling every employee to take the extra money and buy a similar policy in the private market.

McDermott had a quizzical look. Where would the money come from for people who work for a company that doesn't now offer health insurance?

McCrery smiled at me. "I assumed you were saving this for last and we're ready to go into the financing?" I nodded. This is where deals in Washington either hold together or fall apart.

"This is where Jim's going to jump off my train," McCrery said.

"I don't know that you should make any assumptions about where I'm going to jump," McDermott said.

"I hope I'm wrong," McCrery said.

"But go ahead," McDermott continued, "and explain to me how you deal with the guy who works for a company—fifty people in the company—that doesn't offer him anything."

"Well, bear in mind that right now that employee of that company who's not providing health insurance is not getting anything—literally, nothing," McCrery said. "If he goes out in the individual market and buys his own policy, he's getting no help from the government, nothing, no subsidy whatsoever. He doesn't even get a deduction for the premiums for his health insurance [this has changed: as of 2003, self-employed individuals can deduct their premiums]. So this poor guy is really out of luck. Whereas Jim McDermott's getting subsidized. The taxpayers are subsidizing Jim McDermott's health care— and mine. There is no equity in that. That is a terrible way to construct a system. So I want to—"

"I want to hear about equity," McDermott said.

"I want to dismantle the current system in terms of government subsidies and throw it all back in a big old pot, and then create an equitable system. And what I mean by an equitable system is we basically help those people who need help—low-income people. Jim and I, we make enough money to buy ourselves a decent health insurance policy. I don't need the government to help me pay for my health insurance—that's crazy."

So it would be some kind of sliding scale, I ask, with the tax subsidy tapering off as income rises?

"Yes. Wouldn't be a cliff, it'd be a slope."

What McCrery and McDermott were talking about here would mean scrapping and reallocating the current tax subsidy, under which employers can deduct health care expenses from their taxes, but employees don't have to include the value of these benefits in their taxable income. Since the savings from this decades-old tax exclusion grows as one's tax bracket rises, the arrangement amounts to a $125-billion-a-year subsidy offering the most lavish aid to wealthy executives with gold-plated health plans. Unions love it all the same, because it also underwrites the generous health plans they've negotiated over the years. It's hard to imagine a more popular tax break. Ronald Reagan wanted to revamp it in his original 1985 tax reform, but he lost his nerve. Richard Darman, George H. W. Bush's budget director, wanted to revamp it to pay for Bush's 1992 health plan, but the president wouldn't back him. Did McCrery think the time was ripe to take this on?

"Absolutely," he said.

I turned to McDermott. All my research suggested that the liberal Democrat had to reject this idea, because the unions would staunchly defend the tax exclusion.

"Well, I'm willing to look at his plan with the specifics on paper," McDermott said. "I can't reject it absolutely out of hand because the present system is not perfect, is not doing the job. So I am perfectly willing to look at another alternative."

It was hard to be sure at first if McDermott was open-minded or merely wanted to appear that way. But as he continued, he seemed sincere, and his sincerity seemed born of experience. He recalled a plan he had worked on at the state level, under which Washington State would offer a similar subsidy for uninsured people. The plan had been stymied because the legislature couldn't find the new money.

"You didn't recoup any money," McCrery pointed out, trying to suggest how the reallocation they were discussing could solve this. "You didn't have a pot out there to pull from."

"And that's the problem," McDermott said, nodding. At the state level, you can only experiment so much, because you can't find new dollars.

"But we don't have to come up with new dollars," McCrery said. "We've got present dollars out there [in the current tax subsidy] that we're spending willy-nilly in a very inequitable fashion, in my view, that we can recoup and redistribute."

"I would not reject his idea," McDermott said, as if he had made a decision. This was a big deal—so big that McDermott would later ask me if I was planning to publish this before election day. He was relieved when I told him no.

"That's good to know," McCrery said. "The reason I assumed that he would is that labor unions generally are very much opposed to this idea."

"Because they're fearful," McDermott explained. "They're like business. Business is afraid the taxes are going to go up, and the labor unions are afraid that the benefits are going to go down."

The union politics are simple, McDermott added. Suppose the government said it planned to take away the subsidy that underwrites current health plans. "How are they going to go to their members and say they stood for that?" McDermott asked. "That's where the dilemma is."

"I'm glad to hear Jim describe it that way," McCrery said. "I think if we educate the union members as to the advantages of an individual-based system wherein they are cashed out in the form of wages, they won't be so fearful. They might even like it. The union bosses will not like it because we are essentially taking away one of the goodies that they can claim to have provided to their members. But the union members themselves, once you explain to them, look, you're going to get $10,000 more in wages. Now you'll have to pay taxes on those wages and that's the big difference, but then under the market that we foresee, you can go out and buy a pretty darn good health insurance package for $5000—I think they might say, 'Whoa, maybe there's something to this.'"

I asked if something like this reallocation of today's tax subsidy—which policy analysts of all stripes tend to favor, but that prompts political pros to roll their eyes—could actually happen. McDermott said it was the toughest piece of the puzzle. Agreeing on a benefits package was simple by comparison.

"But the financing question," he continued, "is fraught with the human emotional problem of, 'I have this now, if I let go of it, why should I trust a politician? Why should I trust Jim McCrery and Jim McDermott that they're going to give me something as good as what I've got right now?' Creating that uncertainty was a big part of the Harry and Louise ads [in which a homey couple dispensed insurance industry propaganda in the guise of common sense], and the whole undercutting of the Clinton program. A standard political technique is to create disbelief or uncertainty about something—and the thing is gone in a minute."

"It's a lot easier to beat something," McCrery added, "than it is to pass something."

"That's absolutely right. And that's why I say, Jim, put the plan on the table and I'll look at it." McDermott conceded that if they were starting from scratch, and someone proposed a health subsidy that favored upper-income Americans the way the current tax system does, he and Ted Kennedy would be shouting about its injustice, not turning a blind eye, as they do now. "That's why I can't reject what he's talking about," McDermott said. "Because I know the present system is not fair."

Stop for a moment and look where we are. McDermott, the Democrat who favors a single-payer system, is open to tax credits, can live with private insurers, and won't rule out revising the $125 billion tax exclusion that is beloved of his party's most loyal interest group. McCrery, the conservative Republican, wants universal coverage, ample subsidies for those who need it, community-rated insurance policies, and a shift toward government funding of individuals (through the tax code) and away from the employer-based system that currently leaves millions insecure or out in the cold. Yes, the devil is in the details. But it's hard to believe that people of goodwill can't get to the finish line from here if they want to. What would that take?

"It's going to take a bipartisan effort," McDermott said. "And it's going to take patience and a certain putting down of ideology to get to a pragmatic solution here."

"Is it doable in your view?" I asked.

"I wouldn't be here if I didn't think it was," he said.

"I'm to the point," McCrery said, "where I am wanting to bring in some Democrats who want to solve the problem, and try to polish a plan and then see who we can sell it to. Just go knock on doors.

"The trust question becomes critical," McDermott said. "Does he trust me? Will I trust him?"

The gulf here is deep, as I learned. "I don't trust the politicians to make the tax credit approach fair," Jay Rockefeller, a Democratic senator from West Virginia, told me. Pete Stark said, "When you've got a party that's committed to destroying Medicare, what's there to negotiate with those clowns?" One senior Republican legislator told me that certain Democrats "have a higher calling than keeping their word to a Republican." Senator Bill Frist of Tennessee told me (before he became Majority Leader) that some on the other side want the problem to get worse so they can fix it more nearly on their terms.

"That's the real question," McDermott was saying, "because why should I waste my time going to a meeting at McCrery's office if he's just going to play the same old goddamn game and jerk me around. I mean, we've got so little time. You're only going to go to a place where you trust the guy. That's crucial to making this happen."

"Yeah," McCrery said, pointing his finger at the couch they sat on. "Would you come to this interview?" They laughed.

"We wouldn't be having this interview if I didn't trust you," McDermott said. "Yes, I trust him. I mean, you can't underestimate because this is a people business. It's not just ideas and it's not just numbers—it's the people have got to be able to work together. And there's been a hell of a lot of things that have separated us.

"Now," McDermott said with a wink, as the session broke up, "we have to go to meetings of our respective caucuses and plan how to beat the crap out of each other."

———

Despite the political squabbling and hard choices needed to finance such a plan, McDermott and McCrery think a deal remains possible. Tom Scully, who runs the Bush administration's Center for Medicare and Medicaid Services (and who helped draft the 1992 Bush health plan as a top aide in George H. W. Bush's budget office), told me that while the plan involves a "tax credit," it could be implemented as a simple, user-friendly transfer payment. How might this work? States might be asked to certify six or seven private insurance companies to offer the agreed-on basic benefit plan with a community-rated premium. Low-income people would be informed they have access to this plan. An eligible citizen would walk into Blue Cross of California or Colorado and show that based on their earnings they qualify for a health tax credit of, say, $4000. The person would never see the cash directly; the insurance company would apply to the government for the payment on their behalf. The Department of Treasury would transfer the $4000, and if the cost of the policy were $5000, the beneficiary would pay his additional $1000. In effect it would act as a kind of health care voucher. But the tax credit rhetoric matters. "Politically, the refundable tax credit is attractive," said Stuart Butler of the Heritage Foundation, an analyst who has helped pioneer the development of this concept over the last decade. "As I point out to the merriment of some liberal audiences, a refundable tax credit is a subsidy to poor people that Republicans can happily vote for as a tax cut."

As McDermott and McCrery's dialogue suggests, the big question is whether the left will be open to market-friendly approaches, and the right ready to pony up money equal to the problem. Such a plan would cost about $80 billion a year today. (We'll discuss funding in Chapter 10.) Where do things stand? In the House of Representatives, many on the left still prefer a single-payer program, about which two things can be said. First, as a matter of politics, it's not going to happen. And second, as a matter of policy, it *shouldn't* happen. A system that relies this intrusively on centralized government control of medical prices, practice patterns, and service delivery is not the right model for a sector that will experience an explosion of beneficial innovation in the next thirty years.

Moreover, the left should realize it can achieve its social objectives through a plan like the one we've sketched here. The logic is plain. Universal coverage won't happen without both political parties. And as much as liberals might wish it, they're not going to persuade Republicans to outlaw the insurance industry and adopt a single-payer system. It's time liberals made peace with the notion that a regulated market of competing private health plans can be the vehicle for getting everyone covered. Yes, it means that unlike other advanced countries, we'll have billions of "health" dollars siphoned off by middlemen and marketers. But if liberals think of it as a jobs program, they'll learn to love it. After all, billions in "school" spending now gives a livelihood to countless excess bureaucrats in dysfunctional urban districts, and I haven't heard a liberal complaint. More importantly, over time, if the GOP caucus can be persuaded of the wisdom of Jim McCrery's vision, health insurance will become more like a regulated utility. If everyone's covered, and insurer "cherry picking" is dead, the left should be happy.

Business might be, too. Its support is plainly crucial for reforms like this to happen. McCrery isn't the only one who thinks CEOs want these costs off their payrolls. "It is not an impossible thing to do," Bill Bradley told me. He hoped via his 2000 plan to launch a major dialogue with CEOs on this kind of evolution. "It is in the self-interest of the business community because they finally wouldn't have to worry about these costs," Bradley said. Norm Pattiz, the chairman of broadcasting giant Westwood One, agreed. "Companies are more concerned about multiples of cash flow," Pattiz said. If businesses didn't have to bear the share they do today of society's overall health costs, the extra earnings they would show, multiplied in the stock market by their firms' price-to-earnings ratio, would represent enormous value creation for American business. "Anytime you can take a dollar and arbitrage that dollar into ten or twenty dollars by not spending it on things like health care," Pattiz said, "that's a powerful economic influence. More and more people who run companies now come from that school."

What about conservatives? There are promising noises. "The extent to which the left believes that the right is opposed to universal coverage is overstated," Ed Gillespie, the Republican party chairman, told me. "I don't know many conservative Republicans who don't favor having everyone have health insurance. It's the means by which you do it that is the argument." Rick Davis, John McCain's adviser, said the GOP's calculations have changed as well.

> It wasn't long ago where you would sit in meetings with smart Republican strategists who would say, "We don't want to talk about health care because that's not on our playing field. The voters won't believe anything we tell them because they've long since figured out that whatever we're selling they're not buying." Hillary Clinton changed that dynamic. That whole debate around her health care plan really created an opening for Republicans so that they now believe they can at least fight to an even finish if not create some advantage from time to time on issues of health care.

In crass political terms, this new mind-set is vital. One senior Republican committee chairman told me that the longer the GOP holds its House majority, the more Republicans come to realize that health "pork" is just as good as any other—and that the hometown Medical Industrial Complex is grateful when they deliver.

When it comes to stepping up to the costs of covering everyone, of course, the current administration has shown little interest. I told Mitch Daniels, the White House budget director until June of 2003, that basically I just wanted the current George Bush to give us his daddy's health plan—not the one he has offered, which is one-seventh as generous. "I can see why that would disappoint you," Daniels said dryly. But that wasn't Daniels' final word.

> I can look at what you're talking about here [the well-funded tax credit approach] and say, as an advocate of limited government, this doesn't necessarily bother me because arguably it is less intrusive, less compli-cated than what we do now. There are many more dollars attached to it, but the two [more money and "big government"] should not be just casually equated. . . . I'm imagining that we would cash in a lot of things [in terms of other programs being reduced] . . . if you shifted to this kind of a system. To me that's a great bargain. If it costs more in total that's fine, too.

The Heritage Foundation offered a plan not long ago that would get to universal coverage, but liberals were so turned off by its tax-based approach that they didn't bother to look at the fine print, which included a hefty $55 billion in new funding to achieve its goal—more than some Democratic presidential candidates are pledging for this purpose. With the Two Percent version priced at $80 billion, Heritage at $55 billion, and the GOP noises I've noted in the air, there's a discussion to be had.

In the end, the "grand bargain" we need on health care requires Democrats to accept the existence of a private insurance industry and Republicans to accept the need to help everyone buy a decent policy. It's about liberals agreeing that innovation shouldn't be regulated out of U.S. health care, and conservatives agreeing that justice has to be regulated into it. The uninsured may seem invisible, but today their ranks are equal to the combined populations of Oklahoma, Connecti-cut, Iowa, Mississippi, Kansas, Arkansas, Utah, Nevada, New Mexico, West Virginia, Nebraska, Idaho, Maine, New Hampshire, Hawaii, Rhode Island, Montana, Delaware, North Dakota, South Dakota,

Alaska, Vermont, and Wyoming. Would America conceivably turn its back on the citizens of these twenty-three states if they lacked basic health coverage? That is what we've been doing for decades. If, as we've now seen, a single-payer liberal Democrat and a conservative Republican can sit down and find their way to rough consensus on the idea that a fix is possible, can't the rest of us?

6

MILLIONAIRE TEACHERS

It's two hours into the school year, and already Vince Eisman is full of regrets. As the kids play kickball at recess, the new fourth grade teacher at Coliseum elementary school in central Los Angeles is kicking himself. Where did the time go? The "What was the most exciting thing about your summer?" exercise had taken much longer than expected, and he'd barely gotten started on his classroom rules of behavior before the break came. Still, Eisman—instantly christened Mr. "Ice-man" (a name that will stick) by one 9-year-old—is hopeful. Though they score around the sixteenth percentile on state achievement tests, his twenty students—nearly all black and Latino—seem eager, with hands raised and faces bright. He'd heard horror stories about disconnected or drugged-out parents, but several introduced themselves this morning and urged him to "work 'em hard." Over the buzz of playground chatter, Eisman, 30, is excited, overwhelmed, and self-critical all at once. "Maybe I should have done the rules first," he says. "I didn't get anything done like I'd planned."

For one of L.A.'s toughest schools, Eisman was a catch. Few new teachers are finishing a master's degree in Roman history with a thesis on Augustan poetry and propaganda. Eisman had originally planned to teach college. His wife kept telling him he was great with young kids, but Eisman feared they wouldn't be stimulating enough. To test the waters, he spent a year subbing in k–12 classes while teaching two night courses in Greco-Roman history at community college. The college students seemed burned-out and flaky. The kids were a blast, and working with them stretched him like nothing he'd done before. Eisman got accepted by a "district intern program" that crash-trains uncertified newcomers in L.A., faxed his résumé to schools, and was hired within days. He packed up his wife and baby and set off for pricey Tinseltown to live, somehow, on $32,000 a year.

Eisman's classroom is in a portable, prefab "bungalow," a monument to the district's failure to plan for rising enrollments. It smells of disinfectant. He and his wife spent days scrubbing off mold left by the previous occupant. Posters of Martin Luther King Jr., Willie Mays, and Sidney Poitier dot the walls. Another poster reminds students to report any weapon they see. His kids work in groups, "interviewing" each other about their vacations.

"Are you gonna stay here?" a boy named Mikhel suddenly asks. They've been abandoned by so many teachers, Eisman explains later. Not to mention family members. "Yes," Eisman tells Mikhel, "I'm here for good."

Urban America better hope so. No one should need much convincing that schools in the nation's poor neighborhoods are in crisis. Students attending them are a full three grade levels behind students in higher-income areas, according to a recent Department of Education study. "The numbers tell a sad and alarming story," concluded *Education Week* in a special report a few years ago. "Most 4th graders who live in U.S. cities can't read and understand a simple children's book, and most 8th graders can't use arithmetic to solve a practical problem."

There are probably a hundred things we need to do for these schools, and ten big things that could make a difference, but if you could focus on only one thing, the most important would be teacher quality. The teacher question is so vital that the Hart–Rudman Commission, the same group whose report presciently stressed America's vulnerability to major terror attacks, defined teacher quality as an issue of *national security*. Two million new teachers must be recruited in the next decade—700,000 of them in urban districts—thanks to a coming wave of retirements and rising enrollments. That means that fully two-thirds of today's teacher corps will turn over. Replacing them with top talent and not simply warm bodies is a tall order, especially in urban districts, where half the new teachers quit within three years (depressingly, studies suggest, it's the smarter half). With research showing that half the achievement gap facing poor and minority students is due not to poverty or family conditions but to systematic differences in teacher quality, the question of teacher recruitment in poor schools is more than just the biggest issue in education. It's the next great frontier for social justice.

To focus on teacher quality is not to be a "teacher basher," or to denigrate the thousands of talented and dedicated teachers who have been working their hearts out for years under awful conditions to make a difference for poor children. But as good teachers in these schools have told me with passion, the scale of the need is immense. The incompetence of many of their colleagues is appalling. And the obstacles to solving the problem are deep.

These obstacles start with the nation's schools of education, our major supplier of teachers. One study found that of every 600 people who enter a four-year teaching program, 180 finish, 72 become teachers, and only 40 are still in the classroom several years later. The ed schools are largely viewed as third-tier backwaters on campus, filled with faculty that hasn't been near a classroom for years. The schools typically feature self-contained curriculums and extra requirements for education courses, all to avoid losing revenue to other parts of the university.

One result: Three in four elementary school teachers, half of middle school teachers, and a third of high school teachers majored only in education, not in the subject matter they actually need to *teach*. "Out-of-field" teaching is widespread, and disproportionately affects poor children. The numbers are staggering. One federal study of grades 7 to 12 estimated conservatively that 18 million children were being taught core academic courses by teachers who lacked even a minor in the subject—including one in four math students, four in ten life sciences students, more than half of history students, and six in ten physical science students. Only 41 percent of U.S. students are taught math by teachers who majored in math, versus 71 percent internationally. Guess which kids in America don't get taught by the math majors?

Moreover, the state competency requirements that graduates of such programs must meet are a mockery, with standards that are "appallingly low," in the words of Rod Paige, President Bush's Secretary of Education. Only 29 states require candidates to take a test in the area they plan to teach. Nearly all are so easy to pass that they keep only "illiterates" out of teaching, as the late Albert Shanker, the legendary president of the American Federation of Teachers, once said. Yet even these minimal standards are routinely waived to allow the issuance of "emergency credentials," so that in our biggest cities as many as half of new hires, and up to 25 percent of the full teacher corps, aren't properly trained or credentialed. The most severe shortages exist in specialties like math, science, and bilingual and special education, where people trained as teachers find their skills command a premium outside the classroom. "Why is it that there are still incompetent people in classrooms?" asked Sandra Feldman, the president of the American Federation of Teachers. "Because there's a tremendous shortage, and because people who are not competent in the first instance are hired to babysit. It's tragic."

I got a glimpse of this tragedy shortly after Roy Romer, the former three-term governor of Colorado and chairman of the Democratic National Committee, became school superintendent in Los Angeles in 2000. In one meeting I sat in on, Romer's staffers explained that many L.A. elementary school teachers weren't able to teach reading, a major problem for the literacy program the district was rolling out. But in math, they told Romer, the situation was even worse. In eighth grade and above, they explained, the math teachers were better because they tended to be math majors. But the early grades were a mess. And training the teachers to teach math was more complicated. All teachers knew how to read, after all—they just might not know how to teach it. But many early grade teachers had real math phobias.

"What's the content level for third grade math?" Romer barked.

Multiplication tables, division, that kind of thing, came the reply.

"What percent of math teachers in grades 3 to 5 are adequate?" Romer asked.

The staffers looked at each other a little helplessly. "Forty to fifty percent" are adequate, they finally offered.

"Excuse me," Romer erupted, "but how can the most technically advanced nation in the world have a situation where maybe 40 percent are adequate? Any logical person coming in from Mars would say, 'What gives here?' I'm really genuinely curious. What is the culture of the society that lets this happen?"

The question hung there. "What do we plan to do about it?" Romer asked. A training program for math teachers starts next March, one staffer explained. Romer suddenly looked weary, as if registering that this was eight months away. He took his glasses off and rubbed his eyes. "Any chance we could have bright math kids in senior high school teach the elementary school kids?" he asked. The staffers exchanged ambiguous glances. "Ah, that's probably too embarrassing to do," Romer said, shaking his head.

Other inanities make matters worse. Fifty state bureaucracies certify teachers, a patchwork scheme that often forces even previously licensed arrivals to jump through crazy hoops, like pricey night courses. Districts often won't pay such incoming teachers commensurate with their seniority. As a result, many women (who still make up 70 percent of the teacher corps) leave the field if their husbands relocate. The situation is so bad that big cities routinely recruit overseas. New York has recruited in Canada, Austria, and the Caribbean; Philadelphia in India and Spain; Los Angeles in the Philippines; Houston in Russia. Chicago in recent years has interviewed in twenty-five countries, many less developed than the United States.

Add to the mix the fact that teachers with seniority and talent often high-tail it out of troubled schools as fast as they can, and the grim bottom line emerges: The neediest children in America routinely go from kindergarten to sixth grade and beyond with a brand new, untrained rookie "teaching" them each year. What could be more unjust?

Yet if it's possible, things will soon get worse, because many of the best teachers in the system will shortly retire. Until the 1960s and 1970s, schools got a huge hidden subsidy because many careers weren't open to women and minorities. Now, people who might once have taught science and social studies become doctors, lawyers, and engineers. Teaching salaries that start, on average, at $30,000 and rise to $44,000 simply don't cut it. Though many of today's talented teachers chose their work for love rather than money, it stands to reason that in terms of sheer brainpower, the current teacher corps can't match one inadvertently subsidized by bias. "You take three million of anything," Albert Shanker used to quip about America's teachers, "and you get a lot of average." Today we're getting worse. New teachers simply aren't coming from the top half of the class. Sandra Feldman, herself a product of the era of discrimination, was quite open about the problem. "You have in the schools right now, among the teachers who are going to be retiring, *very* smart people," she told me. "We're not getting in now the same kinds of people. In many places, it's disastrous. We've been saying for years now that we're attracting from the bottom third. This is a hard thing for us to say because we represent all these people."

How would we fix this if we were serious? Broadly speaking, there are two options: (1) improve the skills of the teachers we already have; (2) dramatically upgrade the caliber of the teaching corps through new recruits.

Out of necessity, the first track is where most daily discussion takes place; it's atop the agenda of every serious urban superintendent and union leader. Anthony Alvarado, head of New York City's District 2 from 1987 to 1998, who subsequently served as San Diego's chancellor for instruction, developed the model for progress in such efforts. Alvarado's mantra in District 2 was "teacher development, teacher development, teacher development." He poured money into professional development (from site-based peer coaches in reading and math to special summer institutes), and funded it by controversial cuts in areas (like classroom aides) considered perks for teachers or patronage for district managers. Student achievement rose significantly in District 2, where 60 percent of the children were poor, and early results suggest San Diego is moving in the right direction. There is now a cottage industry and emerging body of academic work on teacher development in large urban settings, and fairly broad consensus among educational leaders on the "culture of learning" being sought. That doesn't mean making it work on the ground is easy; on the contrary, creating a new culture and gaining teacher buy-in is a massive organizational challenge that often fails. It's one reason the job of urban school superintendent is among the toughest in the country. (Alvarado himself left San Diego in 2003 partly because he had become a lightning rod for criticism from the teachers union, which had resisted the reforms that he and superintendent Alan Bersin had championed.)

But what big city superintendents rarely acknowledge—in part because it cuts depressingly against their can-do grain—is that upgrading the skills of existing teachers can only get us so far. Changing the kind of person who goes into teaching isn't high on their agenda because it seems hopelessly beyond what their local budgets and policies can effect. Yet if we were serious as a country, this is exactly what national policy would stress: seizing this moment, at the cusp of a dramatic generational turnover in the teaching ranks, to lure a better caliber of college graduate to our toughest classrooms.

Money will need to be part of this, and we'll get to that. But let's stipulate first that pay isn't everything. Teachers are the only people I've ever met who routinely say, without irony, things similar to what one new teacher confided about her work: "It's so fulfilling, it's awesome!" For many, job security, good health and pension benefits, and summers off each year are worth the income trade-off.

In addition, getting serious about teacher quality will require a host of nonfinancial reforms. For starters, the human resource departments in big districts tend to be so poorly managed that top candidates flee. Then there's the lack of prestige. Tell them you're a teacher at a party, said Jene Galvin, a thirty-year veteran of Cincinnati's public schools, "and you can see the look on their face—like this guy couldn't do anything else or the only thing he could do was teach and the only place he could get a job was in Cincinnati's inner city. That is reality."

In the inner cities, working conditions often scare people off. When a district's de facto recruiting pitch is, "Join us and you'll have the chance to work in dilapidated schools in unsafe neighborhoods under incompetent supervisors," it's hardly surprising when talented people look elsewhere. Harold Levy, chancellor of New York City schools from 1999 to 2002, told me that when the city did a study asking teachers why they had left, the item mentioned most often was,

"I don't like bringing my car into that neighborhood where I have to work."

Discipline is a huge problem, and teachers have few ways to get the most disruptive kids, who ruin the learning environment for everyone, out of class. Then there's sheer volume: A high school social studies or English teacher commonly teaches 225 kids a day, in six classes of 35 or more. "Those numbers after a while wear you down, and so many of them are high-need," said Steve Steinberg, a fifteen-year veteran in L.A. "That's why the best teachers end up at the best suburban schools."

Pockets of improvement exist. Connecticut, for example, has made a systematic effort over twenty years to raise pay and professional standards at the same time, and urban children there score better than in most other states. Under Harold Levy, a "Chancellor's District" of low-performing schools in New York City received special attention, and teachers were offered a 15 percent pay hike to take on the challenge. Though Levy told me in retrospect that 15 percent wasn't enough to staff these schools properly, the schools showed twice the rate of gain of others in New York on reading and math. The New Teacher Project, started by Michele Rhee and Wendy Kopp of Teach for America, has worked with a number of cities to attract midcareer professionals to the classroom; in New York City, these "teaching fellows" accounted for one in four new hires in 2002, a remarkable achievement.

But here's the point: If we're honest, none of these developments, promising as they seem, can be brought to the scale of today's need. In other words, just as it is true that salary isn't all that matters, it is equally true that nonsalary measures alone will never suffice to attract and retain hundreds of thousands of talented new teachers for poor districts. When it comes to the shortage specialties, and the nation's toughest schools, there's no avoiding this reality: If we're serious, we need to talk about money.

This shouldn't come as news. In 1970 in New York City, a starting lawyer going into a prestigious firm and a starting teacher going into public education had a differential in their entry salary of about $2000, said Harold Levy. Today, between salary and bonus, that starting lawyer makes $145,000, while starting teachers in New York City earn roughly $40,000. "Why would we think the laws of supply and demand have been repealed with respect to public education and with respect to the labor market here?" Levy asked me. "We have teachers who have to supplement their income by being waiters and waitresses. That's obscene."

Roy Romer explained his dilemma when it came to staffing L.A.'s toughest schools. Senior teachers have the right to pick congenial assignments in more upscale neighborhoods, and Romer knew he couldn't force someone to teach in the inner city if she didn't want to; she'd simply leave the profession. But what frustrated Romer is that he didn't have the money (or the ability, under the union contract) to offer substantial pay differentials to encourage talented teachers who might be willing to take the plunge.

———

Conservatives I've talked with agree that these children deserve better; they also appreciate that market forces largely determine where the top talent goes. Look at Table 6.1, which compares teacher salaries in some major U.S. cities with those offered in nearby suburbs. When the suburbs (1) pay more, (2) have better working conditions, and (3) serve easier-to-teach kids who bring fewer problems to school, we're essentially relying on missionaries to bring quality instruction to urban America. How many more years need to pass before we admit that the missionary "plan" isn't working?

Yet conservatives rightly worry that pouring more money into today's system subsidizes mediocrity, rather than luring new talent, especially when union rules make it next to impossible to fire bad teachers. "Dismissing a tenured teacher," one California official has said, "is not a process, it's a career." The effort can involve hundreds of thousands of dollars, years of legal due process, and a paperwork burden that becomes a lifestyle choice. Since few administrators want to pursue dismissal when the odds seem so long, bad teachers are shuffled scandalously from school to school. "The only way to get them out of the school system is if they take a kid and shove him up

**Table 6.1 Teacher Salaries —
Urban Versus Nearby Suburban Districts**

2002–2003 Contract Year

District	Starting Salary	Maximum Salary
New York, N.Y.	$39,000	$81,232
Scarsdale, N.Y.	$41,488	$106,305
Chicago, Ill.	$34,538	$63,276
New Trier Township, Ill.	$39,608	$94,545
Philadelphia, Penn.	$33,249	$69,056
Upper Merion, Penn.	$35,025	$84,605
Washington, D.C.	$31,892	$62,175
Montgomery County, Md.	$36,841	$82,263
Cleveland, Ohio	$32,684	$69,325
Shaker Heights, Ohio	$34,521	$79,595
Boston, Mass.	$38,934	$74,613
Newton, Mass.	$36,866	$77,077
Los Angeles, Calif.	$39,974	$70,145
Santa Monica/Malibu, Calif.	$39,021	$78,442

Source: District personnel and human resources offices; local union contracts.

Note: Starting salary is for a certified teacher with a bachelor's degree. Maximum salary is the highest possible based on a ten-month, normal length day contract. To be eligible for this maximum, a teacher typically will have a doctorate degree and at least fifteen years of experience. The maximum may also include bonuses for longevity or merit.

against the wall," one former school board member told me, "and even then it's not easy to do." While national data are not available, in a recent five-year period only 62 of California's 220,000 tenured teachers were dismissed. Partly that's because performance evaluation is a charade, with only a handful of teachers receiving "unsatisfactory" ratings each year. To be fair, unions say that it's not always their fault. In many cities, teachers are on probation for the first few years, meaning they can be fired with few hassles. When poor performers aren't dismissed it's because districts are desperate. "They're holding their breath up to a mirror to see if it's there," said Sandra Feldman. "They're putting warm bodies in classrooms and then beating up on the unions because the [dismissal] process takes too long."

The right conclusion is that there's no way to get top talent without paying up. But that doesn't mean simply throwing money at the problem—we need money wedded to (and, in effect, helping to buy) sensible reforms. The obvious "grand bargain" here would be to make more cash available for teachers in exchange for flexibility in how the money is doled out. That means scrapping the standard "lockstep" union pay scale, under which a biochemistry grad has to be paid the same as a phys ed major if both have the same tenure in the classroom, even though the science grad has lucrative options outside teaching. It also means making it much easier to dismiss low performers that even union leaders agree are blighting the lives of up to 10 percent of urban children. When I first posed this deal to Sandra Feldman a few years ago, she told me that teachers were so underpaid that you'd first need to hike salaries across-the-board by 30 percent—then she'd be willing to discuss serious pay differentials. At the time, I thought, at least that's an offer. You can put a number on it, and start a negotiation. Some educators I told of our conversation felt Feldman was shooting for the moon. But after reflection, and conversations with more urban school officials, teachers, and analysts, I've concluded that Feldman wasn't aiming high enough.

So what if we were serious? What if we owned up to the reality that when Los Angeles raised its starting salaries, as it did recently, from $37,000 to $39,500, or when New York raised them, as it did, from $33,000 to $39,000, and when both cities' salaries top out at $70,000 to $80,000 after more than twenty years in the classroom, this has not and will not have much effect on the career choices of college graduates looking at teaching, and therefore cannot begin to dent the injustice we're perpetuating in poor schools? What would it sound like if we were serious? It might sound something like this:

The goal would be to make teaching poor children the career of choice for talented young Americans who want to make a difference with their lives and make a good living while doing so. Today we have something called Title I through which the federal government provides supplementary funds to poor schools. A serious plan would launch a new program that we could think of as "Title I for Teachers." The federal government would raise salaries for every teacher in poor schools in America by *50 percent*. But this offer would be conditioned on two fundamental reforms. First, the teachers unions would have to let us raise the top half of performers in the teacher corps *another 50 percent on average*. Second, the unions would have to streamline the dismissal process for poor-performing teachers to a fair, swift, four- to six-month period.

This would mean that in a city like Los Angeles—where starting teachers earn $40,000 and top out, after twenty-five years and a Ph.D., at $70,000—there would be a new deal. Starting teachers would earn $60,000, and the best teachers—not all, mind you, but the best—would earn close to $150,000 a year. The *top performing half* of teachers would make $85,000–90,000 a year on average. With the amount they would be able to put aside in savings at these salaries, the aim would be to make America's best teachers of poor children *millionaires* over their careers. We need nothing less if we're to change the way this essential career is viewed by our brightest college graduates.

Some people may say this is crazy. But what is really crazy is that we've waited this long. After all, we've long paid market rates for talent the nation needs when it comes to researchers at the National Institutes of Health or economists at the Federal Reserve—and "combat pay" is a time-honored practice when we ask Americans to take on the toughest assignments.

Rather than be embarrassed to say what they do for a living, teachers of poor children would be held in awe—both for the commitment they've made to one of the nation's most important professions, and for the prestige and rewards their nation has decided this calling merits. We would honor our great teachers the way we honor our great entrepreneurs, our great scientists, our great physicians.

To make this new deal for teachers of poor children a reality, of course, many changes must happen. Teachers and their representatives would need to embrace a new bargain under which the profession becomes a true profession—with the rewards it deserves—in exchange for the kind of accountability and performance assessment that union rules today all but rule out. And money alone isn't the answer. We would also need an array of reforms to support good teaching in the classroom, including safe schools in good repair, career paths that let top teachers take on more responsibility, and new freedom to discipline the few children who spoil everyone's chance to learn.

Critics are sure to raise plenty of questions about such a plan—why this district and not that; how can we assess teachers fairly—and it will be important to discuss the details of how we get from here to there. But the "there" must be nonnegotiable.

This plan to make teaching poor children the most exciting career in America will cost roughly $30 billion a year—a 7 percent increase in the nation's k–12 spending that would buy a 1000 percent revolution in the way teaching is viewed. It would double the federal share of k–12 spending from 7 percent to 14 percent—which is only right, since poor districts can't foot the bill themselves. When we're failing 10 million poor children, the problem is *national*. And a national problem like this will take national resources and leadership to solve it.

There's the plan. We'll also toss in a similar 50 percent pay hike for principals, taking them from $80,000 to $120,000 on average (with the nation's best getting upward of $200,000), because there's a terrible shortage of quality principals as well (this costs only a few billion, since there are far fewer principals than teachers, and I've included it in the $30 billion).

Now, before we get into what it would take to implement this vision, let's stop for a moment and see how it stacks up against other teacher quality "plans." President Bush offers small tax breaks for classroom supplies, nice but symbolic plans to inch up "Troops to Teachers," and an unfunded mandate ordering states to have a qualified teacher in every class by 2006. Senator John Edwards of North Carolina, who's made education a major theme of his presidential campaign, offers rhetoric that honors the spirit of the idea I've outlined while offering $3 billion a year, as opposed to $30 billion, toward this purpose—a resource gap that is typical of other Democratic proposals. Compare this proposal also to the handful of struggling experiments around the country that purport to test the impact of "pay differentials," but that involve amounts far too marginal (usually bonuses of $1000 or $2000) to give teachers and their unions any incentive to make it work.

We know for a start, then, that we're operating at a level that's serious. What do those on the front lines think? To find out I shopped the idea in conversations with superintendents who either today or recently have been responsible for 2.6 million urban schoolchildren, union leaders who've represented more than 1 million teachers, and assorted education experts and teachers. The response was overwhelmingly positive.

"I'd endorse something like that in a hot minute," said Day Higuchi, who was president of the Los Angeles teachers union from 1996 to 2002. Higuchi thought the impact would be substantial.

> Right now L.A. Unified is the employer of last resort. People who can't get jobs elsewhere come here. If we did this, we'd become the employer of first resort and the percentage of credentialed teachers that you can hire initially—teachers in other districts who have a good record they bring with them and a credential—and your more high-powered college students will be taking the job. The flush-out rate is tremendous. At least a quarter of the teachers who try to become teachers in L.A. Unified don't make it through the first year. Half of them are gone by the third year. So if you had an influx of new talent, they would stick.

A similar reaction came from Arne Duncan, CEO of the Chicago Public Schools. "There's very little incentive outside of pure altruism" to go into teaching, Duncan explained. "It would dramatically change the face of the teacher profession."

Rod Paige, secretary of education in the Bush administration and the longtime superintendent in Houston before that, was also impressed with the concept. Although Paige didn't like the idea of it being a federal plan funded with new money, preferring the funds to be shifted from current spending, he went on to say that the federal government obviously has a role; that famous 1983 report, he said, was called *A Nation at Risk,* not *50 States at Risk.* In the end, Paige said, maybe if the plan redirected part of today's 7 percent federal contribution toward something like this, and then added some more to sweeten the pot, it might be a promising way to go. But Paige felt strongly that state and local governments needed to have some "skin in the game" or else it would be a "gravy train."

These reactions suggest that we have the makings of something constructive. My talks with educators on the challenges they see suggest the contours of the conversation we'd need and the sense that a deal is doable. The biggest concerns revolved around two questions: *How* do we decide which teachers are better performers, and *Who* decides?

As a threshold matter, the fact that union leaders felt it made sense to move toward serious pay differentials for teachers was important. When I talked to teachers, superintendents, and even secretaries of education, I said to Sandra Feldman, they said that when they go into the faculty lounge at a school and ask, "Who are the best teachers in the school?" everybody knows, and there's a consensus. Do you feel that's true? I asked her.

"Absolutely true," Feldman said.

"So people know there are differences in quality or impact?"

"Absolutely right." Feldman also agreed that in a sense it was unfair that these better teachers weren't getting rewarded via higher pay now. But you still have to find a way of doing it that most teachers can buy into, she said, and that doesn't seem like cronyism. To Feldman, part of the answer is to raise pay substantially for designated shortage specialties, like math, science, and bilingual education. The other promising path was differentiated roles. A talented classroom teacher might spend part of her time developing curriculum, she said. A great math teacher, where there's a tremendous need, could become a special coach or resource person for the subject at her site. Others might earn designation as mentors.

Ted Mitchell, president of Occidental College and former dean of the UCLA School of Education, said we might reach consensus more easily by not trying to nail down every gradation. "There's a virtue in identifying these teachers by working from the ends to the middle, but not trying to get to a line between 'good' teachers and 'bad' teachers," Mitchell said.

Everybody agrees that there are some groups of bad teachers. Everybody agrees that there is some group of superstar teachers. So let's work at identifying those and let's just acknowledge that in the middle it's probably too hard to make fine-grained distinction in teacher performance. So we're not talking about merit pay for every teacher at the school site and having to make determinations about whether Sally Smith teaching seventh grade social studies deserves a better raise than Paul Jones teaching eighth grade algebra. But if one of them can be acknowledged as a superstar teacher then they go in this other category, and if one of them is regarded as substandard by their peers then we get rid of them.

To gauge conservative reaction I spoke with Chester E. "Checker" Finn, a leading school reformer on the right. Finn is president of the Thomas Fordham Foundation and served as assistant secretary of education in the Reagan administration. "The troubling part is a 50 percent boost for just showing up for work," Finn said, "without any reference to whether anybody you teach learns a damned thing. That's the big problem here."

I told Finn this was essentially the bribe I was offering the unions—making the offer so compelling, thc antc so rich, that it was a clear "win" for them to bring to their members, in exchange for real reform in pay and dismissal practices. To be sure, I told him, I had worried at first, too, about wastefully paying up for mediocrity. But most observers told me the turnover in big districts is so high that within five years you'd have flushed out many of the bad teachers anyway. To the extent that this plan's higher pay lowered turnover, the ability to dismiss poor performers more easily still gave us the chance to lure a new corps of talent under this proposal and start anew.

Finn wasn't done venting. "A lot of them are inept and ineffective and unmotivated and could care less," Finn said of today's teachers. Many Americans, he said, see teachers working five hours a day, 180 days a year with little to show for it in terms of what children are learning. "I don't think you're going to get a real good reception for just paying a whole bunch for showing up without any connection to kids learning or working longer or doing more of something."

"If you wanted to make it really interesting," Finn added, "you'd surrender job security and tenure in return for this raise."

The swap here ought to be you take a risk with your employment and you don't have to be retained if you're not good at what you do. If you are and you get retained, you get paid a whole bunch more money. My version of this has always been that if it's too heavy-duty for current teachers to swallow that trade-off, make this is a whole parallel personnel system for new ones coming in and for the existing ones that want to do it.

How might that work in practice? I asked.

"Any current teacher is free to join this new system on its terms," Finn said, "or stick with the old arrangements in which they have high security and low pay. That's just a political accommodation to an existing workforce for whom this might be too abrupt a shift. Obviously, everybody would opt into the higher pay part if that were the only part. If you're into a mix of higher pay and reduced job security and higher performance expectations, then you have to go through a calculus. Over time you'll get a very different kind of person into teaching under that system."

"It sounds tempting from a union point of view," said Sandra Feldman of a two-track approach. "The more volunteerism you can get in a system like this, the easier it is to sell. But I worry about people working together at a school level. I worry that something like that could create resentment between the people in the different tracks."

Roy Romer was also drawn to a two-track approach. "If you've got to pay this to the existing people with the existing work rules and the existing contract, it's wasted," Romer said.

You've got to say, we're going to divide it. Here's the pasture over here. For those of you who want to stay, fine. This is a new pasture and here's what you've got to do to join this pasture and here's the reward for it. First of all, you've got to demonstrate that you have content knowledge. If you don't have it, you don't get paid for it. Secondly, you've got to accept the fact that this is not a six-hour work day and that there is a commitment to a different hourly schedule and an 11-month year and thirty days for vacation. It's a new annual contract. Third, you have got to assume responsibility for a personal relationship to the students.

They have to have access to you and you have to have concern for them. There is absolute research-based evidence that many kids don't learn because nobody gives them a feeling that they're worthwhile and the safety of an adult who cares for them. I simply say you don't get into this [new high-paying system] unless you commit to it [time-wise] in certain fundamental ways.

Both Sandra Feldman and Harold Levy spoke about the need for poor students to have more time with teachers, a proposition teachers are perfectly open to, Feldman said, so long as they get paid for it, as this plan would assure. Research shows, for example, that disadvantaged kids lose lots of learning in the summer. Good summer schools, Saturday morning and after-school programs, and even Romer-style commitments to individual students might all be ways of getting more from teachers as part of a big new bargain. Both union and district leaders told me they thought virtually every new hire would opt into the new track if it were voluntary, along with perhaps a quarter of the existing senior teachers, meaning that you'd have the bulk of the teacher corps on the new regime within five years.

The role of test scores in teacher ratings spurred predictable debate. Superintendents, along with conservative reformers, wanted test scores given serious weight. At the same time, they recognized current limits to so-called "value-added analysis"—the effort, pioneered by Tennessee researcher William Sanders, to track the impact of an individual teacher on her students each year. In theory, this is the holy grail of "accountability," and thus the dream basis for performance pay. "There's just no reliable way of doing that right now," Sandra Feldman told me. This wasn't only a union view. Joseph Olchefkse, until recently the superintendent in Seattle, has studied the issue, and he felt it would be hard to bring this measure down to the level of the individual teacher. Others think individual value-added measures may soon be practical. Day Higuchi, the longtime L.A. union leader, argued that in elementary school, where children basically have only one teacher, we could constructively measure that teacher's impact if we got the testing right.

Finn and others suggested a blended approach to teacher assessment. "You could have a mixture of value-added analysis at the school level, which is clearly going to be done," said Finn, "combined with some other kind of performance reviews of the individuals within the school." There seemed to be ways to reach common ground here. "It would be a fatal mistake not to include student learning outcomes as the ultimate test of this," said Adam Urbanski, the president of the Rochester Teacher's Union, who has spearheaded union reform efforts for two decades. "It would be equally fatal to use only test scores because you would have a huge invitation to cheating and manipulation—and nobody is better at creative insubordination than school people."

Urbanski, with others, said we need to depolarize the testing argument. Test scores should be part of the teacher assessment, but so should other indicators that educators and the public consider germane—such as dropout rates, graduation rates, peer review, specialized training, classroom practice, and student work. Linda Darling Hammond, professor of education at Stanford University, suggested a process of peer review like that done for teachers granted the elite National Board Certification. It's a process many teachers respect, because other teachers are conducting the assessment. But Romer, with other superintendents, didn't think anything modeled on the National Board system could suffice, because it doesn't include student outcomes. "That's what's happened here time and time again," said San Diego's superintendent Alan Bersin. "You start out with a good idea but it reduces itself to who controls the determination, it becomes a power issue and student issues fall off the agenda. You've got to make this outcome-driven."

"Blended systems are fine," concluded Arthur Levine of Columbia University's Teachers College. "But don't give away the store. If student achievement is the most important thing we care about, that's got to be a major part of the reason for the improvement in salaries."

One promising model that honors the contours of this discussion has been developed by the Milken Family Foundation, under the leadership of Lowell Milken (brother of former financier Michael) and Lew Solmon, a Milken foundation executive and former dean of UCLA's School of Education. Called the "Teacher Advancement Program" (TAP), it features career paths, intensive professional development, ongoing evaluation, and differential compensation. In the 2002–2003 school year, TAP was being piloted in thirty-four schools in Arizona, South Carolina, Arkansas, Colorado, Indiana, and Florida, with thirty-seven more schools slated to begin the program in the 2003–2004 school year (including several in an additional state, Louisiana). Seventy-five percent of the teachers have to vote in favor of the program before TAP will come in to a school. In the first year, teachers are trained in the concept, modify the evaluation criteria to suit their school's needs, and select mentor and master teachers. In the second year TAP starts conducting and honing the teacher evaluations, which occur six to ten times a year; in year three it phases in performance pay. "We do it slowly," Solmon told me. "From the bottom up rather than the top down."

Under the plan, 50 percent of a teacher's bonus goes for the teacher's skills and knowledge, as reflected in the evaluations, which include extensive classroom observation. The other 50 percent is for student "value-added" (30 percent for schoolwide measures, 20 percent for the individual teacher). Mentor and master teachers work with colleagues to improve areas of weakness. For professional development, TAP alters the schedule so that every week there are two to five hours when teachers are out of their classrooms, meeting in cluster groups with mentor or master teachers to solve problems they're having. It's too soon to gauge TAP's impact, of course, and local financial constraints mean its pay scales and bonuses (up to $20,000) offer far less upside than the magnitudes we're discussing. But early signs are promising. In one district in Arizona, for example, the reform has prompted some experienced teachers who appreciate TAP's emphasis on both professional development and on being rewarded for their effectiveness to move from wealthier schools without TAP to poorer schools with TAP, reversing the usual flow.

Moving from the question of "how" to "who," the superintendents all told me that principals need to be the final arbiter of teacher performance—a sticking point with the unions. The problem with giving principals exclusive control, said Sandra Feldman, is that many teachers feel they don't know the first thing about good teaching. Jene

Galvin, the thirty-year Cincinnati schools veteran, thought the millionaire teacher plan was a "home run idea," but said he was with Feldman on the issue of principals. "We don't look at the principals and really believe that they are the experts on pedagogy or classroom teaching or classroom management," Galvin told me. "The reason is they just didn't do it very long." An obvious answer here is to have peer evaluators play a serious role in teacher ratings; in the Milken program, for example, mentor and master teachers do the evaluations along with principals. Galvin's other suggestion was intriguing. He'd require principals to teach, perhaps one period a day. "It links them to their teachers," he said, "and might soften some of the worry that they don't know what the hell they're doing."

"I'm sick of this argument that the principals are bozos," Finn said, when I played back these critiques. But this comment notwithstanding, Finn felt, along with other leaders in the education community I spoke with, that these implementation challenges seemed surmountable. So I asked Finn, if this entire new compensation arrangement were done along the lines we'd discussed, as a parallel track, is it right to say it's an approach he would not feel uncomfortable with?

"No," Finn said, "I wouldn't feel uncomfortable with it, provided that it included the ability for managers of schools to have a whole lot of control over who is working in their school."

All this suggests what the contours of negotiation would sound like, with enough positive noises to think progress is possible. As Chicago schools chief Arne Duncan summed it up, "If people couldn't figure that out, shame on us." At the broader political level, moreover, it turns out that some savvy Republicans think the timing for a plan like this is ripe, once an understandable mental hurdle is surmounted. As things stand, you can't talk to Republicans about teachers without union politics coloring the discussion. After all, teacher unions are big Democratic donors and the chief foes of GOP efforts to introduce voucher programs. The last thing we need is a bunch of rich teachers, runs party logic on teacher pay. All they'd do is contribute more money to make sure Republicans never get elected.

But Rick Davis, a political adviser to John McCain, thinks the issue, and the kind of deal we're discussing, may be inevitable. "Anybody who has looked at teacher pay as an element of the overall problem in education realizes that money matters," Davis told me.

> In the [2000] campaign with McCain we wanted to get out there on teacher pay. It was a very difficult task because we had a hard time figuring out how you pay for it. . . . What everyone liked about Bush's [testing] plan is that it didn't cost them any money. The reality is that it's a good time for this debate. We've exhausted the easy stuff on education. We've got this accountability thing and everyone is going to get tested. By the year 2005 everyone is going to be so tired of standardized testing that there will be a revolt on that. *But we've exhausted, other than the voucher debate, the Republican position on education. So sooner or later we're going to get to teacher pay because we can't be against teachers making money. The American public is going to figure out that their teacher makes less than their garbage collector and they're not going to be for that.* Johnny's teacher should make more than the guy who picks up our garbage. (emphasis added)

My instinct would be to roll out this agenda via a federal challenge. A Two Percent leader would say, "We're putting this pot of money on the table for those communities that can come together around a plan to meet its conditions and make it work." This could reverse the ordinary political dynamics, in which unions and district managers play an inside game without broad public awareness or pressure. Now, instead, parents, local media, and business leaders could ask why unions were balking (if they were) at billions. Rank and file teachers would have a huge stake in the plan's adoption, since they'd stand to lose the chance to earn an extra $20,000 to $50,000 a year. This constituency might help change internal union politics, creating incentives for union leaders to find ways to speedily dismiss poor performers.

There are other benefits. This plan could lure some talent from the suburbs toward higher-paying jobs in the city, which would be a reversal from current norms. It could draw a critical mass of America's best young talent to its toughest neighborhoods, where they'd doubtless apply their energies to problems that go beyond the confines of the schools. "The inadequate development of the human resources of the children of poor families," said economist Arthur Okun in 1974, "is one of the most serious inefficiencies of the American economy." Thirty years later nothing has changed. Corporate America is estimated to spend $80 billion a year retraining high school graduates to work in modern industry. Thirty billion dollars to attract and retain great teachers for poor kids may be the best long-term economic investment we'll ever make. "It's not like there's a constitutional requirement that we only provide 7 or 8 percent of the funding for public education," Senator John Edwards told me. "It's a mind-set."

"Unions are ready to give away more than they have in the past," said Columbia's Arthur Levine.

There are real questions about their future and they're not dumb. My guess is that they're going to be more flexible in all kinds of issues, particularly if they bring a benefit to their members. The harder part of what you're talking about is getting government to put up the money, not getting unions to compromise. Who's getting bad teachers in the United States? Poor people. They don't vote. The reality is we talk about it a lot but we don't care. So why would we pay for them to get good teachers if they're satisfied the way things are?

———

I recently caught up with Vince Eisman, the teacher whom I met on his first day as a teacher in 1999. Now he was 34, starting his fourth year, and he was considered a star. His principal hailed him. He had won local accolades. His colleagues regarded him as a leader. He also told me he was planning to leave the Los Angeles school system at the end of the year.

It was a hundred things, really. "I love teaching in the inner city," Eisman told me. "I've loved teaching these kids." But he's tired. Tired of the lack of parental support. Tired of running out of paper in February and of not having pencils for his class. Fresh budget cuts were making it worse. Eisman had hoped to buy a house, but on his salary it was out of the question. The federal government had a small program that gave teachers dibs on repossessed homes, but they were in such unsafe neighborhoods, the idea was laughable. Eisman's mentor had urged him not to give up on teaching entirely, to at least try it where the whole package wasn't so hard. Eisman planned to move to a rural district upstate, where the quality of life was better, the children less troubled, the houses actually affordable.

I asked Eisman what he was earning. He'd come in at $32,000, I recalled. Now, he said, he was at $47,000. I thought about the plan we've been discussing. What if he'd come in at $60,000, I asked, and was up a similar $15,000 from that? "Would it be different if you were now earning $75,000?" I asked. His tone changed instantly.

"Totally different, completely different," Eisman said. "I would stay teaching in L.A. I love what I'm doing. $75,000 would make my humble little family very content. All those moments when I'm asking myself is this really worth it would be gone."

7

VOUCHERS EVEN LIBERALS

CAN LOVE

When Maria Neri's daughter Tina finished eighth grade a few years ago, her scholarship at a Catholic elementary school in south central Los Angeles ended. The parochial high school where Tina hoped to enroll charges $3500 a year, less than half of what Los Angeles would spend to educate Tina in public school. Maria, 33, earns $600 a month as a part-time teacher's aide; she's looking for a second job, and perhaps a third one as well. Her husband, from whom she is separated, earns $1200 a month as a laborer in a glass factory. He pays his wife's $340 monthly rent, but offers no support beyond that. After paying for food, a phone, gas, and other expenses, Neri had no money left to put toward private schools for Tina. Yet she was afraid to send Tina to the neighborhood public school, where the walls were covered with graffiti and where *cholos,* or gang members, had been involved in shootings that brought police helicopters to the campus. So Neri used her sister's address to enroll Tina at another public school, which, though twenty minutes away, at least seemed safer. But it is far from ideal. Classrooms each have 40 to 45 children, with different grades mixed together. Tina, 16, says the teachers have the students watch movies. Her math teacher was so confused about who Tina was that he gave her an "F" for not completing many assign-ments—a grade he changed, with an embarrassed apology, after Neri confronted him with Tina's completed workbook. "I can see the difference," Neri says. "She's going down." Tina tells her she would go back to Catholic school if they could afford it. "I talk to my daughter," Neri recounts, "and say, 'I'm sorry.'"

Neri's desire to send Tina to a better school is at the heart of one of the nation's most demagogic debates. Vouchers, often touted as a cure for Maria's dilemma, would give parents some or all of the money that government now spends educating their children to use at a school of their choice, not just the one to which they're assigned based on where they live. Depending on whom you listen to, vouchers are either a lifeline or a death knell for public education. "It is quite simply an issue of survival for our nation's poorest students," says Dan Coats, a former Republican senator from Indiana. But Kweisi Mfume, president of the NAACP, calls vouchers a "terrible threat," while Sandra Feldman of the American Federation of Teachers says they mean "a radical abandonment of public schools and public education."

These are heated claims, given how few students are involved in voucher programs today. Fifty-two million children attend grades k–12 in the United States. Only two cities offer publicly funded vouchers. In Milwaukee, whose breakthrough program was passed in 1990, about 12,000 of 104,000 students get a voucher; in Cleveland, they reach 5500 of 77,000 students. Florida's statewide plan served a mere fifty students before being ruled unconstitutional by a state court in August 2002. Privately funded voucher plans in thirty-nine states served 60,000 kids in 2002. Add it up and you get 77,500 kids—around one-tenth of one percent of America's students. Toss in 575,000 children in 2700 charter schools around the country (which also give parents a choice of which school to send their children to), and you're still at *1.2 percent* of schoolchildren. In other words, the voucher debate is taking place utterly at the margins.

As polls prove, an increasing number of minority parents like Maria Neri want a way out. A 2002 poll conducted by the Joint Center for Political and Economic Studies, for example, found that black voters supported vouchers by a margin of 57 to 42 percent; a 1997 poll by the same group found that such support increases dramatically among younger blacks, reaching 76 percent among those aged 18 to 35. It seems immoral to argue that these parents must wait for the day when their urban public schools are somehow "fixed." It's even harder to argue that bigger voucher programs could possibly make things worse.

Yet a political standoff has kept vouchers unavailable to more than 99 percent of urban schoolchildren. Most top Democrats oppose them, saying we should improve public schools rather than drain money from the system. That's no surprise, since teachers' unions are among the party's biggest donors, and send more delegates to the Democratic National Convention than even the state of California. Republicans endorse vouchers as a market-based way to shake up calcified bureaucracies, but generally push low-cost plans that affect only a handful of students. The distrust that fuels this gridlock is profound. Republicans view Democrats as union pawns defending a failed status quo; Democrats think Republicans want to use urban woes to scrap public education and the taxes that fund it.

Missing almost entirely from today's debate is the progressive pro-voucher perspective—which argues that support for education vouchers is perfectly consistent with other efforts to improve urban public schools, like the teacher initiative in the last chapter. Unfortunately, today's political orthodoxy insists these positions can't be coherent—you're either "for" improving public schools, or "for" vouchers that help people escape them. This is a false choice. It says less about the logic of reform than about the poverty of a debate that's strangled by interest groups and ideology on both sides. *Getting serious about recruiting a new generation of teachers while getting serious about vouchers are mutually reinforcing ways to accelerate improvement in poor schools.* Indeed, apart from the lifeline they offer to children who receive them, the very presence of vouchers—and the threat of their expansion—makes it far likelier that the union reforms needed to implement the Two Percent teacher initiative will happen, and happen fast.

The unions and the NAACP notwithstanding, vouchers have a long but unappreciated intellectual pedigree on the left, among reformers who've sought them to help poor children and to equalize funding in rich and poor districts. This "voucher left" has always had less cash and political power than its conservative counterpart or its union foes and has been ignored by the press. But to give urban school-children more hope—and in ways that complement a new national effort to make teaching poor children a career of choice—the voucher left must find its voice.

Finding a productive compromise here means recalling the role of progressives in the history of the voucher movement, and exposing the bipartisan charades that continue to poison the debate over education. It means finding a way for unorthodox new leaders to build a coalition—liberals for whom the moral urgency of helping poor children trumps ancient union ties, and conservatives who reject a laissez-faire approach to life's unfairness. The goal of such an alliance should be yet another "grand bargain": a major multiyear test of vouchers that touches not 5000 but 1 million children—and *increases* school spending in the process. The conventional wisdom says that today's whittled-down pilot programs are all that is politically achievable. The paradox is that only by thinking bigger about how vouchers might help poor children and improve public schools can a more durable coalition emerge.

Jack and Milton

In 1962, John E. "Jack" Coons, an idealistic 32-year-old law professor at Northwestern University, was asked by the U.S. Civil Rights Commission to study whether Chicago schools were complying with de-segregation orders. Coons soon found that what really interested him was a different question: Why were suburban schools so much better than those downtown? Over the next few years, Coons, eventually joined by his students Stephen Sugarman and William Clune, found one answer in what would become a source of enduring outrage: America's property-tax-based system of public school finance created dramatic disparities in the resources available to educate children.

This financial aspect of education's vaunted tradition of "local control" is rarely the subject of national controversy. In part that's because it gives the nation's most powerful citizens an entitlement to lower taxes *and* better schools. Imagine two towns, Slumville and

Suburbia. Slumville has $100,000 in taxable property per pupil; Suburbia has $300,000. If Slumville votes to tax its property at 4 percent, it raises $4000 per pupil. But Suburbia can tax itself at 2 percent and raise $6000 per pupil. Presto! Suburbia's tax rate is half as high, but its public schools enjoy 50 percent more resources per student.

In the 1960s affluent districts routinely spent twice what nearby poorer ones did, and sometimes four or five times as much. To Coons and his colleagues, such inequity in a public service was indefensible. Beginning with the book *Private Wealth and Public Education,* which he, Sugarman, and Clune published in 1970, Coons has denounced the system eloquently. It's worth sampling his arguments, because the left's case for choice is rarely heard. In a 1992 essay, "School Choice as Simple Justice," Coons wrote:

> This socialism for the rich we blithely call "public," though no other public service entails such financial exclusivity. Whether the highway, the swimming pool, the library or the hospital—if it is public, it is accessible. But admission to the government school comes only with the price of the house. If the school is in Beverly Hills or Scarsdale, the poor need not apply.

Coons' point was simple: The quality of public education should not depend on local wealth—unless it is of the wealth of a state as a whole. "Everyone ought to be put in a roughly equivalent position with regard to what the state will do," Coons says.

Coons and Sugarman made a successful case for the unconstitutionality of the school finance system in California's famous *Serrano* case in 1971, beginning a national movement to litigate for school equity. Although it was little noticed then, they cited vouchers as a potential remedy. The idea was to give courts a way to instruct legislatures to fix things without having to mess with "local control." Asking legislatures to centralize school funding entirely at the state level was a political nonstarter. But through various formulas, Coons and Sugarman argued, the state could give families in poorer districts enough cash in the form of vouchers to bring their spending up to that of wealthier districts. And what could be more "local," they reasoned, than giving families direct control over the cash to use at schools as they chose?

Coons and Sugarman, focusing on school equity, thus arrived at a policy that Milton Friedman had been urging through a principled commitment to liberty, and to its embodiment, the market. Friedman's 1955 essay, "The Role of Government in Education," is generally viewed as the fountainhead of the voucher movement. In an ideal world, Friedman reasoned, the government might have no role in schooling at all; yet a minimum required level of education and its financing by the state can be justified:

> A stable and democratic society is impossible without widespread acceptance of some common set of values and without a minimum degree of literacy and knowledge on the part of most citizens . . . the gain from the education of a child accrues not only to the child but to other members of society. . . . Yet it is not feasible to identify the particular individuals benefited or the money value of the benefit and so to charge for the services rendered.

However, Friedman said, if this "neighborhood effect" meant that the government was warranted in paying for k–12 education, another question remained: Should the government run the schools as well? Friedman's insight was that schools could be just as "public" if the government financed but didn't administer them. This notion remains virtually unintelligible to leaders in public education, perhaps because it is so threatening.

Friedman's analogy (adopted by every voucher fan since) was to the G.I. Bill, which gave veterans a maximum sum per year to spend at the college or university of their choice, provided it met certain minimum standards. Likewise, for elementary and secondary schooling, Friedman envisioned a universal voucher scheme that would give parents a fixed sum per child, redeemable at an "approved" school of their choice. Such schools might be nonprofit or for-profit, religious or secular. Parents could add to the sum if they wanted. Government's role would be limited to assuring that "approved" schools included some minimum common content in their programs, "much as it now inspects restaurants to assure that they maintain minimum sanitary standards." To Friedman, market-style competition for students would spur the development of schools that were better tailored to families' needs and cost less than those run by notoriously inefficient public bureaucracies.

Friedman's and Coons' different angles of vision represent the ancient tug between liberty and equality within the pro-voucher camp—a debate the two have waged since Friedman was an occasional guest on Coons' Chicago radio show, "Problems of the City," in the 1960s. Friedman, for example, isn't bothered by issues of school finance equity. "What's your view of inequity in clothing and food?" he snapped when I asked about it, saying such concerns reflect Coons' "socialistic approach." And even if public schools were making every child an Einstein, Friedman said, he would still want vouchers. "Private enterprise as opposed to collectivism," he told me, "would always be better."

Coons is less ideological. In his view, choice would improve the public schools, which he believes would always be chosen by the majority, even with a full-blown voucher system. The prospect of losing students and thus losing funding would force improvements faster than today's seemingly endless rounds of ineffectual education fads. If poor children were getting a decent education under the current system, he added, he probably wouldn't have devoted his life to these issues.

The fate of disadvantaged kids under a voucher regime is where the Coons–Friedman clash is sharpest. Coons would be glad to offer vouchers to all low-income students and to no one else if a consensus for this step could be reached. He fears that under a universal voucher system they could get left behind, as schools competed to recruit richer, smarter, healthier students. The incentives are plain: Such children would be easier (and ultimately cheaper) to teach, and schools could charge wealthy families far more than the voucher amount to maximize profit. Coons and the voucher left therefore insist that any universal scheme include protections for low-income children, as well as for those with learning or physical disabilities. Examples would be increasing the voucher amount for those children to make them more attractive to schools, and letting schools redeem their voucher only if, say, 15 percent of new places were reserved for such children, for whom the voucher would cover tuition. To Friedman, these are unacceptable intrusions on schools' freedom to operate as they like, turning vouchers into "a welfare program, not an education program."

Bipartisan Charades

Because the liberal pro-voucher champions have been opposed by the teachers' unions, they have had little political impact. The muting of their voice, combined with the ease of legislating pilot programs, explains why few urban children have a choice today. At the same time, deceptive arguments made by both teachers' unions and conservative activists keep the broader public confused. Debunking these charades is essential for thinking clearly about how a larger voucher effort might prove useful.

Teachers' unions (and voucher foes generally) rely on five dubious arguments:

There's no evidence that vouchers work.   The trials have been so isolated, unions say, that their results are unproved. That's a nervy case to make when union opposition has kept the trials small. Pro- and anti-voucher forces have funded research in Milwaukee and Cleveland that purports to show why Johnny is doing demonstrably better or worse under vouchers. It's impossible to make sense of these dueling studies, whose sample sizes are so small that results seem likely to turn on whether, say, three kids in Cleveland turned in their homework on time. For now, the "no evidence" argument says more about union chutzpah than about voucher performance.

Vouchers drain money from public schools.   Sandra Feldman told me that the millions of dollars Cleveland uses to give a few thousand children vouchers would be better spent shrinking class size and launching proven reading programs. But this is disingenuous. When Cleveland launched its program, the city provided $10 million in addition to more than $600 million in existing school spending in order to mollify unions, which insisted that vouchers not "come out of the hide" of public schools. It's unfair for the unions to turn around and complain that the cash they insisted on should have gone elsewhere. The truth is that public schools are free to fund such measures now by shifting priorities within their vastly larger budgets. And when broader voucher plans let the amount that public schools receive per student follow students who leave the system, the public school coffers are not drained—schools receive the resources their enrollment merits.

Vouchers are unconstitutional. For years critics have said that if vouchers can be used to send a child to a religious school, it would violate the Constitution's ban on "establishment of religion," but the Supreme Court, in a 5 to 4 decision in June 2002, upheld Cleveland's program against this challenge. The majority ruled that so long as the voucher goes to the parents, to use where they like, and not to any particular type of school directly, it passes constitutional muster. The legal wars will continue, of course, as unions pursue a new era of state-level constitutional litigation. In the end, while precedents can be invoked for either outcome, the better view of confused American jurisprudence in this area is that vouchers are indeed constitutional. After all, no one thinks federal student loans are unconstitutional when students use them to attend Notre Dame. In union hands, this legal complaint always seems suspiciously tactical. It can't be that we're constitutionally obliged to imprison urban kids in failing schools.

The capacity isn't there. Public schools serve 46 million k–12 children; private schools serve 6 million. Since private schools can't accommodate more than a fraction of today's students, opponents say, vouchers can't be a meaningful part of school reform. "Where are these schools going to come from?" Sandra Feldman asked me repeatedly during an interview.

The first response to this argument is to ask, Then what's the problem? If as a practical matter unions feel that most children with vouchers will remain where they are, it's hard to see what the harm is in trying them. A second response is that even relatively few defections from public schools may spark steps to improve them. Districts with innovative charter schools have reported such a reaction.

The larger answer, however, is that broader voucher programs would prompt many institutions and entrepreneurs to add schools and spaces to the "market." This would happen not overnight but over a number of years. The initial spaces would be likely to come from Catholic schools, which account for half the private school slots in the country. Jerome Porath, who for twenty-two years served as schools chief for archdioceses in Los Angeles, Washington, D.C., and Albany, New York, told me that if every student got a voucher worth an amount close to the current per-pupil expenditure, over several years enough facilities could be built or rented "to accommodate everybody who wanted to come." "We'll get out our spreadsheets and figure it out," he said. "You can't think of it in terms of the existing stock of schools," added Milton Friedman. "There will be a flood of new schools started."

Profit is bad.   Voucher foes act as if there were something venal about the profit motive when applied to schools. But public education is already big business. The $420 billion spent each year on k–12 schooling is openly lusted after by textbook publishers, test designers, building contractors, food and janitorial services, and software companies, to name only a few examples. This brings inevitable scandals—for example, the flap in California a few years ago over whether campaign contributions influenced a big textbook purchase. Like health care, defense, and other major public services, schools will always be partly about business; vouchers would simply change who controls the flow of cash. There's no reason to think that the abuses under a voucher system would be worse than the abuses today.

Voucher foes make other unpersuasive claims. They say that vouchers will cream off the most talented children and the most active parents—a worry that seems acute primarily because today's voucher plans remain tiny. They say that private schools will unfairly be able to avoid troublemaking kids by not admitting them—ignoring the fact that public districts themselves often send such kids to special schools of "last resort" (and that, in any event, vouchers are irrelevant to addressing the problem). They say the oversight that will follow public money will make private schools resemble public bureaucracies—ignoring the greater flexibility that most analysts say such schools will retain in hiring and firing, resource allocation, and curriculum design. Finally, voucher foes argue that it is crazy to subsidize more affluent parents who already pay for private school—a seemingly powerful charge until one recalls that such families are now paying twice for schools (once out of their pockets and once through their property taxes), and that vouchers offered only to poor families would avoid the problem entirely.

For their part, conservatives peddle just two hoaxes, but they're big ones:

Vouchers can save lots of money.   Conservatives say this has to be the case, when per-pupil spending in private schools is typically less than half that in public schools today. It's true that religious schools have fewer administrators and lower-paid teachers, and invest less in such amenities as theaters, labs, and gymnasiums. But private schools don't have to take costly disabled and "special education" children; and often public schools must offer extras such as English as a Second Language, breakfast and lunch programs, and transportation. When such differences are taken into account, and hidden subsidies for church space and staff in religious schools are counted, the gap shrinks. Coons says that a voucher's value needs to be no lower than 85 percent of total per-pupil spending in order to stimulate capital investment in new schools. Set it too low, and the result will be simply to fill the handful of empty Catholic school seats.

The right's claim that vouchers will deliver big savings also ignores the case for spending more in many big cities, where dilapidated buildings may collectively require as much as $50 billion in repairs. Some public school bureaucracies—Washington, D.C., and St. Louis come to mind—seem so hopeless that it would be senseless to pour new money in until management has improved. But despite run-down buildings and a higher proportion of special-needs students, cities such as Philadelphia and Baltimore spend far less per pupil than do the suburbs near them.

The freer the market, the better the result.   Conservatives find the left's worries over disadvantaged kids almost superfluous. The beauty of markets, they say, is that the existence of such customers will call forth a supply of schools to serve them. This faith is misplaced, as markets like the one for health insurance prove every day. Profitable insuring means shunning poorer, sicker customers while competing for those who are wealthier and healthier. This isn't a criticism of markets; it's a reminder that markets allocate resources without regard to social goals. Only sensible regulations (like Coons' on vouchers) can assure that private incentives are used to meet public objectives.

New Voices, New Politics

Disingenuous rhetoric; visceral distrust; maximum posturing; minimal progress. Political debates escape this kind of dead end when grassroots pressure makes the status quo untenable, or when leaders emerge with fresh ways of framing the issues. It's possible that urban schools will fall so far that the poor revolt; or that crime, bred by ignorance, might worsen in ways that force society to act. There's a better path to hope for, however, if new leaders can help us to think differently about today's predicament.

Arthur Levine, the president of Teachers College at Columbia University, suggests how powerful a Nixon-to-China voice on vouchers can be. A self-described liberal Democrat, he has devoted much of his career to urban schooling. He's a lifelong voucher foe who feared they would undermine public schools, and yet a few years ago Levine called for a "rescue operation" that would give vouchers to 2 to 3 million poor children at the worst urban public schools. "For me," Levine said, "it's the equivalent of Schindler's list." He's not a "convert" to vouchers, he explained, but a practical man who sees this as part of the answer for a desperate situation. "It's just not happening fast enough," he said, "given the scale of the problem."

Levine's stature commands influence as his fellow liberals struggle to square old convictions with bleak urban realities. Take John Brademas, the former president of New York University and before that a Democratic congressman from Indiana who wrote key federal education laws in the 1960s and 1970s. When I asked Brademas about vouchers, he could barely contain his anger, lecturing me passionately on why they were at bottom a right-wing plot to destroy public education. When he took a breath, I asked: What about Arthur Levine? You can't lump him with the school-bashers. "I know, I know," he said, sounding torn. "I'm not saying I'm not keeping the intellectual door open a crack."

Like many Democrats, Brademas remains profoundly suspicious of the motives of most voucher advocates. Howard Fuller, the former Milwaukee superintendent who now chairs the Black Alliance for Educational Options, said there's a way to solve this problem. A man came up to Fuller after a speech and told him, "Everything you said makes sense, but I'm a liberal—I can't support these right-wing ideas." "Then join us," Fuller replied. "It won't be controlled by the right wing because we'll have *you*."

If Levine represents the new educational conscience of the left, Lisa Graham Keegan is an iconoclast of the right. Keegan, 44, is president of the Education Leadership Council, an organization of reform-minded, conservative state school chiefs. She served as Superintendent of Public Instruction in Arizona from 1995 to 2002. Keegan made her name as a state legislator in 1994 when she came within a few votes of getting a sweeping voucher bill enacted. An eleventh-hour compromise with voucher foes instead brought passage of the nation's broadest charter school law, whose progress she subsequently supervised. As a Republican innovator from Barry Goldwater country, and an education adviser to John McCain in his 2000 presidential campaign, Keegan has long been viewed by party regulars as a comer. Yet she talks about schools, equity, and taxes in ways that sound more like Ted Kennedy than Ronald Reagan.

Keegan told me that using a property tax base for school finance is "pernicious" and "wholly unfair." Local financing made sense 200 years ago, she argued, when limited transportation and communications meant towns had no choice but to be self-sufficient. Today, however, Keegan views things more cynically. "This is about lower tax rates for the wealthy," she said, "not about local control."

The facts support Keegan's view. In thirty-five states, the property tax burden in poor districts is more than twice as high as it is in rich ones. The federal mortgage interest deduction then adds insult to injury, giving better-off homeowners a back-door school subsidy (helping them live near better schools) that is seven times greater than federal aid to poor schools. An analysis by the National Center for Education Statistics shows that even after decades of litigation and programs meant to aid poor schools, most poor schoolchildren still live in districts that spend less per student than their state's average; one in five poor students gets between 10 and 30 percent less. In many places the gap is more dramatic.

Failing to acknowledge these realities, Keegan said, undermines legitimate GOP doubts about whether more resources can improve schools. "It's disingenuous for conservatives to say money doesn't matter," Keegan argued, "and then turn around and talk about preserving local control." Keegan wants a system of "student-centered funding," in which revenues raised from sources other than a property tax would be distributed by the state on an equal per-pupil basis via vouchers. To pair fairer financing with freer competition for students, Keegan says, each camp must part with something precious: The right has to relinquish local control; the unions have to yield their public school monopoly.

Keegan, like Levine, is helping make the world safe for colleagues to speak their minds. "I always felt squeamish about my own concerns on the equity issue," said Clint Bolick, the litigation director of the conservative Institute for Justice, which represented Milwaukee and Cleveland in their court battles over vouchers. "I felt it was a ruse to raise taxes." New Jersey, where Bolick grew up, has seen big tax increases through two decades of equity litigation, with little to show for it in student achievement. "The kids were the de facto plaintiffs," he said, "but the unions were the de facto beneficiaries." Newark schools are a shambles, for example, despite spending a whopping $13,000 per pupil; in Bolick's view, it's a cautionary reminder about throwing good money after bad.

Yet with a nod to Keegan, Bolick said, "we can't be saying that geography should be determining educational opportunity or funding." It may be, he muses, that while liberals won the court battles that gave poor parents a right to more equitable school financing, conservatives will supply the way to implement the remedy. Bolick thinks those fighting for equity in school finance and those fighting for vouchers will join forces before long, in part because the experience of championing urban children tempers ideology. "What started for me as a public policy issue and a philosophical issue," he explains, "has become a heart and soul, 'bleeding heart conservative' issue. Seeing these kids has been a transformative experience."

A Grand Bargain?

If leading liberals are willing to question the public school monopoly, and prominent conservatives can hear the call of social justice, the voucher debate has a chance to move forward. The sensible first step is a much bigger road test. Here's the idea I put to various players in the debate: Suppose everyone came together and said, let's take three or four big cities where we agree the public schools are dysfunctional. (Leave out dens of mismanagement like Newark or Washington, D.C., where spending is ample but ineffective.) In these cities, we'll raise per-pupil spending by 20 or 30 percent, giving the left the resources it says urban schools need. But we'll implement this increase only via a universal voucher system that finally gives *every* kid a choice, not just a handful. In a city that now spends $6000 per pupil, for example, every child would get, say, a $7500 voucher.

Depending on the cities, the federal government could fund this boost for $1 to 2 billion a year. The feds would guarantee to bankroll it for ten or fifteen years, to give entrepreneurs (both nonprofit and for-profit) the incentive to make investments in new schools, and thus get a true test of competition's impact. Following Jack Coons' advice, we'd also toss in sensible regulations, such as one requiring that any school that wants to take the voucher has to reserve a certain portion of seats (say, 15 percent) for which the voucher would suffice as full tuition, so it's not simply a way for schools to jack up prices or shun poorer kids.

How did such a "grand bargain" play? Jack Coons, the "egalitarian," said it sounded great. So did Clint Bolick, the conservative Republican, though he thought the spending increase would mean "some of my fellow conservatives would have apoplexy." Senator Lamar Alexander of Tennessee, who served as secretary of education in George H. W. Bush's cabinet, signed on. So did Rod Paige, education secretary in the current Bush administration. Polly Williams, who led the drive to enact vouchers in Milwaukee, was hesitant about extending vouchers to families who weren't poor, so we posited a fix: Give them only to kids eligible for the federal school lunch program. We would move pretty far toward universal coverage this way, since, sadly, two out of three urban children qualify for school lunch assistance.

William Bennett told me he would take this deal in a second, adding that he had heard something like it before. Bennett said that when he was education secretary in the Reagan administration in the mid-1980s, Albert Shanker said to him, we'll buy vouchers, but you've got to make it $6000 per kid, which back then was a lot of money. Shanker added that the vouchers could only go to children attending the lowest-performing 10 percent of schools. "I said, 'Deal,'" Bennett recalled. "He called me back and said, 'We can't do this.'" He couldn't bring his union along with him.

What about the NAACP? To date, the organization has welcomed philanthropic efforts, but when public funds are at issue, it stands by the unions. Julian Bond, the chairman of the NAACP, has called vouchers "pork for private schools." Yet when I asked Kweisi Mfume, the NAACP president, about this proposal, he didn't hesitate. "I don't have a problem with that at all," he said. Mfume said NAACP opposition has not been ideological, but based on three concerns: The association doesn't want programs that leave nearly every child out; it wants accountability to the public on student performance; and it

wants an honest approach to higher costs—such as those for transportation—that must be paid to make the system work for poor children. The pilot programs in Milwaukee and Cleveland fail, he said,
especially on grounds one and three; the bargain I sketched addressed
them. "If our concerns are met, I'm open," Mfume said, even if that
meant taking a different stance from the unions. (Mfume's representative denied later that he had taken this position, but I have my notes.)

"It's a bad idea," Milton Friedman said at first, arguing that any increase in spending would "fuel the racketeers in the education business." On the basis of his beliefs, Friedman has a point: If you think
spending is already too high, raising it further creates big profit opportunities for operators who can take the vouchers and run schools
much more efficiently. Fueled by systematic federal overpayments,
many Medicare HMOs faced such scams a few years ago.

But outliers like Washington, D.C., aside, it's not clear that urban
schools are overspending. Given that, wasn't it worth running a little
risk to get a substantial voucher test under way? It seemed that Friedman wouldn't sign on, but toward the end of our discussion, he re-
lented. "I'll tell you what I would go for," he said. Friedman has always
believed that so many families would flee public schools if given a
voucher worth even half of today's per-pupil spending that resources
for each child remaining in the current system would rise. (If ten public school children have $5000 spent on each of them, and three leave
taking $2500 each, spending on the seven remaining would rise about
20 percent, to just under $6100.) So Friedman said he would approve
of a 20 percent increase in per-pupil spending for those who remained, so long as the voucher was worth only half that. Since Friedman thinks this increase will come over time anyway, he's not
compromising his ideals. His principled accommodation is to put his
money where his beliefs are and increase spending up front as part of
the deal.

But look where we are. Philadelphia spends about $8000 per pupil
(versus $10,000 to $14,000 in affluent suburbs nearby). By Mfume's
logic, the NAACP would accept a citywide voucher at $9600. Fried-
man can live with $9600 of funding for current public school pupils
but would want a voucher for departing students at $4000. At this

point, everybody's in the same room (indeed, since our conversation, Friedman has said publicly that he is open to the voucher being fully equal to current per-pupil spending). Surely there's a deal to be made here—and a chance, therefore, to help children while meaningfully evaluating voucher efficacy, addressing questions about everything from student achievement to private profiteering.

What about the unions? "I would go high on per-pupil spending because the stakes are high," Lamar Alexander told me, "and to expose the hypocrisy of the unions. If I told the NEA [National Education Association] that we'd double it in the five largest cities, they wouldn't take it."

Was he right? I met with Bob Chase, then the president of the National Education Association, in the union's headquarters in Washington. (Chase left office in 2002.) He made the familiar case for why vouchers were ineffectual today and would be a threatening distraction for public schools if tried more broadly. Only 25 percent of the adult population has children in the schools, he explained. We need to help the other 75 percent understand why financial support of schools is important. In this regard, I sketched the deal—a handful of cities, higher spending, but only through vouchers. My tape recorder captured the staccato response:

"Is there any circumstance under which that would be something that . . . "

"No."

". . . you guys could live with. Why?"

"No."

"Double school spending . . . "

"No."

". . . in inner cities?"

"No."

"Triple it . . . "

"No."

". . . but give them a voucher?"

"'Cause, one, that's not going to happen. I'm not going to answer a hypothetical [question] when nothing like that is *ever* possible."

"But teachers use hypotheticals every day," I said.

"Not in arguments like this we don't. . . . It's pure and simply not going to happen. I'm not even going to use the intellectual processes to see if in fact that could work or not work because it's not going to happen. That's a fact."

Sandra Feldman was similarly unwilling to consider such a plan. If new money is available for cities, both said, it should be spent to improve the existing system. They'd fund pay raises to attract teachers to work downtown, turnaround programs for troubled schools, and general urban programs for health, nutrition, and parenting skills. But they refuse to recognize that pay raises—or smaller class sizes, or any specific reform—could happen under this voucher test, if that's what schools felt was needed to attract students.

Liberty, Equality, Vouchers

If you believe that for both moral and pragmatic reasons choice deserves a serious test, the path to progress follows a simple logic. A progressive hand is needed to attain the potential benefits of vouchers without risk to the poor. Many conservatives are open to such efforts if they enable larger voucher trials. Given the troubled state of urban schooling, the Democratic Party should be the natural home of this progressive influence. It is not, because teachers unions loom large in Democratic fundraising and campaigns. Yet the Republicans' commitment to minorities will probably never be trusted to carry this issue alone. And, not unreasonably, Republicans will not boost spending for urban schools without tying such increases to systemic reform—the same framework we've used, on a far larger scale, in our millionaire teacher initiative.

How to break the impasse? Conservatives need to accept that sound policy in this case is also smart political strategy. Teacher union intransigence is sustainable only so long as minority leaders stand with them. Richer and more ambitious voucher plans are the only way to split them off.

Put yourself in the place of an urban minority leader and you'll see why. "Follow my leadership on schools," a Republican typically says.

"After three years, in the handful of schools that your state musters the courage to call 'failing,' I'll give a few children a little voucher that might give a fraction of one percent of your constituents a shot at paying for Catholic school."

Why on earth would an African-American or Latino leader in any big city, who stands shoulder to shoulder with the teachers unions on everything from extending health coverage to raising the minimum wage, break ranks with her union allies for a token sham like that?

Thinking bigger thus makes progress likelier. "That's why I've taken the more radical side," explained the Rev. Floyd Flake, a voucher advocate and former Democratic congressman from New York. "It's the only way to force the debate." And thinking big is the only way conservatives can tell minority leaders what they need to hear from them: "I want you to embrace this; I know it isn't easy; so it has to be *real.*"

If unions are not open to measures like these, they may soon be in for worse. Many big city superintendents who are active, lifelong Democrats privately agree that the unions are the biggest obstacles to sound reform. These administrators fantasize about schemes to get big chunks of their system out from under debilitating restrictions and industrial union tactics.

In short, we may not be far from a tipping point. At some point, a talented presidential candidate—maybe in 2004, maybe later—will decide that if the unions in effect require him or her to tell poor families they're trapped, while also resisting sensible reforms (like serious pay differentials) that could lure top young graduates to teach in our toughest schools, they're more trouble than they're worth. And when that candidate discovers that a message of commonsense reform resonates powerfully with voters precisely because it is at odds with current union practice, well—you can see where this goes.

At some level even the unions know their stonewalling is indefensible. "I would never argue with an individual parent who wanted to figure out a way to get his or her child into a better situation," Sandra Feldman told me. "But to me, as a matter of public policy, that's not a good argument. The objective is to make the schools good—not to escape them."

But what if the ability to escape might help make the schools better? And what if testing this proposition can't make anyone worse off? Yes, big voucher trials may require an act of faith, but it wouldn't be the first calculated gamble in American education to pay off. A much smaller federal government rolled the dice on land grant colleges in the 1860s with only a foggy notion of what they'd do; the research they sparked made U.S. agriculture the world's most productive. The G.I. Bill helped to spawn the postwar middle class. The moral urgency of today's voucher gamble is much greater.

Why Not Both?

For all of these reasons, Democrats should see large-scale urban voucher trials as an opportunity, not a threat. Republicans should see that funding these trials generously is good politics and good policy. And leaders in both parties should look past today's orthodoxy to see that generously funded voucher trials can work in tandem with our Two Percent teacher initiative to radically speed progress in poor schools.

Imagine the situation five years afterward, if both plans were launched. In cities leading the implementation of the teacher initiative, the teacher corps is being transformed, with half of all teachers already working under the new "higher pay for greater professionalism" track, parents excited about the new energy in the classroom, and test scores heading up. Teaching as a career enjoys a "buzz" on college campuses not seen in decades, and is getting unprecedented attention in the press and popular culture. In cities not yet pursuing the teacher initiative, school officials, business leaders, and community groups are rushing to put together plans to apply for the federal money that will let them embark on this same road.

In a handful of cities, meanwhile, generous (and closely watched) voucher trials are under way. Both existing and newly formed schools are using the extra cash to vie for students with better-paid teachers, upgraded facilities, and innovative after-school programs. Several models seem to be producing higher student achievement.

In all districts, the larger presence of choice on the horizon is making change happen faster. Where the teacher initiative is rolling out, union leaders find it's really not so painful to change some practices in order to implement hefty wage increases for everyone they represent—especially when the price of intransigence may be to see their city become the next big voucher trial. In fact, the flood of top college graduates into teaching is raising morale among union leaders, making them prominent spokespeople for an exciting way to combine a passion for public service with a comfortable living.

In cities with voucher trials, meanwhile, superintendents say the fact that parents have options is forcing unions and schools to change much faster, in ways that complement their district's systemic, standards-based improvement efforts.

These ideas aren't panaceas, of course—there is no such thing for schools in poor neighborhoods, at least not until we can figure out how to remove the word "poor" from that phrase. But we'd be moving past today's bipartisan charades. We'd be taking luck, and equal opportunity, seriously. And with some hard work and a few breaks, we might just change the life chances of millions of disadvantaged kids.

8

UNCLE SAM
(NOT YOUR BOSS)
GUARANTEES YOU
A LIVING WAGE

P at Williams came home exhausted from another ten-hour day in April 2001 to find the note in her mailbox that would swallow her life's savings. The gas company had cut her off because her account was $477 overdue. The 46-year-old single mother had been working at or near the minimum wage in Shreveport, Louisiana, for two decades. The nursing home where she worked as a nurse's assistant paid her $5.55 an hour, though she'd been there ten years and had taken college courses to become certified. She'd started cleaning offices at night for $5.15 an hour—the federal minimum wage—because she couldn't make ends meet. Not that she could on these two jobs. Williams earned $10,067 in 2000. She also received $2300 from the earned income tax credit, the federal subsidy for the working poor, but she was eligible for this much only because she was taking care of her 7-year-old grandson more than half the year. Without that child in her keep, her tax credit would have been just $27, and Williams figured she'd be on the streets. As it was, the unpaid bills piled up: Williams owed $142 to the electric company, $55 to the phone company, $23 on the student loan for those nursing classes, and $40 for her burglar alarm, a necessity in her crime-ridden neighborhood. Williams dreamed about the breathing room she might have if she could make $7 an hour. But an unexpectedly cold winter had blindsided her. The check she sent to the gas company wiped out most of the tiny nest egg she'd managed to put aside over the years. "It's devastating," she told *The Wall Street Journal.* "You think you're moving forward, but you're just moving backwards."

Few observers would dispute that this is the case for millions of unskilled workers—the maids, nursing assistants, custodians, security guards, food service workers, and child and elderly care providers whose earnings have sagged for two decades while the incomes of college graduates have leapt. Economists say this growing gap between the well-off and the working poor—a change from the days when the proverbial rising tide lifted all boats—is due largely to the way technology has reshaped work to benefit Americans with more skills. The lagging federal minimum wage hasn't helped; at $5.15, it's worth less now, adjusted for inflation, than it was in the 1970s. Union membership decline and rising payroll taxes have also helped erode living standards at the bottom; so, too, to some degree, have trade with less developed countries and an influx of unskilled immigrants. Even in the boom of the late 1990s, which helped many unskilled workers get a toehold in the job market, millions of working-age poor people either never found work or worked too few hours at wages too meager to escape poverty.

These trends converge in ways that mock the value of work. Roughly 15 million Americans dwell in poverty despite living in homes headed by full-time workers, up 50 percent since 1975. Millions more are so depressed by dim earnings prospects that they've stopped looking for work altogether. "Employment opportunities for the less skilled are not what they used to be, so people just leave the labor force," Robert Topel, an economist at the University of Chicago, has said. The portion of male high school dropouts who have simply dropped out of the workforce (or who can't find jobs despite trying) has doubled since the mid-1970s. It can't be a coincidence that this wage and employment meltdown for the unskilled has been matched by rising crime, illegitimacy, drug use, and prison rolls, which together have spawned vast urban wastelands and a generation of ghetto kids with few models of normal social life revolving around work. Welfare reform, meanwhile, has turned several million welfare mothers into an equal number of working poor mothers, helping explain why visits to soup kitchens more than doubled from 1997 to 2001. Jobs for the unskilled, as Barbara Ehrenreich eloquently showed in her 2001 bestseller *Nickel and Dimed,* simply don't pay enough to live on.

What to do? The usual catalogue of remedies is well-meaning. Improve education and job training. Reform labor laws, which now let employers fire unionizing workers with impunity. Lower the rate of legal immigration while shifting the immigrant mix toward better-skilled workers who don't compete with the native-born working poor. The trouble, if we're honest, is that these steps could take years, even decades, to make a dent; or that they address too small a piece of a broad problem to be sufficient. Meanwhile, the debate over a "living wage," as we've seen in Chapter 1, is caught in an unproductive rut. The right wants to kick out social supports and force people to work, without acknowledging that abysmal wages for the unskilled leave them prey to the same social problems as when they were on welfare. The left cries for mandated "living wages" far in excess of what many less skilled workers are worth to employers, thus assuring they won't be hired.

Isn't there anything we can do *now* that doesn't consign today's luckless workers to lives of not-so-quiet desperation—and thereby complete the unfinished agenda of building a decent society, in which work truly pays?

Enter Edmund Phelps, a mild-mannered 71-year-old economist at Columbia University. Phelps first came to prominence in 1968 when, along with Milton Friedman, he fathered the theory that there is a "natural" rate of unemployment below which inflation is sure to take off. Phelps has devoted much of his time since then to figuring out how to lower this expected jobless rate and improve chances for less blessed workers. The seed was planted for much of this work in 1969, when Phelps, then at the University of Pennsylvania, wrangled a coveted sabbatical year at Stanford's Center for Advanced Study. Another scholar at the center that year was John Rawls, who was writing *A Theory of Justice*.

"I had heard the name John Rawls," Phelps told me. "I was told he was something of a prophetic avant-garde moral philosopher and it was important to understand him." So when Phelps arrived in Palo Alto that summer and saw there was an open office next to Rawls, he took it. "He gave me some stuff to read," Phelps recalled.

> I didn't know quite what to say. It was some stuff about the veil and what these blindfolded individuals would choose to do behind the veil. It got me starting to think, what if they knew that there was a one-quarter probability that they would be blue-collar workers and a one-quarter probably of being something else?. . . [But Rawls] didn't want the people behind the veil of ignorance to know what the chances were of being a blue-collar worker or white-collar worker or ditch digger or whatever. . . . He wanted people behind the veil of ignorance to worry a lot about what would happen if they were in that bottom group.

It turned out Phelps had identified for Rawls the main objection economists would later raise to his theory—Why assume that people in the "original position" would be so risk-averse? But Rawls' ideas left a profound impression on Phelps. They got Phelps wrestling, unlike many in his profession, with how efficiency (so beloved of economists) could be made to coexist with equity. "It heightened my interest in the high incidence of unemployment at the low end of the labor market," Phelps told me, "and in the problem of low wage rates."

> From an early time, I read Rawls as making a deep case for redistributive wage subsidies. High wages would be taxed a bit on top of the usual taxes [needed] to pay for national defense and the other basic needs of government in order to provide some wage subsidies at the low end. To this day that's what I think Rawls is basically about.

The years 1969 and 1970 were tumultuous ones on campus. The offices at Stanford where Phelps and Rawls worked were firebombed by radical protesters. Phelps saw Rawls' work as a kind of response to the radicals, who held that capitalism was run only for the benefit of rich and powerful interests. In Rawls' vision, as filtered through an economist's sensibility, America could continue with the capitalist enterprise that had been so rewarding for the majority while at the same time taking modest steps to pull low-end workers up to a more adequate level. By involving them more fully in society's market economy, Phelps reasoned, you might ultimately dissolve America's underclass.

The concerns awakened in Phelps that year percolated for nearly three decades as he built an international reputation in areas such as growth and macroeconomic equilibrium. But Phelps never shook his quiet obsession. He finally outlined his ideas fully in a 1997 book, *Rewarding Work*.

Phelps's appeal lies in a nonideological approach that frees him to debunk everyone's favorite bromide. Phelps can't understand, for example, why liberals always say the answer is to boost various welfare payments, when that only deepens an already corrosive dependency. As proof he offers an astounding comparison: In 1990, the lowest-earning tenth of the American workforce took home $15 billion in wages; meanwhile, total public assistance for health care, housing, food stamps, and related aid benefiting these same families topped $180 billion. Phelps's point: It's not healthy for so big a swath of society to feel responsible for so little of its own upkeep.

But that doesn't mean you pull the rug out. Indeed, Phelps shames conservative purists for their devotion to laissez-faire, which he says not only caricatures the thinking of right-wing heros like Adam Smith, but offends all notions of justice. Smith and his progeny, Phelps explains, championed public subsidies to spur the common good (in education, for example). And since the sinking pay of less skilled workers comes from broad forces beyond their control, Phelps argues, it's immoral to leave such workers languishing—not to mention shortsighted, given the social pathologies that poorly rewarded work breeds.

Phelps's big idea is to guarantee $9 to $10 an hour for full-time work via a sliding-scale tax credit to employers. The "grand bargain" here requires the left to stop trying to place the full burden of a living

**Table 8.1 The Phelps Wage Subsidy—
$9 "Living Wage" Illustration**

Wage Cost per Hour	Subsidy per Hour	Gross Wage per Hour
6.00	3.00	9.00
7.00	2.29	9.29
8.00	1.65	9.65
9.00	1.12	10.12
10.00	0.71	10.71
11.00	0.43	11.43
12.00	0.24	12.24
13.00	0.13	13.13
14.00	0.06	14.06

wage on employers, while the right accepts the need to have government fund the rest. Business should love it, because workers could be hired for as little as $6 an hour, with government putting up $3 to match it. Since the social benefits of work (in terms of less crime, welfare dependency, and so on) exceed less skilled workers' productivity (which limits what employers can offer in wages), it makes sense for society to subsidize the difference. As Phelps explains:

> The philosophy behind the employment subsidy system is that the private benefit of employment does not fully capture—and hence the paycheck of less productive workers does not fully reflect—the whole of the *social* benefit from these people's becoming employed workers. That social benefit is the private benefit going to their employer plus the external benefit to the rest of society from their position as participants in the business life of their community and the country, earning their own keep and supporting their children and setting an example for others growing up in their neighborhood.

A glance at Table 8.1 shows how Phelps's plan would work to create a national living wage of $9 an hour. Say the official minimum wage facing employers is $6. Under his plan, employers would receive a $3-an-hour subsidy from the government (implemented via a rebate against their payroll taxes, perhaps) for every full-time worker they employ at this rate. The system would be designed so that the wage subsidy is passed through to the employee, who would see only the $9 wage in his or her pay. As the wage rate rises, Phelps's subsidy tapers off, reaching zero around $14, just above the median wage. The idea is to get less advantaged workers into entry-level jobs, while helping work pay decently and making it possible for workers to get raises without losing their full subsidy.

There are obviously many permutations through which we could combine the Phelps subsidy and the official minimum wage; the ultimate policy choice involves a balance among (1) the amount we think is reasonable to spend as a nation for these purposes; (2) the new effective minimum wage we want to reach; and (3) what portion of achieving that new minimum we think should be borne by private firms and what portion should be borne by government (a choice that also affects how many low-wage jobs are created). Phelps's $3 plan, for example, costs about $85 billion a year atop today's $35 billion earned income tax credit (which we would shift to help fund the Phelps subsidy, since the EITC has a similar intent but leaves many low-wage workers—especially those who are childless—outside its coverage). We could apply the same $3 Phelps subsidy to today's $5.15-an-hour federal minimum wage and create an effective minimum of $8.15 for the same national "price"; and we could raise the minimum wage to $7 (as most liberals want) and put a $3 dollar Phelps subsidy atop it to get to a $10 wage for this price, too. Alternatively, we could raise the minimum to $7 and apply a $2 Phelps plan to reach $9, but for a cost of only about $35 billion a year atop today's EITC. These scenarios suggest how the levers work.

My preference is for the 6 plus 3 equals 9 plan, but the precise numbers are open to discussion. I came to this exercise with three goals that had to be balanced. First, I originally wanted to reach a living wage of $10 an hour, because I don't see how people can live on less than that (especially in big cities), and because I thought $10 an hour made for the cleanest political rallying cry. My second aim was to keep the minimum wage facing employers relatively low, so as to encourage the greatest possible creation of entry-levels jobs that give unskilled workers a way into the workplace and a chance to rise.

Third, I had to make sure that whatever resources I devoted to a Phelps-style subsidy left me room to fund the other priorities we have within the Two Percent Solution. Balancing these goals left me at 6 plus 3. I realize a 7 plus 2 option might have more appeal—conservatives will like that the federal cost is far less, liberals will be happy to put more burden on employers, and some states are already close to a $7 minimum wage anyway. But this should be a bargain between left and right that best serves public policy, and if the higher public cost "buys" several million additional low-wage jobs for unskilled workers, in my view, it's worth it. In the end, even though I'm short of my $10 goal, $9 an hour plus basic health coverage (from Chapter 5) is how we'd be defining the decent minimum in America. This is a dramatic improvement over the $5.15 to $7 or so minimum we see today (depending on the state) with no health coverage at all. Assuming that a full-time worker puts in 2000 hours a year at a $6 federal minimum wage, such workers would earn an extra $6000 a year and have health benefits. For tens of millions of struggling families that will seem like morning in America, indeed.

After raising the minimum wage to $6, I'd also index it (and the Phelps subsidy) to inflation, as Alaska, Washington, and Oregon have done. The reason: Once we've decided what America's decent minimum should be, why would we purposely let it erode for no reason? The best thing indexing would do is banish the absurd debate ("Why not make the minimum wage $50?" versus "Why not bring back slavery?") we're now forced to endure each time around. For businesspeople, modest and predictable annual hikes from a low base are better than not knowing when Congress will jerk their labor costs around on a whim. For liberals, an assured boost means less time fighting for basics and more time asking why our economy leaves so many full-time workers on the edge, even after the minimum is indexed. In the end, partisan Democrats may have to make the biggest "sacrifice" by embracing automatic indexing. As things now stand, with Congress needing to act, Democrats are guaranteed a politically potent brawl every few years that boosts turnout and reminds voters which side they're on.

Unlike similar-sounding income support schemes—like Milton Friedman's "negative income tax," George McGovern's $1000-a-head "demogrant," or Daniel Patrick Moynihan's Family Assistance Plan—Phelps's subsidy is available *only for those who work*. Phelps makes the subsidy available only to low-paid work in the private sector; most government wage scales, Phelps reckons, are already padded, since they operate outside markets. Phelps also limits his plan to full-time workers. "If the idea is to promote independence and self-sufficiency," he says, "then you want to restrict it to people who are serious about that as a goal." Unlike today's EITC—which, to limit its cost, is targeted on families with children—Phelps's scheme doesn't leave out millions of disadvantaged and underemployed single males, who are society's biggest troublemakers and are most in need of help to improve their prospects for getting married and supporting a family.

So how have people in power responded to this idea? A senior Bush White House economic adviser told me (not for attribution) that a Phelps-style approach was precisely what we would do "if we were serious." Union officials I spoke with, like Dean Tipps, California chief of the Service Employees International Union, focused more on organizing to convert low-wage jobs into middle-class jobs—a vital effort, except that it's hard to think such organizing can reach the scale of today's need, or work in low-wage industries in which profit margins are perennially thin. Other labor leaders, reflecting years spent across the table from employers, have a threshold reluctance to the Phelps employer-based approach. "I have a lifelong predilection not to give employers money to subsidize wages," said Tom Donahue, former president of the AFL-CIO. It lets them off the hook, he said, for paying a decent wage themselves. But Donahue also acknowledged that at some point higher mandated wages cost jobs. Donahue told me that while his instincts led him to prefer that any bigger subsidies go to individuals via EITC expansions, he wouldn't want to oppose the Phelps approach, because reframing the debate around what the nation needs to do to create a decent reward for work is "exactly where we need to go."

Left-leaning economists, such as Jared Bernstein of the Economic Policy Institute, think getting to $9 an hour would be great, but they worry, with Donahue, about letting business shift costs to government that they should bear themselves. They also fret about "leakage," the prospect that businesses will game the system to capture the subsidy and pad their profits rather than passing it through to employees (by lowering every low-wage worker's pay to the minimum, for example). That's an argument, they say, for giving subsidies to poor workers directly. Phelps replies that only by subsidizing the employer can you get the new job creation at the low end that brings unskilled Americans into the economic mainstream. Phelps also argues persuasively that because his sliding-scale subsidy preserves wage differentials at every level, employers won't be able to force everyone down to the minimum. More desirable workers who were worth a differential before a subsidy regime is in place (say, the $6.75 versus the $6.00 worker) would still be worth more to employers afterward, and would be competed for, just as in a pre-subsidy labor market.

As with any such program, the potential for fraud is obviously a concern. Firms might try to classify part-time workers or independent contractors as full-time workers to get a subsidy, or cook up other such schemes. But that's not much different from the way firms illegally call workers independent contractors today to avoid payroll taxes. Fraud and cheating are illegal, just as they are all throughout our complex tax system, and strong enforcement and severe penalties would be needed. Conservatives also rightly raise the question of how this plan would deal with immigrants; it can't be the case that you can get off the bus from Mexico and be entitled to a $9-an-hour job. They're right, of course, and so eligibility would have to be restricted to American citizens, or perhaps to those legal immigrants who have been here for some period of years. Contrary to what many conservatives assume, however, just one in four poor workers are recent immigrants. About a quarter of America's poverty-level work is a function of being an open society; there are millions upon millions of Pat Williamses in our midst.

The main objection to Phelps's idea is cost. Yes, analysts across the political spectrum seem to say, Phelps may have the answer—it's too bad we can't afford it. As mentioned, the Phelps plan would cost roughly $85 billion a year atop today's EITC. That's a fortune compared to today's political debate, but it's less than a penny in the two cents on the national dollar we've been discussing. Phelps in fact argues that any new financing would be transitional; before long, he says, the wage subsidies would pay for themselves, given the cuts in myriad welfare, police, and court costs that would come as work became the norm, along with shrinking unemployment benefits and higher tax revenues from workers and corporate profits. Phelps makes a good case, but we'll be conservative here and pay for it all anyway when we finance our Two Percent plan in Chapter 10. (If Phelps is right, the country will then have $85 billion a year for other uses.)

Money aside, in the end a Phelps-style subsidy really amounts to a new economic philosophy, a way to marry the efficiency of direct cash payments with the notion of work as the organizing principle for a robust federal commitment to a minimally decent life. It invites public debate to move past isolated and uninspiring squabbles over food stamps and housing vouchers and transportation assistance and child care credits, and shift to an explicit discussion of how we should define and pay for a minimally decent life for Americans who work. *Nine bucks an hour plus health care!* The paradox is that even as this approach honors conservative instincts, it is simultaneously more radical and lefty, because it socializes the cost of the progressive guarantee rather than trying to load it on business, as liberals usually prefer.

The case for serious government action to make work pay via something like the Phelps subsidy draws its ultimate legitimacy from the CEO compensation scandals we've seen these last few years. The conceit, of course, is that top CEOs rake in more than $20 million on average because that's what "the market" demands. If you want Michael Jordan in your lineup, the logic runs, you have to pay what it takes to get him. The reality, however, is that CEO pay is set through a clubby, rigged system in which CEOs, their buddies on board compensation committees, and a small cadre of lawyers and "compensation consultants" are in cahoots to keep the millions coming irrespective of performance. Once this veil is lifted, and we realize that CEO pay is set largely by the exercise of institutional power designed to insulate CEOs from market forces, there is no philosophical or ideological reason not to use the same power on behalf of low-wage workers. Why should we honor market wage-setting only at the bottom, regardless of the social consequences? Why shouldn't we say instead that there's nothing "right" about full-time work that produces poverty, any more than it's "right" that cancer should run it's course without intervention?

The argument generally made against policies like an indexed minimum wage, or wage supplements such as the Phelps plan, is that they represent unacceptable and even dangerous attempts to tamper with markets.

Now we know better. Combining the power of market incentives to get disadvantaged folks into jobs with the power of American decency to help these jobs pay a living wage doesn't depart from modern capitalism's norms. It democratizes them. After all, if the boss wouldn't dream of having his paycheck determined entirely by the free market, why should the rest of us?

9

PATRIOT DOLLARS

The fourth leg of the Two Percent agenda—after health care, education, and a living wage—is campaign finance reform. This raises a question: Why? It's not directly concerned with providing a decent minimum, as are the proposals for health coverage and wage subsidies. It's not directly concerned with equal opportunity, as are the proposals to attract great teachers for poor children and bigger tests of school choice. It's also not a big-ticket item requiring tens of billions of "Two Percent" dollars. But the way campaigns are financed warps public debate, and makes it systematically harder for proposals favoring poor workers and poor children to be heard. A more democratic market of political ideas is needed to secure a permanent place for the Two Percent issues on the national agenda.

Bruce Ackerman, the Sterling Professor of Law at Yale University, was thinking this way himself in the early 1990s while teaching a class called "Theory in Practice." He'd guide students through Rawls, some of the other greats, and his own writings. Then he'd have the class write essays that applied these ideas to real-world problems. The problem he chose in 1991 was democratic politics. Ackerman usually wrote a little thought-starting paper to get the young minds whirring. That's when "patriot dollars"—his campaign reform idea—hit him. It was a marriage of the professor's longtime concern with making politics more democratic and his attraction to market-based solutions outside the usual liberal paradigm.

Ackerman had hit upon an eclectic way of framing the problem. He started from the premise that the standard liberal argument—that we're spending "too much" on campaigns—was absurd. The money spent in a presidential election cycle is peanuts compared to the billions spent on broadcast advertising by commercial advertisers. Instead, what Ackerman found corrosive was the imbalance between private money and public money and the way this tilts debate. "The more big money shapes the direction of American politics," Ackerman says, "the less democratic politics can serve as a primary legitimator for economic inequality. If economic inequality is to remain (relatively) legitimate in our society, democratic politics must retain its integrity as a sphere of (relative) equality." Yet as we've seen more recently, McCain–Feingold's ban on "soft money" for the national parties isn't changing this tilt at all, but is merely diverting big private money into other channels such as state parties and single-issue groups.

Any constructive response to the influence of private money has to involve some form of public financing, which conservatives generally oppose, in part because they're able to raise more private money. ("Welfare for politicians," they cry. "Why should taxpayers have to pay for a campaign they may oppose?") But Ackerman the liberal also finds the typical proposals for "clean money" wanting. "The old reform agenda," he writes, "hands a pot of money to bureaucrats who are supposed to dole it out by referring to criteria established by a statute." The "central misconception" of this approach, he says, is "its fondness for bureaucratic solutions to the resource allocation problem."

Ackerman's answer—which came to him as he scribbled his thoughts that night to get his students thinking—was simple: give every registered voter a $50 voucher that he or she can spend to support candidates or political organizations in federal elections. Ackerman would issue voters a special "Patriot" ATM card. Each election cycle the government would automatically credit their Patriot accounts with fifty dollars each. Candidates and organizations that met some minimal threshold of legitimacy would be eligible to solicit and compete for the funds. Citizens would "vote" their dollars from any ATM machine, where new software will have facilitated this use.

You can see instantly the beauty of this idea. Instead of limiting political "speech" (which most plans to cap private money do, perhaps
unconstitutionally), it increases it. Instead of having some central bureaucracy manage public funds, it lets individuals make their own
choices. And here's the clincher: Fifty dollars for each of America's
roughly 100 million voters means that $5 billion in new campaign
cash gets injected via the grassroots—more than offsetting the $3 bil-
lion raised largely from special interests in the 2000 campaign cycle.
"It transforms campaign finance from an inegalitarian embarrassment
into a new occasion for civic responsibility," Ackerman told me. Before long coffee shops and bars might be filled with folks debating
how to use their Patriot dollars wisely.

In addition, candidates might put at the center of their campaigns
issues that don't get attention now, because they appeal to millions of
voters who have no voice in today's money-primary. Recall how former
senator Bob Kerrey explained the reality in Chapter 2. When he
needed to raise money, Kerrey explained, "I'm not going to ask somebody for money who gets a minimum wage. I ask somebody who is
college educated whose income is over $250,000 a year—and then I
have to say things like, 'Why don't you get rid of the estate tax, why
don't you lower the capital gains tax, why don't you make our tax system less progressive, blah-blah-blah.' Same thing on corporations." Under a system of Patriot dollars, a candidate who wanted to talk about,
say, America's 42 million uninsured might find a large constituency
ready to vote their $50 to assure that such a candidacy was viable.

Such a system might serve to create a more democratic market of
political ideas. It's hard to believe, for example, that the 2000 Republican presidential field would have narrowed so long before an actual
primary under the Patriot system. John McCain might have been as
well funded as George W. Bush within weeks of his New Hampshire
upset.

There are details to be worked out, of course. How should funds be
split between primaries and general elections? Among House, Senate,
and presidential contests? What kind of private "seed financing"
would be permissible in order to raise awareness of a candidate who
could then appeal for the Patriot dollars? What safeguards are needed

to make sure people can't effectively sell their Patriot dollars—as happens, for example, with food stamps? Ackerman devotes much of his book, *Voting With Dollars,* written with his colleague Ian Ayres, to ways to protect against such potential abuses, and dealing with Patriot's other nuances. Legislators would obviously have to work through these challenges. But the first step is to focus on the big idea.

Come Clean

One objection I heard from conservatives, even if they were open to the notion that Patriot dollars might broaden debate in positive ways, was that the amount seemed arbitrary. Why $50 a voter, and not $500? Ackerman told me that his aim was to have a 2 to 1 ratio of public to private money. Count the amount of private money spent in the last election, Ackerman said. Multiply that by two and divide by the number of voters and that's the amount for the Patriot dollar accounts for the next go-round. "The democratic process should be controlled in large part by a democratic distribution of money," said Ackerman of his rationale. Obviously this would be a political negotiation. But remember, Ackerman stressed, "we're not repressing speech, we're just adding on."

I asked Christopher Shays, the Republican congressman from Connecticut who has been a leader on campaign reform, what he thought of Ackerman's idea. Shays was coauthor of the Shays–Meehan reform bill, the House counterpart to McCain–Feingold. "Conceptually, I think there's a lot of merit to the idea," Shays told me. Shays supports public financing of campaigns, and thought Ackerman's notion of implementing this via individuals might change the way conservatives viewed the matter. "The question is, could you try it in a smaller way?" Shays said. "The one value to having states do things is that they become your laboratory." Ackerman told me he thought that was a sensible idea—though he naturally wanted a big state like California to take the lead.

In one focus group conducted for this book, we raised the Patriot dollars idea, and some in the group liked it. Others questioned whether people would use them. "I mean, people don't even vote," one man said. "That's like voting twice. You're going to vote with your $50 and then vote with your regular vote." Ellen Miller, the former head of Public Campaign and the Center for Responsive Politics (who told us in Chapter 1 that thirty years of reform efforts had come to naught), had the same concern. "It assumes an engaged public and that's a huge assumption," she told me. "On the other hand, if they got $50 to bet on a candidate, people do like to bet in this country and so it might actually serve as a way to engage them more in the process."

I said to Miller that one could make the argument that if we had a system like this and people didn't vote their dollars, then we'd get the debate and the government we deserve. Why should we be more paternalistic?

"I don't buy that argument," Miller said.

If I am a candidate and I say to the public in my district, "I deserve your $50 because I'm the candidate who will bring you health care. I am the candidate who will bring jobs to your district." They have ample evidence to say, "the last candidate who came around said that and they didn't do anything." The question is whether people are engaged enough for this kind of system to work. Has America become too cynical about politics to engage in this kind of fashion? I don't know the answer to that. The [Patriot dollars] system rests on that.

Miller prefers "clean election" laws, like those that have been enacted in Arizona, Maine, Massachusetts, and Vermont. A number of other states are considering them. Under these laws, candidates get a flat public grant based on some formula after demonstrating a threshold level of political viability. In 2002, for example, Janet Napolitano of Arizona became the first governor elected running "clean." To do so, she had to collect more than 4000 $5 qualifying contributions from registered voters, and agree to abide by overall spending limits and to raise no private money (save for a modest amount of seed money). Under the system she then got $2.3 million in "Clean Money" public funding. "This is just a different world altogether," Napolitano, previously the state's attorney general, told the Associated Press during the race. "You can really just focus on voters, and do a much more grassroots campaign." If a privately funded rival goes over the clean spending limits, most such laws immediately increase the public grant so that "clean" candidates can match them dollar for dollar.

Nearly three in four state senators elected in Maine in 2002 ran clean, as did about six of ten members elected to the House. In Arizona, about a third of the state legislature won clean, more than double the number in 2000. In Massachusetts, however, the system has had problems. Voters passed a "clean elections" ballot measure, but the legislature balked at funding it. This uncertainty led Robert Reich, the former secretary of labor and a public-financing advocate, to "go private" out of perceived necessity in his unsuccessful 2002 gubernatorial campaign.

Two Tracks?

The common theme between Ackerman's idea and the clean elections approach is to establish a viable way for candidates to fund races without special interest money. Jonathan Rauch, an author and columnist for *National Journal,* an influential Washington, D.C., magazine, has offered an original framework that could incorporate either Patriot dollars or clean elections in ways both liberals and conservatives would find appealing. Rauch laid out his idea in a 1997 cover story in *National Journal,* "An Immodest Proposal to Blow Up Our Campaign Finance System." Years later it remains the most illuminating piece ever written on the subject.

Rauch's idea is to join two proposals that each party wants but can never get the other to agree to: (1) public financing for candidates who agree not to take private cash, and (2) instant disclosure of all private contributions—but no other rules for such giving at all. His plan offends everyone. Liberals loathe the idea of scrapping the web of campaign laws meant to rein in special interests. Conservatives hate the idea of using tax dollars to fund campaigns.

But Rauch argues persuasively that such recalcitrance dooms us to tinker at the edges of a failed system. The reforms initiated after the

Watergate scandal in the 1970s were supposed to take money out of politics, but campaign costs have more than doubled over the intervening twenty-five years. All of those White House coffees, Lincoln bedroom rentals, and Republican Pioneer soirees are the depressing culmination of a long bipartisan march to excess. In retrospect, Rauch says, we shouldn't have expected anything different, because the premises of today's system are naive and flawed. We thought assorted "caps" (like limits for individual contributions, now set at $2000) would limit overall spending and insulate politicians from dependence on narrow interests. Instead, like water that flows to where it's not blocked, smaller contributions were "bundled" into big ones by savvy firms, and wealthy self-financed candidates like Ross Perot proliferated. Uncapped gifts of so-called "soft" money and "independent expenditures" became the megaphone of choice for special interests.

We've also acted as if this political money was an evil to be stamped out, not a reality to be managed. Rauch, anticipating today's inevitable end run of McCain–Feingold, says that this is silly. "Politicians need to raise money to run for office, and one way or another they will get it," he writes. "Groups need to influence the government, and one way or another they will spend money to do so."

The grown-up fix, Rauch contends, is another "grand bargain"—this one marrying public finance with private deregulation. Candidates who reach some qualifying threshold would get enough public cash to run a competitive campaign (a scheme that could encompass either Patriot dollars or the clean election plan). In exchange, they'd pledge not to take or seek private contributions. Private spending by groups, parties, and candidates, meanwhile, would be instantly disclosed and reported. Mandatory electronic filing could make such data instantly available to the press and on the Internet.

All other rules would be scrapped.

The result? Instead of pretending to control things via complex rules that lawyers now help candidates skirt, we'd make the question of how candidates are financed an issue in every campaign. Politicians would have to decide if they want to play the money game or go the public route. Voters would have to decide what level of sleaze they think matters. Real-time disclosure means they'd know that their in-

cumbent congressman, for example, is taking a bundle from the tobacco lobby or the Sierra Club or his rich wife. If they know the facts
and elect him anyway—hey, that's democracy.

There are other pluses. Rauch thinks his scheme would put the focus back on ethics (what politicians *should* do) rather than legality
(what they *can* do). That alone would improve public debate
overnight. After all, Washington has been convulsed in recent years
by fundraising "scandals" that actually turned on which phone lines
and offices presidents and senators used to make fundraising calls.
Does anyone outside Washington really think any of this is the issue?

Moreover, by keeping the political parties as the clearinghouse for
private money, Rauch's plan could strengthen them. As Senator Mitch
McConnell, the Kentucky Republican who is the leading foe of Mc-
Cain–Feingold, has rightly argued, the soft money ban couldn't take
money out of politics, but it could take the national parties out of
politics. That money isn't drying up: It's bankrolling state affiliates
and interest groups who flood campaigns with ads promoting their
own pet peeves, not the less parochial agendas of the national political parties.

"I've always liked Jonathan Rauch's approach to it," Ellen Miller
told me.

> It's a great bottom-line strategy because I think it will appeal enor-
> mously to Republicans. It would [also] appeal enormously to incum-
> bents because they think they can raise more of this money and it gives
> them choices. . . . I am perfectly comfortable in a system that has no
> limits as long as there is an alternative way to run with public financ-
> ing. I've always seen this as the end game. No one [in the liberal reform
> movement] has ever wanted me to talk about it.

No one has ever wanted me to talk about it. That, in the end, may be the
problem. The left's quixotic dream of getting money out of politics altogether muzzles bold yet pragmatic efforts to inject public money in
ways that would be acceptable to conservatives and to the public, and
would assure candidates a viable way to run without special interest
cash. That's what we should be seeking. McCain–Feingold hasn't

begun to get us there. Its great virtue—indeed, McCain's singular achievement—was to prove that a constituency for reform can be aroused.

Polls, and the focus groups I conducted for this book, confirm how passionately Americans feel about the system being rigged, and how dramatically they feel this skews our politics. In a *Newsweek* poll in 2000, for example, 57 percent of Americans called it a "major problem" that political contributions had too much influence on elections and government policy, versus 10 percent who felt this was "not a problem." Eighty-five percent in a CBS News poll that year felt the system needed either "fundamental changes" or had to be "completely rebuilt." A CBS News/*New York Times* poll in 2000 found that people believed party leaders and contributors had far more say in determining presidential nominees than average voters. A 2000 poll sponsored by the Committee for Economic Development, a business group, showed that 78 percent of business executives think the current campaign finance system has spawned an arms race for cash that is out of control. In addition, 75 percent of business leaders said they believe political contributions give them an advantage in the shaping of legislation; and 51 percent said they feared adverse legislative consequences for themselves or their industry if they turned down requests for political contributions from high-ranking political leaders and/or political operatives. In the face of these public sentiments, the fact that campaign finance doesn't rank high among the issues voters mention as important to them (as opposed to, say, health care or education) may say more about how jaded citizens are than about their interest in a better system. One 1997 poll, after all, showed that people thought they were more likely to see Elvis than see real campaign finance reform.

Ackerman's Patriot dollars, in a two-track system à la Rauch, is an easy idea for people to understand and could get us where we need to go. All that remains is for a critical mass of leaders to break out of ingrained ways of thinking to put these commonsense solutions before the public.

10

FINDING TWO CENTS

Time to review the bidding. We've discussed ideologically androgynous ways to fund health care for everyone for $80 billion a year; a plan to make teaching in poor schools the career of choice for talented young Americans at $30 billion; and a wage subsidy to establish a de facto living wage of $9 an hour for $85 billion. We've also detailed a plan for bigger trials of generously funded school vouchers that costs about $2 billion, and a "Patriot dollars" campaign finance reform for $3 billion. Recall that our Two Percent Solution means we have 2 percent of America's roughly $11 trillion GDP in 2004 to play with, or $220 billion a year. Adding up our agenda so far brings us to $200 billion, so we've still got some room left.

I'm going to exercise the author's prerogative and plunk down $10 billion to help make preschool universal in America, and another $10 billion a year as the federal contribution to the $100 billion construction and repairs backlog in the nation's school districts—and do both of these things without giving you the full chapter and verse. If you need lengthy convincing that every child in America should have the chance to attend a high-quality preschool, or details on how much this helps their subsequent educational achievement, and how other advanced nations invest far more in this critical area than we do, there are studies galore that present the compelling case (a good place to start is "Preschool for All: Investing in a Productive and Just Society," issued in 2002 by the Committee for Economic Development). It will likely cost $25 to 35 billion a year in new money to make preschool universal; $10 billion is a federal contribution that should help state and local governments come together and finish the job. As for school construction, the average school building in American cities is forty years old; poor children routinely go to schools that are overrun with rats and sewage, or that feature collapsing ceilings, ventilation systems that leave kids shivering or sweltering in class, and worse. Congress's General Accounting Office has documented this disgrace, as have numerous state lawsuits. It's hard to imagine a clearer way to tell these children they don't matter than to tolerate their shameful school facilities.

There it is: For two cents on the national dollar we have a country where everyone has basic health coverage; every full-time worker earns at least $9 an hour; poor children have great teachers in fixed-up schools where they show up ready to learn; and we've created a way for politicians to run for office (if they want to) without special-interest cash. In short, we've "taken luck seriously" by being serious ourselves about equal opportunity through education; by creatively democratizing money in politics; and by assuring a minimally decent life for citizens of the world's richest country. And we've done this while leaving intact the incentives through which capitalism delivers its miracles of growth and innovation.

All we have to do now is pay for it.

Financing such deals is where the trouble always comes, of course, because it means taking things away from constituencies who won't let them go without a fight. "Getting those numbers is hard," Senator John Edwards told me. "Having spent some time on it myself, I'm telling you it's very hard."

Yet here as well, there is something liberating about thinking bigger. Most Washington fights are an "inside" game, in which powerful lobbies square off in arcane disputes that few citizens can comprehend. Our Two Percent Solution, by contrast, involves such big goals, and creates so many millions of new "winners," that its ambition may help surmount the normal angst of resource reallocation. But be warned: As with any funding package that's ultimately successful, there is something for everyone to hate.

Enough throat-clearing. Take a deep breath and join me in the heady world of macro-resource allocation. All we need, it turns out, are seven commonsense reforms—plus a bonus for those willing to climb over an extra political hurdle in the pursuit of sanity. The general theme of our funding plan is "stop and shift"—as in, *stop* unjustified or indefensible subsidies and spending patterns; and *shift* from less effective to more effective ways of achieving a similar result. There will be no shortage of special-interest naysayers attacking these measures. But decide for yourself if, taken together, these trade-offs seem a fair way to promote *the national interest* via our Two Percent agenda (savings are shown in 2004 dollars).

1. Stop giving unjustified subsidies to big corporations (or, more precisely, "end one-quarter of corporate welfare as we know it"). (Annual savings: $25 billion.) Analysts of all stripes—from the libertarian Cato Institute to Ralph Nader to *Time* magazine's award-winning investigative team of Don Bartlett and Jim Steele—estimate that between $90 and $125 billion goes annually for "corporate welfare." Even granting that, as with "pork barrel" spending, one man's corporate welfare is another man's vital jobs program, there's a limit to sanity here. A stunning $70 billion in digital broadcast spectrum was handed over to existing broadcasters in 1996 as part of a plan to transition to high-definition television. The Mining Act of 1872 lets companies purchase the rights to federal lands for $5 an acre or less and mine valuable minerals without paying a penny in royalties. (In 1994 a Canadian company got rights to such lands containing $10 billion in gold reserves; taxpayers got less than $10,000. In 1995 a Danish firm patented land in Idaho containing more than $1 billion in minerals for a price of $275.) For years government has given away, royalty free, the fruits of research conducted in the biotech, computer, aerospace, and pharmaceutical fields. The Partnership for a New Generation of Vehicles spent billions from 1993 to 2002 helping Detroit (which hardly needed the handout) develop environmentally friendly cars; the leading innovators during that time were Honda and Toyota, who didn't participate in the program.

Then, of course, come farm subsidies, most of which go to wealthy farmers and corporate farms. Ten percent of farm subsidy recipients collect two-thirds of the money; in a recent year, leading corporate farm aid recipients included billionaire David Rockefeller ($352,187); media mogul Ted Turner ($176,077); NBA player Scottie Pippen ($131,575); and five Fortune 500 firms—Westvaco ($268,740), Chevron ($260,223), John Hancock Mutual Life Insurance ($211,386), DuPont ($188,732), and Caterpillar ($171,698). Brian Riedl of the Heritage Foundation calculated that Congress could have guaranteed every full-time farmer a minimum income of more than $32,000 for a family of four for only $4 billion a year—one-fifth of the cost of the new corporate subsidies in 2002's farm bill. Ralph Nader rightly calls such firms "welfare kings." He and former Bush budget director Mitch Daniels (now there's an odd couple) have looked for ways to work together to slash business pork, suggesting reform's bipartisan appeal here.

I'm a pragmatist. It's too much to expect Washington to end corporate welfare—but it's not too much to ask Washington to end *a quarter* of corporate welfare. John McCain and Richard Gephardt have suggested a commission modeled on the military base closing commission that helped Congress make similarly tough political calls at the end of the Cold War, via a comprehensive package that comes to Congress for an up-or-down vote. Leaving three of every four dollars of corporate pork untouched should give the lobbyists plenty to brag about even as this helps fund our Two Percent.

2. Stop subsidizing extra health coverage for Americans who already have good coverage (and use the money to help subsidize basic coverage for those who have none). (Annual savings: $35 billion.) As Congressmen Jim McDermott and Jim McCrery discussed in Chapter 5, employees don't pay taxes on compensation they receive in the form of employer-paid health insurance. This subsidy comes to about $120 billion a year, 70 percent of which goes to the highest-earning one-third of Americans. I propose we include as taxable income employer health contributions that exceed the average that employers provide. (The Congressional Budget Office estimates these averages were $500 a month for family coverage and $200 a month for individuals in 2001; they would be indexed for inflation.) Unions, as we saw, are the major foes of this change, because the subsidy helps underwrite the generous health plans they've negotiated. If such a lavish subsidy were tilted toward higher-income Americans in any other context, Democrats would be screaming about the injustice. My wager is that if this change were part of a comprehensive package that achieved the Two Percent Solution's many progressive goals, including universal coverage and a national living wage, union leaders would see their way to participating in its financing. Their members, at least, haven't closed the door: The Two Percent poll (which we'll discuss in Chapter 12) showed that two-thirds of union households would be willing to pay more in taxes to address the problems of the uninsured and poor schools. (Another plus of this measure is that capping the current federal subsidy would help restrain the galloping growth of health costs.)

3. Shift one of every six dollars going to bureaucratic programs serving the poor to help fund a living wage and health benefits for poor workers.   (Annual savings: $30 billion.) In 2004 governments at all levels will spend about $175 billion on means-tested benefits for low-income Americans to help them get food, housing, job training, child care, and other services (this amount does *not* include the earned income tax credit, education aid, or more than $200 billion for health care, mostly via Medicaid). The federal share of this sum is $140 billion. I propose we shift $30 billion—roughly one in five dollars of the federal share, or one in six of the total—to the Two Percent agenda. Much of the rest goes to the elderly, disabled, and others who cannot work, and these sums can't safely be consolidated into programs aimed at workers. But a 15–20 percent shift is doable, and would achieve liberal goals with less bureaucracy in ways conservatives can support.

4. Shift half of current federal aid to poor schools to the Two Percent teacher initiative.   (Annual savings: $5 billion.) The so-called "Title I" program sends about $12 billion a year to poorer districts. Educators told me that much of it is spent ineffectively. One superintendent said it's viewed as a local "entitlement," a de facto jobs program used to hire teachers' aides whose impact on student learning is dubious. Since our Two Percent agenda includes a $30 billion teacher compensation initiative, and $20 billion for universal preschool and construction, it's only right to honor the concerns raised by Title I's critics and insist that half of Title I's current funding be redirected to our new priorities. This shift also signals federal determination to help slash the infamous and wasteful administrative "blob" in education. Only about a third of our k–12 spending goes to teacher salaries in America, as opposed to 70 percent in other advanced nations. "We have lots of bureaucracy around the edges that sucks up the money that should go to teachers and to decent class sizes," said Linda Darling-Hammond of Stanford University. Reallocating a chunk of Title I as part of a new teacher-centered federal agenda makes sense.

5. Shift $25 billion now given as "backstop compensation" to health care providers for serving the uninsured (and use it to fund expanded health coverage). (Annual savings: $25 billion.) If every American has health coverage, there's no need to continue the $25 billion in subsidies going to hospitals and other providers who handle a disproportionate share of uninsured patients. Academic health centers in big cities will oppose this shift because they are major beneficiaries of these subsidies, and it's likely that when the uninsured get covered, they won't use these centers' emergency rooms or facilities, where they often wait hours to be seen. These health centers may therefore need to reengineer their cost structures, or lobby for explicit subsidies for medical education not hidden in various Medicare and Medicaid reimbursement schemes. If patients go elsewhere once they are insured, that's a legitimate form of consumer pressure on these facilities.

6. Middle Eastern oil liberation tax (or, "Stop Pretending Cheap Gas Doesn't Really Cost Us Much More"). (Annual revenue: $60 billion.) I propose phasing in over several years a new 60-cent-per-gallon gas tax to help fund our Two Percent Solution and reduce our dependence on Middle Eastern oil. After all, how many wars should we fight in the Persian Gulf before we get more serious about energy conservation and independence? It's worth taking a moment to lay out the case here.

For starters, I know from focus groups conducted for this book that higher gas taxes are unpopular. People were more than willing to cancel the as-yet-unimplemented parts of George W. Bush's 2001 tax cut to help fund a Two Percent plan; indeed, most assented to that idea in an instant. But when higher gas taxes came up, they literally moaned. This public sentiment helps explain why the last time energy taxes were discussed, as part of Bill Clinton's 1993 deficit reduction plan, we ended up with a hike of only 4.3 cents a gallon, and Bob Dole even made repealing that little levy an issue in his 1996 presidential campaign.

But pandering isn't inevitable. In the early 1990s, Ross Perot and Paul Tsongas were calling for a new 50-cent-per-gallon tax phased in over five years. The "big three" automakers and oil giants Chevron and Conoco were on board. Why? They'd come round to the view held by every other advanced nation: The environmental, economic, and national security costs of cheap oil make higher taxes to reduce consumption a smart way to fund government.

To the rest of the world, our price complaint must look a little silly. After all, at roughly $1.50 a gallon (putting aside the temporary spike to $1.75 during the 2003 conflict with Iraq), gas prices are lower today in real terms than they were in 1950—and nearly 45 percent lower than after the last embargo's price peak in 1981. Thanks to these bargains, Americans slurp as much oil as ever. And despite perennial warnings about fickle foreign supplies, we imported 61 percent of the oil we consumed last year, up from 33 percent in 1975.

In France and Germany a gallon of gas costs around $4.00; in Japan, about $3.50. Taxes there account for 55 to 70 percent of the pump price; in France, per gallon taxes run more than $2.80. Here, by contrast, federal and state taxes together average 42 cents a gallon, less than 30 percent of the price. Thanks in part to their policy of high-priced gas, our industrial competitors have made stunning strides in energy efficiency and independence. France now gets more than 70 percent of its electrical energy from nuclear power. In Japan, oil imports in 1980 were 5.5 percent of GDP; by decade's end, they'd fallen to 1 percent. The industrial restructuring that enabled this drop left Japan producing two and a half times its 1975 output with, in effect, the same tank of gas.

It's not that the United States has made no progress. Economywide energy efficiency is up by more than 40 percent since 1975. Average auto fuel efficiency has risen from 16 to 20.4 miles per gallon over the same period. Still, the average fuel economy of the *new* car fleet has fallen every year since 1986, from a high of 25.9 miles per gallon to about 23.8 today. And American drivers still consume about two times more gasoline per capita than people in other advanced countries. That helps explain why worrisome carbon emissions per capita are more than twice as high here, too.

Why is gas guzzling such a problem? Economists say it's because of the societal costs our energy gluttony brings, costs that aren't reflected in what we pay at the pump. The smog clouds (and seasonal health alerts) in Los Angeles and Denver are just the most visible reminders that our car-centered culture takes a toll on the environment. Outsized reliance on foreign energy supplies brings the risk of sudden, dramatic recessions when they're interrupted. To avoid such economic crises, we'd apparently prefer to fight—in the Persian Gulf, that is—than switch, via higher gas prices, to less perilous dependence.

At roughly a billion dollars per penny in annual revenue, a 60 cent gas tax would pay for a nice chunk of the Two Percent Solution, while still leaving gas prices 20 percent below their 1981 high, and about half what motorists abroad pay. A higher gas tax would also substitute a market-based approach to auto efficiency for today's mixed signals, through which low prices urge consumers to buy SUVs, while mileage-minded regulators tell the big three to build compacts.

The chief (and valid) objection to higher gas taxes is that they fall most heavily on those with less income. But our Two Percent agenda has already addressed this concern by enacting a big new wage subsidy for low-income workers. (Even if we conservatively assume that lower-income people buy as much gas proportionally as higher-income people, that means 10 percent of the new $60 billion gas tax will hit the lowest-earning 10 percent of Americans. This $6 billion in taxes should be compared with the $85 billion in new wage subsidies we've targeted toward low-income workers.) Rural politicians moan that gas levies unfairly hit their long-distance drivers harder than city folk. But while a 60 cent tax would cost the average U.S. driver an extra $350 or so a year, the regional variation is only plus or minus a hundred bucks. When it comes to aggregate benefits distributed by the federal government, the per capita variation among states is already about $1500. That's ten times as much, and no one's complaining.

The truth is that every tank of gas today contains fresh proof of the "consume now" ethic that pervades our culture. In 1991, the Germans enacted with little fanfare a 50 cent gas tax to help rebuild the former East Germany. In 1993, Americans found four cents on top of $1.20 gas almost too much to bear, even while we bequeath our children dirtier air and the continued risk of war over oil. A decade later, it's time to have a grown-up conversation about using sensible energy taxes to achieve America's social, economic, environmental, energy, and national security goals.

7. Cancel a portion of President Bush's tax relief for America's highest earners.   (Annual savings: $70 billion.) The bulk of President Bush's tax cuts have gone largely to the best-off Americans. Scrapping about one-third of these tax cuts (which represents only a portion of the relief given to the nation's highest earners) would generate roughly $70 billion a year on average over the next decade to help fund our Two Percent Solution. Bush's tax cuts also feature a number of "sunsets" and "phase outs" designed to make them appear smaller than they are likely to be; if the tax cuts are in fact made permanent, as many Republicans want, then less than one-quarter of the tax cuts would need to be cancelled to achieve the same $70 billion annual savings. (Beyond the Two Percent agenda, the balance of these tax cuts might separately be revisited to eliminate the outsized budget deficits they will help create).

The rationale here, as we've discussed, is straightforward. Given the unmet needs we're seeking to address, tax relief for those already well off shouldn't be a national priority. Fortunately, we know that marginal tax rates at today's levels are consistent with high economic growth because they were slightly higher under Bill Clinton. Indeed, they rose from 36 percent to 39.6 percent for the best-off Americans after 1993, and the period afterwards nonetheless produced the longest expansion since World War II.

———

Let's pause at this point and see where we are. Our target is $220 billion a year. These seven measures give us $250 billion. In other words, we're done, or more than done, meaning that some of these changes (like the gas tax) can be sensibly phased in over a few years.

But there's one more big category that ought to be on the table: the defense budget. At the time this book first appears, Democrats will almost certainly be afraid to touch it, and Republicans will not be so inclined. For that reason I've made sure we can fund our Two Percent Solution without touching defense. Yet as Richard Nixon said in another context, "We could do it, but it would be wrong." We can't talk honestly about sane opportunities to reallocate national resources without talking about defense.

The Bush administration inherited a $300 billion defense budget. It has called for increases that would take us to $470 billion by 2007. We will already have reached nearly $400 billion with Democratic assent by 2004. As Lawrence Korb, a former Reagan defense official now at the Council on Foreign Relations, points out, $400 billion will be more than the next twenty nations in the world spend combined, and 15 percent higher in inflation-adjusted terms than we spent on average during the entire Cold War (when we weren't the only superpower). We spend $15 billion a year on our arsenal of 6000 nuclear warheads alone. Europe, which now boasts a greater collective GDP and population than the United States, spends $200 billion less each year on defense; on a per person basis, that means our NATO allies are spending half as much as we do. Going to $470 billion will mean the Pentagon budget would be 50 percent bigger than its average during the Cold War. Is this necessary or wise in the age of terror—where the gravest threats come not from a rival Russian superpower rolling into Germany, but from a few thousand determined radicals who want to kill us, or from small rogue states who spend a tiny fraction of what we do on defense?

The Bush administration itself felt differently when it first took office, after a campaign in which George W. Bush had called for less Pentagon spending than Al Gore. Secretary of Defense Donald Rumsfeld's laudable aim was to reform the Pentagon in Nixon-to-China fashion, as only Republicans can. Yet Rumsfeld had hit a storm of bureaucratic, congressional, and interest group opposition by September 2001. In the wake of 9/11, therefore, Bush and Rumsfeld decided that reform was a luxury; better to throw money at everything, they reasoned, since the public would obviously support it, and worry about rationality later.

Beyond the U.S. military's peerless technology, firepower, and skill, however, this spending spree masks dramatic waste and disorganization that cries out for attention. As one Bush cabinet official told me privately, "Not too far down the road Rumsfeld will get back on the track of rationalizing defense spending so that it doesn't go into a runaway mode." Consider, by way of example, two areas the GOP would be pouncing on if similar issues were presented in budgets for education or health:

Procurement. Reinvestment as weapons age is obviously essential. The question is how much, how fast, and for what? With the services led by former fighter pilots, submariners, and tank commanders, it's no surprise they're eager for fancier versions of the usual machines. "Despite the absence of a superpower challenger," writes Michael O'Hanlon of the Brookings Institution, "the [Bush] Administration proposes replacing most major combat systems . . . with systems costing twice as much—and doing so throughout the force structure." But the logic of buying higher-tech weapons that often cost many times more than those they replace can be suspect. As one general told me, "As a rule, we're not buying improvements in relevant capability that are anywhere comparable to the massively higher price tags these successor weapons carry."

More disturbing is evidence that "we are buying systems without a clear idea of how to use them," said Andrew Krepinevich of the Center for Strategic and Budgetary Assessment. Take the services' plan to buy three new tactical warplanes. Such planes need to operate from forward bases in places like Japan, South Korea, Guam, and the Middle East. The problem is that new technologies are making these bases vulnerable. Satellite systems will let U.S. foes monitor these ports and airfields; the spread of ballistic missiles means that an enemy (say, North Korea) can credibly threaten to take them out in a crisis. The fix, in theory, is theater missile defense, but who knows if billions more will ever make such systems work? Given this emerging reality, should we really let the Pentagon pour more than $300 billion in coming years into fighters destined to be sitting ducks?

Tooth-to-tail.   According to Business Executives for National Security (BENS), a Pentagon watchdog group, the imbalance between combat and support forces—the military's "tooth" and "tail"—has reached troubling proportions. BENS estimates that 70 percent of defense dollars now go to "the tail." That's upward of $200 billion a year. It's not money well spent. Studies show that in many functions that could be privatized—like housing, payroll processing, travel, and inventory management—the Pentagon wastes up to $30 billion compared to more efficient private sector practices. "Such excessive overhead is inexcusable," says former BENS chief Thomas McInerney, a retired Air Force lieutenant general.

To be sure, the Pentagon can't control many things that push costs up: new duties like environmental cleanup and the drug war; or soaring health costs, driven by the presence of more troops with families in the volunteer force. Though excess base capacity was shaved by 20 percent through several rounds of closures, pork-barrel politics still saddles the services with countless bases and depots they don't need.

Advocates for Bush's defense hikes rightly note that we've cut the military from its Reagan-era peak while deploying it on dozens more smaller operations like Haiti and Bosnia; and now we've had a showdown with Iraq and the ongoing fight against terror. Under Reagan, military spending peaked in 1986–1987 at 6.2 percent of GDP and 2.2

million active duty troops; we're down to 3.3 percent and 1.4 million troops today. But as the recent Iraqi conflict demonstrated, technological advances have made our smaller force far more lethal. And, as Korb puts it, we're not going to war against Ronald Reagan's military in any event. Spending as a share of GDP doesn't suggest anything but the capacity to do more if we think that's wise. There's a good argument that defense is the kind of fixed cost that shouldn't rise in tandem with national income; after all, you don't buy a new security system for your home every time you get a raise. The key is assessing our potential threats and developing force structures and capabilities to meet them, something experts across the spectrum say we didn't manage to do during four separate "major reviews" in the 1990s. "They're delaying the hard choices again," one general told me after one of these exercises. "There's a real need for dramatic change in our armed forces but everyone's keeping their little piece of the pie. It almost makes me ill when I read these reports."

Yet Bush has proposed to raise spending to levels 50 percent above the Pentagon's Cold War average, and Democrats have assented without a peep. President Bush's frequent cry that this "sends a message" to foes that America will stay the course against terror seems especially wrongheaded. Does Bush truly imagine that terrorists like Osama bin Laden are deterred by the size of the U.S. defense budget?

Commonsense leaders in both parties should challenge our current course. The first sensible step would be to establish a standing congressional committee to monitor the post–9/11 defense buildup. Unprecedented mountains of cash are being handed to a Pentagon that Bush's own budget office says has not properly accounted for more than *a trillion dollars* in past years, and in an era when corporate misbehavior justifies extra scrutiny. Harry Truman provides the model. In February 1941, outraged by what he was hearing about rip-offs by contractors in the war buildup, Truman proposed and was assigned to lead the Senate Special Committee to Investigate the National Defense Program. Over the next few years, Truman exposed shocking waste, fraud, and mismanagement, often thanks to leads from patriotic defense industry employees troubled by what their bosses were doing. Truman landed on the cover of *Time* and earned national acclaim. "The man from Missouri," his senate colleague Claude Pepper recalled later, "had dared to say 'show-me' to the powerful military–industrial complex and he had caught many people in the act." It doesn't detract from the remarkable accomplishments and professionalism of our armed forces to say that a few $400 hammers and $800 toilet seats will make Bush's defense budget as open to question as it deserves to be.

Beyond that, an affirmative case for a saner defense budget must be made. It will need to be linked to detailed priorities in procurement, research and development, and war-fighting capabilities, but an overarching argument will help Americans make sense of the stakes. So let's consider the following bonus spending cut option:

Adopt an Eisenhower-style "8-7-23" defense plan.   (Annual savings: $50 billion.) "Make no mistake," our commonsense leader would say. "National security is job one. And to make sure that no power can threaten us, I believe we must spend far more than any conceivable rival. Insuring that margin of safety won't come cheap. America will spend 8 times more on our military than China, 7 times more than Russia, and 23 times more than Iran, North Korea, and Syria combined.

"But here's where I differ with the president, and lock arms with President Eisenhower, who knew something about saying no to military profiteers who exploit public fear to line their pockets. It was Ike, after all, who put the importance of being a *smart* hawk into perspective.

"Listen to Ike: 'Every gun that is made, every warship launched, every rocket fired signifies, in the final sense, a theft from those who hunger and are not fed, those who are cold and are not clothed.'

"Well, I like Ike. And I believe, in the Eisenhower tradition, that being strong doesn't mean winking at corporate wish lists just because they wave a flag, or kowtowing to contractors peddling yesterday's arms for tomorrow's threats. That's why I insist we spend 8 times more than China—but not 9 times more, as the president wants; 7 times more than Russia, but not 8 times more; and 23 times more than Iran, North Korea, and Syria combined—but not 26 times more.

The rough result would be a military budget of $400 billion, not $450 billion. That's $100 billion more than when Bill Clinton left office, and 15 percent above the Cold War average."

To be sure, Republicans have an easier time making this case. "I am a hawk but a cheap hawk," Newt Gingrich used to say. "I don't think we ought to salute waste just because it is in uniform . . . Our goal should be to downsize the Pentagon until it seems to be at most a triangle." But one way or another, the case must be made. We can fund our Two Percent agenda without defense savings, but if Ike were here he'd say there was $50 billion to be had without compromising our security. If defense is part of the mix, we've reached $300 billion in potential annual savings, meaning our fearless leaders can horse-trade or "mix and match" as they see fit to reach the $220 billion we need.

Two Percent Solution — Summary

($billions 2004)

What We're Buying

Universal health coverage	80
High-poverty teacher initiative	30
Richly funded voucher trials	2
Universal preschool contribution	10
School construction and repair	10
Low-income worker wage subsidy	85
Patriot dollars	3
Total	*220*

How We'll Pay For It

Cut one-fourth of corporate welfare	25
Limit health tax exclusion	35
Shift programs for poor to direct aid	30
Shift federal school aid to teacher plan	5
End uninsured subsidy for hospitals	25
60-cent-per-gallon higher gas tax	60
Cancel some tax cuts for best-off	70
Bonus: Eisenhower defense plan	50
Total	*300*

A common critique of funding plans like the one I've laid out is that they look "easy on paper," and of course that's true. But a better way to think about the trade-offs is to consider what it means if we *can't* reallocate two cents on the dollar for the goals we've discussed. If that's the case, we're doomed to symbolic posturing rather than serious reform on health care, schools, wages, and more. . . .

> Because corporations need 100 percent of their current
>   corporate welfare, and 75 percent just won't do;
> Because it's more important to give extra health subsidies to
>   people who already have good coverage rather than help 42
>   million Americans with none get the basics;
> Because it's essential to deliver help to poor Americans through
>   bureaucracies that may not work effectively but that are nice
>   jobs programs for people who vote a certain way;
> Because we need to give billions to hospitals for taking care of
>   the uninsured even if everyone has insurance;
> Because our leaders shouldn't have to risk teaching citizens how
>   cheap gas undermines America's security, environment, and
>   economy;
> Because we can't be safe unless we spend more on defense than
>   the next twenty nations combined;
> And because our overriding national priority should be lowering
>   taxes on wealthier Americans to levels below those that
>   applied during the longest economic boom in our history.

When put this way, is it really unthinkable that we might reject undeserving claims on federal largesse and attention and take real steps toward renewal?

II

FIXING

EVERYTHING ELSE

Shortly after one of our conversations on the Two Percent agenda, Mitch Daniels, President Bush's first budget director, sent me an email. "One question I didn't get around to asking," Daniels wrote, "is: Presuming the nation made the two percent commitment, even if it were achieved largely through a shift in resources rather than a pure expansion of government spending, what is the plan when the entitlement crunch arrives? You've pointed out that we can afford this now, but probably not then . . . so if we embark on this approach, do we have a problem when all the new bills start coming due?"

It's a crucial question—perhaps *the* crucial question—and so naturally it was also the first question my wife asked when I began bleating on about the Two Percent Solution at home. My answer comes down to a political judgment. If we get everyone "in the boat" now (in terms of defining the social contract in ways we've discussed), we'll figure out how to ride the age wave together. If we don't get everyone in the boat now—and so don't get serious about health coverage, poor schools, the working poor, and more—then once the boomers hit the fan, we'll be so busy coping we may not think about pulling anyone new in again for twenty years.

Yet the question of how to manage and finance Social Security and Medicare once the boomers retire remains the $25 trillion question, because that's the amount of unfunded promises that exist in these programs today. While we don't have room here to detail every way to strengthen these programs, we need to broadly examine the challenges they face and the big fixes that seem sensible, in order to be confident that the Two Percent Solution is sustainable. Our habits of Mutually Assured Demagoguery have made it hard to have a constructive public discussion on these questions, or honest talk about the spiraling health costs that go beyond the elderly programs and that affect us all. The fiscal reckoning ahead will change this.

Ponzi's Revenge

Start with Social Security, which currently sends $470 billion a year in checks to 45 million Americans, providing nearly two-thirds of retirees with half their income, and lifting 10 million of our oldest citizens out of poverty. As we discussed in Chapter 3, the system is hurtling toward an explosion of red ink; and, absent reform, most younger workers won't come close to getting back a reasonable "return" on what they paid in. Beyond eye-glazing numbers, fears of "insolvency," and reckless rhetoric on all sides, Social Security's dilemma will soon prompt the renegotiation of a social commitment in which every American has a hefty financial and moral stake.

Thinking sensibly about the future of the nation's most successful government program requires an unblinking look at its past. Today's troubles are the legacy of seventy years not only of undisputed gains, but of pervasive myths and unintended consequences that the defenders of Social Security's chastity prefer to ignore. The question of how to provide security for the elderly without starving the nation of resources for other priorities has been a tension in Social Security from its inception. Its founders in the 1930s felt that the large transfers from young to old implicit in a "pay-as-you-go" system funded by workers were justified, given that seniors in Depression days were often desperate. Even then, however, they recognized the trade-offs. "The pattern cannot be larger than the cloth," wrote the program's advisory council in 1938; protection of the aged could not come "at the expense of . . . impairing such essential services as education and public health or of lowering of the standard of living of the working population." "No benefits should be promised or implied," that early report added prophetically, "which cannot be safely financed not only in the early years of the program, but when workers now young will be old."

FDR himself stressed the notion of limits as the flip side of largesse. "This act does not offer anyone an easy life," he said in a 1938 fireside chat. It would "furnish that minimum necessary to keep a foothold; and that is the kind of protection Americans want." Indeed, Phillip Longman, in his 1996 book *The Return of Thrift,* argues that Social Security was enacted largely in the drive to beat back costlier demands for universal old age assistance championed by the physician and reformer Francis Townsend, whose 10 million followers made him the one-man AARP of his day. Limiting Social Security's benefits to those who had contributed payroll taxes was the ingenious (and palatable) way to cap government's exposure, even as it gave Roosevelt the illusion of insurance he needed so that "no damn politician" (as he famously said) could ever scrap his plan.

In both senses, this "contributory" design worked. In 1940, fewer than 1 percent of the elderly received Social Security. Even as late as 1953, fewer than half the elderly got benefits, since they'd either retired before the system started or hadn't contributed long enough to qualify. Only in the go-go sixties did America's policy hubris fully flower, sparking the hefty expansions that contained the seeds of today's reckoning. But those were heady days. In 1967, the economist Paul Samuelson wryly quipped that "the beauty about social insurance is that it is actuarially unsound," relying on a growing population and rising real incomes to pay each generation of retirees more than they paid into the system. "A growing nation," Samuelson concluded, "is the greatest Ponzi game ever contrived." Robert Ball, a program official and advocate who has figured in these debates for half a century (and remains a player today), captured the spirit when he wrote that "a 'minimum income for all' might have been a stirring objective when it was proposed by Sidney and Beatrice Webb about 1910, but we can do much better than that in the United States in 1966."

For retirees, the pleasant surprises had just begun. In 1972, benefits were increased across the board by 20 percent. Then, in a step Richard Nixon would call his biggest economic mistake, they were indexed to inflation. Ironically, raising benefits each year by the consumer price index was conceived as an effort to cap the benefit bidding wars that had become a bipartisan preelection ritual. The dawn of the great inflation of the 1970s, of course, wasn't brilliant timing. A disastrous and inadvertent "double indexing" in the new benefit formula made matters worse, showering billions in mistaken windfalls for several years. (When this error was finally fixed in 1977, the extraordinary "Notch Baby" lobby was born, furious at being denied their "entitlement" to this excess.)

In the late 1970s, benefits were tweaked again to rise automatically in tandem with real wages, thus promising each successive cohort of retirees higher real benefits. All told, in the 1970s benefits grew *ten times faster in real terms than did the number of Americans aged 65 and over.* The "replacement rate"—a measure of the share of preretirement earnings replaced by Social Security—jumped from 34 percent in 1970 to 54 percent in 1981. This spiral brought the system's finances to the brink of crisis, prompting the big bipartisan fix of 1983. Those reforms raised payroll taxes, taxed benefits for the first time, and trimmed future costs by inching the retirement age toward 67 between 2003 and 2025. Still, typical workers retiring in the mid-1990s got three times more in real terms than did their grandparents in 1940.

What is the moral of this story? After decades of expansion, FDR's "foothold" has grown enough to make the trade-offs foreseen by the system's founders ripe for revisiting. Only a grinch could grumble about the most effective anti-poverty program in history; but only a fool would fail to ask whether the Ponzi scheme is sustainable, and at what price. Today, more than $15 billion in Social Security goes annually to households with retirement incomes of more than $100,000 a year; $45 billion to those in the $50,000 to $100,000 range. "We have to go to seniors and say, 'Look, we can't keep this up,'" said former Nebraska senator Bob Kerrey. "Yes, poverty is a concern. But please don't tell me that every American over 65 is foraging in the alley for garbage, or eating dog food. They're going to Vegas with their COLAs

[Social Security's annual Cost of Living Adjustments in benefits] while kids don't have computers in class."

Kerrey is right: Thanks to our aging population, longer life spans, generous benefit hikes, and sluggish growth, the one thing certain about Social Security is that before the baby boom retires it will change. Call it Ponzi's revenge. As we saw in Chapter 3, there were seven workers paying into the system for every retiree in 1950. In 1990 there were five; by 2030 there will be fewer than three. Life expectancy, meanwhile, has increased by 14 years since Social Security was enacted, while the retirement age has yet to budge from 65, meaning benefits are drawn far longer. Financially, these trends mean that the "pay-as-you-go" nature of Social Security, in which today's workers are taxed to fund the retirement of their parents, simply cannot continue without big tax hikes or cuts in projected benefits for tomorrow's workers. The current estimate is that Social Security will start paying out more each year than it takes in 2018. After that date it will add billions to the annual deficit, instead of helping mask deficits in the rest of the budget, as the program's surpluses do today.

Unfortunately, the forces leading the charge for inertia have the upper hand, thanks to the Three Great Myths of Social Security that they, and petrified politicians, refuse to debunk:

1. You're just getting back what you paid in.   Consider the facts (as documented by Eugene Steuerle of the Urban Institute). Early generations of beneficiaries paid in little and rode the rising benefit wave. The result? The average one-earner couple retiring in 1960 got back eleven times what they paid in (after accounting for inflation and interest). By the early 1980s, owing to the growing payroll tax bite, that average couple had to scrape by on four times what they paid in, but in absolute dollars those retirees (many still collecting) enjoy the biggest windfalls Social Security will ever bestow. How big? On average, on lifetime payroll contributions of $65,000, they receive an astonishing $280,000 in benefits, for a net lifetime "profit" of about $215,000 (in 2003 dollars). People retiring in 2000 will still receive 1.2 to 1.4 times their contributions. But many boomers retiring in 2010, and the bulk of the Generation X'ers who come after, will face lifetime *losses*.

2. Social Security is "progressive."   It's one thing to pay windfalls, quite another to save your biggest bonanzas for retirees with the highest incomes. But this fact—that Social Security is regressive within generations—is not well understood. It's commonly argued that the regressive payroll tax through which the system is financed is more than offset by the progressive tilt of its benefit structure, which gives lower-wage workers a higher percentage of their preretirement pay. But as Eugene Steuerle has stressed, the system still transfers larger amounts of money the richer you are. (A two-earner couple retiring in 2000 with one high wage and one average wage will receive $400,000 in lifetime Social Security benefits; a couple with one average wage and one low wage will receive $300,000.) This isn't a paradox, because the benefit formula is based on wages. A lawyer who gets a 25 percent "replacement rate" on his eligible earnings will collect more money over his retirement than a dishwasher who gets 50 percent of his. This trend is compounded by Social Security's spousal benefit, which gives spouses 50 percent of the worker's benefit regardless of income level, so that more money goes to better-off spouses. To be sure, the (smaller) parts of Social Security that provide disability benefits and aid to survivors are indeed progressive. But when it comes to its major retirement component, Social Security thus resembles our other great regressive entitlement, the mortgage interest deduction, which offers a big housing subsidy to someone like Bill Gates, while Gates's maid, if she rents, gets no subsidy at all.

3. It's OK, there's a trust fund.   Remember how awful it was when you realized there wasn't a Tooth Fairy or a Santa Claus? Well, brace yourself for another rude awakening: The Social Security trust fund is an accounting fiction. While it's true that about $100 billion more comes in today via Social Security taxes than gets paid out in benefits, that "surplus" is immediately invested in Treasury bonds, in effect loaning the money to Uncle Sam to mask the deep deficits in the rest of the budget. The so-called surpluses building up in this trust fund are thus nothing but IOUs. Making good on them as the boomers retire won't be pretty, since by that time we'll be paying out far more in Social Security than payroll taxes bring in. The tragedy is that today's "surpluses" were designed by congressional reformers in 1983 to add to national savings, in hopes of boosting economic growth before the big bills came due. Instead, they became an easy way to evade hard choices in the rest of the budget. For the record, the head-in-the-sand crowd insists these trust funds (there's one for Medicare, too) are as "real" as any private retirement account holding Treasury bonds. Maybe it's time we switched to a clearer label: the "Pass the Huge Tax Hike to the Kids" Funds.

The force of these myths in preserving the status quo adds generational insult to injury when it comes to government priorities already dramatically skewed to favor the elderly at the expense of children and long-term growth. The federal government spends about eight times more on seniors as on children under 18. (Even when you factor in state and local spending for public education, the ratio is still three-to-one.) Fear of the mighty seniors lobby takes so many benefits off the table that both political parties must slash forward-looking investments in research and development and infrastructure to show even bogus paths to budget balance, while half of eligible kids are told we can't "afford" their Head Start programs. One in six American children—nearly 12 million, at last count—live in poverty, a higher rate than any other age group. Republicans and Democrats, meanwhile, who differ little on these arrangements, swear on the stump every two years that "this campaign is about the future."

What is to be done? We need first to be clear on our goals. We want to assure that we can finance a reasonable floor of protection for retirees, since many depend on Social Security for much of their income. Next, we want to help younger workers avoid getting so little "back" on their payroll taxes, a situation they will rightly find politically and economically intolerable (though, to be fair, "return on investment" is not the full way to think about Social Security; it's insurance against disability as well). Finally, we want to raise national savings, and thus investment, to fuel the additional growth to help pay for all those graying boomers. National savings will be increased if Social Security (and the budget as a whole) runs greater surpluses, or at least smaller deficits.

The debate thus far has been predictably unhelpful. The Republican Party has pledged, most recently in the 2002 election, "to oppose any proposal that would cut benefits, raise taxes, or raise the retirement age." Democrats hold these positions, too. Sounds great, except that to keep Social Security solvent we'll soon have to do some of the following: cut projected benefits, raise taxes, and raise the retirement age. It's comforting to know both parties have categorically ruled out anything that might solve the problem—and to see them bristle at the notion that any scoundrel would suggest otherwise.

Most of the controversy has been over "privatization," with the left saying that this will unravel the very notion of social insurance and the right saying it will offer younger workers the chance for higher returns. But both sides are being unusually disingenuous, even by Washington standards. First, the left won't admit that Republicans are not talking about fully privatizing Social Security. The most any GOP plan seeks to do is give workers a chance to put 2 percentage points of today's 12 percent Social Security payroll tax into accounts they own, invest, and control. Such plans are also pushed by farsighted Democrats like former senator Daniel Patrick Moynihan, who, before his death, feared a replay of the politics of welfare reform, in which liberals spent years holding the line against any change while those wanting to scrap the program defined, and then won, the debate. "If you don't open this up and do the few things you have to do," Moynihan told me, "you'll lose the system." Worse, the left assails such plans by comparing them unfavorably with so-called "current benefits" under the system, when every honest observer knows these "current benefits" can't be financed in the future without economy-killing tax hikes.

But conservatives, obsessed with the higher returns young workers could earn on their own, duck the question of how to get from here to there, in effect promising a free lunch. The trick in switching midstream from today's "pay-as-you-go" to a partially prefunded private retirement system is that one generation has to pay twice: first for the retirement of its parents, and then for its own, since younger folks in a private scheme will start paying for themselves. Usually such plans require at least a trillion dollars in these "transition" costs. Chile paid for the change in part by using the 5 percent of GDP budget *surplus* they were running when they switched. No such luck here. Conservatives either can't do the math or simply fear admitting that they can't have Bush's tax cuts for the wealthy and also fund their proposed transition to partial private accounts.

Here's the critical point: Whether you're for or against partial privatization, we're still going to need a financing mechanism that can close a gap that amounts to roughly 1.8 percent of payroll over the next seventy-five years (the equivalent of $5–10 trillion in current dollars, depending on whose numbers you believe). So here's a radical thought: Instead of getting bogged down in ideological wars, why don't we take a commonsense step that in one stroke fixes the system's finances, and leaves the privatization fight for another day? Luckily, there's an arcane but powerful little reform that can do the trick—the public finance equivalent of nuclear fission.

Fixing Social Security in One Easy Step

What am I talking about? It has to do with the way benefit levels are calculated for Social Security recipients when they're first eligible for the program. Changing this initial level has a powerful systemwide effect, because it means that even with annual cost-of-living adjustments, a person's benefits will always be lower than they would have been, at least in theory, under today's clearly unsustainable system. Yes, this will be politically controversial. (Everything serious is, if you hadn't already noticed, since we've reached an era when hard choices are unavoidable.) But this step was enacted by Great Britain under Margaret Thatcher, and the Brits are now in far better shape than the other advanced nations in terms of funding the boomers' retirement.

In simple terms here's what needs to be done. Today, initial Social Security benefits are calculated as a percentage of a worker's average monthly earnings over his or her career. To update those earnings into present-day dollars, they are "indexed" by the increase in average *wages* in our economy since that time. The other way to update those earlier earnings would be to index them to the change in economy-wide *prices*. Since wages rise faster than prices over time (because wages reflect not only inflation but also the increased productivity of our workforce thanks to advances in technology and education), the wage-indexed number is higher, and so initial benefits based on that calculation are higher, too.

I know what you're thinking: Why would we ever change to price indexing, other than from some Scrooge-like desire to lower future benefits? Well, to be sure, we probably wouldn't think about it if we weren't on the cusp of the biggest financial crunch in American history. But we are. And there's a defensible policy rationale as well. For starters, the system hasn't always been wage-indexed. From 1935 to 1975, in fact, there was no indexing at all; Congress simply enacted changes to benefit schedules it deemed appropriate on an ad hoc basis. In addition, under wage indexing, every new cohort of retirees is guaranteed a higher level of real benefits in retirement than the previous generation. For example, the typical worker scheduled to retire in 2020 is scheduled to receive monthly payments 20 percent higher in real terms than today's retirees. Scheduled benefits for today's teenagers are scheduled to be 60 percent higher in real terms. When we had a younger population and rising productivity this was affordable. But in the era ahead it is simply not affordable—except at the cost of imposing a tax burden on our children that's unacceptable, or eliminating big chunks of government activities that citizens rightly expect. Besides, on what moral theory should we guarantee seniors— already the wealthiest segment of the population—ever-higher real benefits, when many other Americans may be struggling to get a foothold? A change from wage indexing to price indexing would mean that every new cohort of retirees will get benefits with purchasing power at least equal to what retirees get today (and probably a little higher, since we wouldn't phase it in for a few years). What they won't get is the unaffordable promise of perpetual real increases—because there are other priorities for nonelderly Americans that also need to be paid for during the boomers' golden years.

The upside is that a shift to price indexing closes the entire fiscal gap in Social Security, and even leaves a bit of extra cash with which we could add progressive benefit increases for low-income workers and widows (currently not treated well by the system). If this is later combined with personal account options that were progressively funded, such a redesigned system would be sustainable and offer a better deal for the low-earners who deserve special concern.

There are variations on pure price indexing worth considering as well—for example, trimming some of the benefits going to better-off seniors, or indexing the retirement age at which full benefits become available to reflect today's longer life spans. Adopting such measures would lessen the need to go to full price indexing to close the system's financing gap. The important point is that "fixing solvency first" via price indexing or related measures could free us to have the kind of discussion that is impossible today, when the financial question is routinely muddled with the question of privatization. Democrats want government to fund new private accounts on top of Social Security to help middle- and low-income families build nest eggs for retirement. Republicans want to let workers divert a small piece of their payroll taxes into private accounts to help toward the same end. Why not both? If solvency has been solved, we can have a cleaner conversation about building wealth for retirement in ways that produce a common-sense synthesis of liberal and conservative ideas.

Since this price indexing option is well known, why haven't our leaders done it? Or even seriously discussed it? Because on an issue that's easy to demagogue, this is the biggest, fattest, soft-pitch-down-the-center-of-the-demagogic-plate of them all. Price indexing initial benefits (as well as the other options noted) will be assailed as a huge "benefit cut." So it's hard to see it happening until we're near the edge of crisis, when both parties hold hands at midnight and take the leap. The problem is that it would be much better if we make changes to Social Security sooner, so people have time to adjust their expectations and plans. If young people became a constituency for reform it could speed things up. This isn't a brief for "generational war," but at this point, a little generational self-defense wouldn't hurt.

Medicare: "The Hard One"

If that seemed like heavy lifting, catch your breath: Social Security is viewed by all experts as "the easy one" compared to Medicare. After all, as we saw, "fixing" it is basically a financial question. Medicare, by contrast, is part of a byzantine health sector in varying stages of crisis that is responsible for one-seventh of the nation's economic output. It also involves the delivery of complex services (not merely checks) by several million health care workers and a gaggle of major industries. Medicare's coming overhaul will therefore be a tortuous process that showcases the big questions of self-government as few issues can. Can a democracy summon the will to fix looming problems without a galvanizing crisis? Can the center govern, and put flesh on reforms that harness private interest for public good? Or will the Medical–Industrial Complex foil them with high-minded objections that mask bottom-line greed? Is rational reform a hopeless quest anyway in a capital ruled by cash, fear, and lust for power?

The beginning of wisdom on Medicare's woes involve a paradox: The program costs too much and covers too little. At roughly $250 billion, Medicare, like U.S. health care generally, spends far more per person than do other advanced nations, and without better outcomes to show for it. Costs are slated to rise from 2.5 percent of GDP to 5 percent by 2030. Medicare's share of federal spending will similarly double, from 12 percent to 24 percent. How can this surge be funded? Medicare's 2.9 percent payroll tax could double to keep the trust fund that covers hospital services solvent. Trillions of general fund dollars could be diverted, stealing the equivalent of a shiny new Pentagon or ten education departments from our kids' discretionary budget choices each year. If you don't like these options, you're left shifting more of the burden to seniors, millions of whom will already be struggling thanks to inadequate savings and pensions, as well as Social Security benefits that (even before potential trims) won't rise as fast as health costs. For many of tomorrow's elderly, these numbers spell shrunken living standards that are hard to square with the growing rage for early retirement. The only thing certain is that something's got to give.

For all of these frailties, however, Medicare remains one of government's undeniable success stories. By pooling health risks across 40 million seniors, it has brought security to a segment of the population that was deemed uninsurable prior to 1965. The trick now is to adapt this success to an aging population in the face of pricey new health technologies.

Unfortunately, the debate isn't framed this way. Instead, almost all public discussion of Medicare's long-term problems involves the "solvency" of its hospital "trust fund," set to "go belly up" in 2029. Making this trust fund solvent—and this applies to Social Security, too—involves trimming program costs or raising earmarked payroll taxes to keep projected revenues and expenses in synch over some extended period. Yet defining the problem as one of restoring solvency to a segregated set of programs rules out important questions of overall resource allocation in advance. Is it wise or necessary, for example, for us to let Medicare double before long to 5 percent of GDP, at the expense of other social needs? Or does that prospect make the search for more efficient modes of health delivery not just important, but a kind of national emergency? Where, to put it another way, is the Head Start trust fund? Or the trust fund to ease the plight of the working poor, or to improve teacher quality in inner cities? The frustrating paradox of public finance on the eve of the baby boomers' retirement is that earmarked trust funds that benefit the elderly tacitly banish such questions, even as their coming "bankruptcy" remains politically indispensable in forcing action that might help address them.

Yet as Robert Reischauer of the Urban Institute points out, these "insolvency" worries are only one of the "four I's" plaguing Medicare, since the program is also inadequate, inefficient, and inequitable. Unlike most private plans and public coverage across Europe, Medicare doesn't pay for prescription drugs and offers poor catastrophic coverage. As a result, most retirees need supplementary Medigap or employer-provided "wraparound" policies that can push yearly out-of-pocket costs past $3500. Meanwhile, the program's unmanaged fee-for-service care spawns excess tests and procedures, while Medigap coverage of co-payments and deductibles sends folks racing to the doctor for a sniffle. Then there's Kremlin-style central pricing, which once left Florida hospitals flooded with MRIs (by over-reimbursing for the machines after actual costs had dropped), while giving anesthesiologists (paid by the hour) a stake in keeping you under.

But the least understood feature of Medicare today is its simple unfairness. In 1998, for example, Medicare spent more than $7000 on each senior in Louisiana and the District of Columbia, versus about

$4300 in Minnesota and Oregon (the national average was $5500). According to Dr. John Wennberg of Dartmouth Medical School, a leading student of regional health costs, only a tiny portion of these variations can be explained by cost-of-living differences for supplies, wages, and the like. Instead, they're driven by local differences in the numbers of doctors and hospital beds, and the associated "practice style" this breeds—a self-interested case of supply driving demand. The effect has been to transform Medicare into a crazy quilt of indefensible cross-subsidies that remain invisible to taxpayers.

What to do? Centrist Democrats and Republicans have moved toward consensus in recent years on structural reforms for Medicare that harness market forces for public purposes. The approach is called "premium support," modeled largely on the health plan now serving more than 8 million federal workers and their families. It would phase out today's centrally administered price-setting system, and the archaic distinction between the program's separate parts "A" and "B" (for hospital care and everything else). It would change Medicare to a consumer-based system that gives seniors a range of plans to choose from, makes payments to those plans on their behalf, and includes incentives to pick plans that manage care cost-effectively. If seniors preferred a plan that costs more than the federal payment they're entitled to, they'd add more out of their own pocket. Government would regulate the health plans' financial soundness and marketing, and guard against plans that undermine the whole system by trying to skim off the healthiest patients. If it sounds familiar, there's a reason—it's the same "managed competition" approach underlying the health plan discussed by Congressmen McDermott and McCrery in Chapter 5. President Bush offered a version of this idea in early 2003, and while liberal Democrats blasted it during congressional debate over the summer, more market-minded Democrats have in recent years endorsed such a scheme if done with proper safeguards.

To be sure, the debate over Medicare's inevitable evolution will be fraught with battles, driven in particular by liberal suspicions of any market-friendly approach. How much regulation, for example, is needed to assure that seniors make safe, informed choices? Should the federal payment on behalf of each beneficiary change as needed to cover an assured package of benefits, as the Democrats prefer? Or should it instead be a defined contribution that limits federal budget exposure while providing the impetus for further health delivery efficiencies, as the Republicans want? One key will be to figure out how to adjust the payments made to health plans to reflect a person's risk profile, without which the problem of skimming off healthy seniors (which lay behind many Medicare HMO scams in the late 1990s) could leave the sick or the poor in jeopardy. Another key will be to harness the political imperative to add prescription drugs to the program as a way to force broader reforms that might make costs more controllable in the long run. Ultimately, successful reform via premium support means finding a way to assure that *limiting the growth in the voucher or subsidy actually limits the growth of overall health costs, rather than simply shifting an ever-increasing share of the burden to individuals.* Only if this goal can be achieved will liberals' proper concerns be addressed in ways that avoid intrusive and distorting price controls throughout medicine.

But we should be clear that cost savings may only appear down the road. Even if you think, as I do, that premium support assigns government a role it's likely to perform better than it does central pricing, and even if competition seems indispensable for curing many of Medicare's indefensible inequities, it's probably not possible to have the right benefit levels, protect needy seniors, and also bank savings anytime soon. Even advocates like Robert Reischauer, Bob Kerrey, and Bill Thomas, the conservative chairman of the House Ways and Means Committee, told me you can't feel confident about achieving such savings. It's a matter of faith in the long-term impact of competition. We know that the alternative—unmanaged fee-for-service, with the downsides of central pricing—can't be the answer. But since one of our chief goals in Medicare is to control long-term costs, does this mean premium support is senseless?

A few years ago, I might have said yes. Now, humbled by the difference between the results experts often expect from policy and what actually happens, I'm less sure, and less worried. No one (least of all me, as a White House budget aide) thought Bill Clinton's 1993 economic package would lead to stunning surpluses by decade's end.

Well, surprise. The same lesson applies here. You push policy in the right direction, and come back and tweak when you need to. Even if savings do occur, Medicare accounts for only one in six dollars spent on health care, meaning that if we stay on course to hit 20 percent of GDP by the early 2020s, we need to start a national assault on aggregate health spending in the next few years (on which more in a moment). Democrats, as we've discussed, will need to lead that charge, if they want government to have cash for any other social purpose. But there's more important work to do first.

For me, that work is universal coverage. Getting a premium support structure in place can help us move in this direction, because it would be easy to bring new people into this system, and it's the only model under which Republicans will join the cause rather than resist it. As we discussed in Chapter 5, universal coverage won't happen without the support of both political parties. And as much as liberals might wish it, they're not going to persuade Republicans to outlaw the insurance industry and adopt a single-payer system modeled on Canada's. They can, however, realistically hope to turn health insurance over time into more of a regulated utility, as Republican Jim McCrery envisions. In this way, premium support in Medicare, by introducing a system of smartly regulated regional health insurance markets or exchanges, can help pave the way for a distinctively American form of universal coverage.

National Health Costs: The Seminal Challenge

So what about health costs? The truth is they're the seminal challenge—and one that has been utterly neglected. The expected rise in health costs from today's 14 percent of GDP toward 20 percent of GDP as the baby boomers retire represents the biggest challenge to social justice and sane governance in the next generation. The reason, as we've seen, is that public budgets will be so squeezed by health costs that it will become increasingly difficult to fund other existing public commitments, let alone take on new ones.

Slowing this cost growth without sacrificing health care quality is the single biggest leverage point in public finance, and one that would bring a huge benefit for society. America today spends far more per capita on health care than every other advanced nation, yet we do not have better public health outcomes (on measures like life expectancy, infant mortality, and so on). We also know there are dramatic regional differences in the use of health services, yet again experts say that areas with higher usage and spending see no improvement in health outcomes. These international comparisons and regional benchmarks suggest that it should unquestionably be possible to shave serious sums from projected health costs without compromising quality. The impact would be dramatic. One percent of GDP is worth more than $100 billion a year in today's dollars, a large chunk of which rests on public budgets. It may not be too much of an overstatement to say that if we can make the health sector more efficient, we can save the world (or at least free up enough resources to fund universal health coverage, upgrade dilapidated urban schools, raise teacher pay, and lift subsidies for the working poor in perpetuity). The issue needn't be framed in terms of "liberal" goals, of course, since health costs will be in competition with missile defense as much as with Head Start.

Yet it has been virtually impossible to get the question of aggregate health costs on the national agenda since the demise of the Clinton health plan in 1994. Liberals, still reeling from that debacle, prefer to focus (albeit timidly) on expanding coverage, and tend to be in denial about the coming collision between health costs and other causes they cherish. Conservatives care about the long-run cost outlook but for political reasons don't want to appear miserly. The main way the cost issue has been expressed in public life has been via the surge of managed care (itself partly reflecting a failure of public action), followed by the backlash against the temporary cost restraint that HMOs delivered in the mid-1990s. Since 2000, fresh double-digit surges in health costs, deeply troubling to business, have made the moment ripe again for a serious debate. Behind closed doors, moreover, a critical mass of senior officials on both sides of the aisle worries deeply about the imminent showdown between health costs and the rest of government.

In the shorthand of economists, the question is whether we can lick "Baumol's disease" in health care. In the 1960s, William Baumol, an economist at New York University, offered his famous theory of "cost disease," which posits that labor-intensive parts of the economy—symphonies, live theater, and schools, for instance—are immune from the technology-based productivity gains that the rest of the economy enjoys. A string quartet in Mozart's day is a string quartet today; you can't use three musicians or replace them with robots. Wages in these sectors rise with marketwide compensation. But without the offsetting productivity gains that goods-producing, capital-intensive sectors enjoy, says Baumol, cost increases in the "productivity immune" sectors will always be above average.

The general assumption has been that the health sector suffers from this cost disease, and health care's ever-rising share of GDP seems to have borne this out. Yet we know that technology plays a major role in health. In addition, an emerging movement is working to reengineer health delivery with a view to radically streamlining costs even while boosting quality. Its advocates say that best practices and protocols can purge enormous waste *and* poor medical care from the system simultaneously. It's what "managed care" could mean in the best sense, and one of its most enthusiastic pioneers and evangelists is former treasury secretary Paul O'Neill.

In 1999, when O'Neill was CEO of Alcoa, the Pittsburgh-based industrial giant, he convened the health stakeholders in the region to form the Pittsburgh Regional Health Initiative. The coalition includes forty-two area hospitals, four major insurers, several hundred doctors and nurses, and dozens of corporate and civic leaders. PRHI aims to "perfect" the local health care system using the same process that Toyota famously used to revolutionize auto manufacturing, techniques that Alcoa later adopted with great success. To date, PRHI has focused on three areas. The first is patient safety, with a goal of reducing medication errors and hospital-acquired infections, long an industry scourge. Pittsburgh is now the only community in the country where competing hospitals have agreed to share sensitive data on medication errors and infections (usually closely held because of litigation fears), and work together to bring the numbers to zero. PRHI's second goal is to achieve the world's best patient outcomes in several clinical areas. Hundreds of area physicians have produced sophisticated databases to compare patient outcomes and collaborate to improve care in cardiac surgery, hip and knee replacement surgery, repeat cesarean sections, depression, diabetes, and radiation oncology. Finally, area providers are adopting the methods of the Toyota Production System, redesigning organizations in ways that let employees at all levels learn from errors and problems, and improve health care delivery processes quickly, frequently, and at low cost.

"With the right deployment of ideas," O'Neill told me, "it is possible to accomplish things that most people would say cannot be done." O'Neill believes this reengineering holds the potential to shave health costs from 14 percent of GDP to 7 percent while *improving* quality. It's an audacious and inspiring goal, one that also runs up against the reality that every dollar of "medical waste" is someone's dollar of income. Yet if such efforts could even shave a few points off projected health cost growth, the social payoff would be tremendous. O'Neill rightly recognizes the stakes. "One of the reasons I was reluctant to come back to government," O'Neill told me while he was serving in the Bush administration, "was because I thought what I was doing there [with PRHI] was maybe more important than anything I could do in the government. If we can get a demonstration that something really important and measurable is happening, the implementation could move pretty fast across the country."

Though it's too soon to judge PRHI's progress, O'Neill's Pittsburgh work could become a model for the national, Manhattan Project-style effort we need on health costs, a project that will require presidential involvement and leadership from the business and foundation communities. It will also require a change in the way we discuss "controlling health costs"—a change that at last moves us away from *cost shifting* toward systemic *cost re-engineering*.

After all, everyone says they want to control health costs. But what nearly everyone really means is that they want to shift their health costs to somebody else. Business, for example, says health costs are out of control—but one of their major coping strategies is to support a new prescription drug benefit in Medicare. That's because if the feds pick up the tab for these drugs it will get business off the hook for billions they're now expected to pay for their retirees. It's perfectly rational, but it's also a cost shift. To employees and their unions, cost control means employers picking up the tab and not passing it on to them. To state governments, cost control means getting the feds to pay more of the bill. All of these efforts are understandable. But all of them involve cost shifts. And in the end, cost shifts aren't about solving the problem; they're about making health costs somebody else's problem—a situation that will always favor those with more raw political and economic muscle. True cost-effectiveness in health care requires a new kind of national conversation—the kind that O'Neill and others have started.

Such an effort is the indispensable complement to a national push for universal coverage, which will raise costs in the short term. But this sequencing—get everyone in, then rein in costs—is the right approach. Until all Americans are in the system, serious cost containment efforts end up being implemented in ways that disproportionately hurt people who are uninsured. After all, that's how we've rationed care for decades.

———

In this section of the book we've seen how a Two Percent agenda that blends the best of liberal and conservative values can make dramatic progress against our biggest domestic problems. Yet that's only the first step. Plenty of well-meaning blueprints languish untouched on dusty shelves. It's time to turn more concretely to the contours of a Two Percent Society. Is the public ready to consider such an agenda? Is the press, the primary shaper of public opinion, prepared to play its part? What will the broader public culture of a Two Percent nation sound and feel like—and can America find its way there fast enough? As we're about to see, when you hide behind a mirror and start listening for the answers, there are grounds for hope, especially if our leaders rise to the occasion.

PART THREE

The Two Percent

Society

12

IS THE PUBLIC READY?

In an antiseptic conference room in a modern office building in Orange County, California, eleven casually dressed women were seated around a table. Behind them, outside the window, the late afternoon sun reflected off a glass-sheathed building, sending a sharp shaft of light across the industrial park tableau. On a white flip chart on an easel by the table three phrases were listed: 40 million uninsured; 15 million working poor; 10 million poor kids in failing schools. The man at the head of the table asked a question.

"It's pretty clear," the focus group moderator said, "that if you're somebody who doesn't have health insurance or if you're somebody who's near the poverty line, or if you've got children in a school that you believe is failing, that you would have a stake in this. For people who don't fall into those categories, do you have a stake in solving these problems? Or is this just something we should deal with because we care about the people who are in these circumstances?"

I was watching this from behind a one-way mirror. I came to Orange County for two guided conversations with swing voters because political consultants told me I should. Anyone can serve up a plan, they said, but you need a way to help politicians sink their teeth into this Two Percent agenda, a reason to take it seriously. Do a couple of focus groups, they counseled, and use what you learn to shape a short national poll that gives an early, statistically valid sense of how the public would react. That will give the political community something concrete to chew on. Not that it's the be-all and end-all, they cautioned. "I don't think this is going to be the kind of issue that is going to be driven by the electorate," said Rick Davis, John McCain's political adviser. "They will follow if it's led by somebody." That seemed right to me. But in gauging how to lead citizens toward a Two Percent Society, it helps to have a sense of how ready they are to follow. Thanks to a grant from the Annie E. Casey Foundation, I retained Peter D. Hart Research, one of the top Washington firms that do such work. And so there I was, munching peanut M&M's behind the mirror.

"Do you have a stake in solving these problems?" the moderator asked.

"All three of those things right there will affect the future of the country," said one woman, pointing to the flip chart.

"Exactly," said another. Others were nodding.

"How?" the moderator asked.

"Well, if you have children, in covering the health insurance, if they have improper nutrition, it's going to affect their brain. And they don't have the right shots and that type of thing. Students failing school, that speaks for itself. And the working poor . . . "

"Tell me what you mean, 'it speaks for itself,'" the moderator said. "If I don't have school-age children . . . "

"If Johnny can't read in grade twelve, there's really not a lot of hope for him as far as being a contributing member of society."

"That's going to cost us," added another, "because then he'll be on welfare because he can't get a good job."

"It's going to cost us more financially," agreed another. She said it was also unfair, because this person's lack of education means he wouldn't get a good job, and then he'd pass on few opportunities to his own children. The cycle would be perpetuated.

"What's going to happen to the economy thirty years from now when you've got all these kids that can't read?" chimed in another. "The future is in technology. We're going to be left behind."

"That's what I was just going to say."

"You don't get people educated, I think they're going to get out there and get frustrated with the low-paying jobs. And then a lot of times the crime is going to go up."

"And drugs, violence."

A similar-sized group of men, who came in for their separate session later (researchers often split the genders, I learned, because women apparently clam up around domineering males), had similar reactions. Four hours listening to real people offered insights into constructive ways to frame these issues, some of which have been sprinkled already throughout our discussion. It seemed clear that most people wanted the country to tackle these problems, were open to addressing them via the Two Percent ideas, and wanted to learn more. As every politician and political consultant would expect, however, there were also internal contradictions in the ways people thought about things and huge information gaps—a reminder of how hard it is to move the nation, and how indispensable the education aspects of leadership are. People were also deeply distrustful of politicians and alienated from a system they saw as rigged by and for special interests. "No one is paying the politicians to care," went a typical explanation of why we haven't addressed these problems to date. Another person said she'd support the Two Percent Solution only if offered by a candidate who said he would serve one term—that's the only way you could trust them. (The focus groups also supplied some comic moments. At one point the moderator asked the men if there was any leader who could come to the public and say, "We need to do this as a country," and it would make a difference in how they viewed this agenda. One man paused thoughtfully and said, "Yes, but he's dead." Robert Kennedy? I thought. Martin Luther King? No. "Sonny Bono," he said.)

To develop the survey component of the research, Peter D. Hart Research, which is a Democratic firm, collaborated with the Republican firm of Robert Teeter, giving my survey the same bipartisan imprimatur as the NBC News/*Wall Street Journal* poll, which Hart and Teeter have long conducted. This credibility is important. It's easy to design a poll to produce the illusion of runaway public enthusiasm for anything; an axiom among pollsters holds that the way questions are structured determines the result. For a first-timer like me, however, the process of "taking out the bias" was an education. For example, in one draft question we asked whether the federal government was doing enough about "the roughly 40 million people who lack health insurance." Sorry, the pollsters said; that 40 million number has to go. I was stunned. It was a fact, I felt; and no one trying to address the issue would ever speak about it without citing the 40 million. Yet to public opinion gurus, such a question is loaded; no one wants to say we shouldn't be doing more when so many people are affected.

Since resources were limited, I focused on testing three of the Two Percent agenda's biggest-ticket items: American-style universal health coverage; the teacher initiative; and the wage subsidy for the working poor (which together account for $195 billion of our $220 billion plan). My expectations were low; after all, nothing like this ambitious agenda has been on offer, and none of the public education that would need to accompany it has been done. I was prepared to be pleased with 40 percent support for the ideas, and ready to make the case that the right kind of leadership could bring another 10 to 20 percent of Americans on board. As it turns out, I was too pessimistic.

Should government do more?   We started by asking whether the federal government should be doing more, doing less, or was doing the right amount about these problems. Fifty-four percent said the feds should be doing "much more" about "people lacking health insurance"; 48 percent said "much more" about "poorly performing public schools in low-income communities"; 40 percent said "much more" for "people who work full-time but earn low wages and live in poverty." When, as researchers typically do, you add up the "much more" and "somewhat more" responses for a measure of general support for a bigger federal role on a problem, the totals were substantial, and the hierarchy of concern remained the same. Seventy-four percent said the federal government should do more about the uninsured; 68 percent on poor schools; and 65 percent on the working poor.

Would you pay more in taxes?   Next, since we didn't have time to test all the funding mechanisms discussed in Chapter 11, we used people's willingness to pay more in taxes as a way to gauge how ready they were to bear some burden to address these problems. Regarding the uninsured, 55 percent were willing to pay more in taxes versus 39 per-

Table 12.1 Two Percent Solution—Overall Poll Results

Percent

	Uninsured/ Universal Coverage	Poor Schools/ Teacher Plan	Working Poor/ Wage Subsidy
Should feds do more?	74	68	65
Are you willing to pay more taxes to address? (Yes/No)	55/39	59/35	38/53
Initial reaction to Two Percent proposal (Favor/Oppose)	69/29	59/36	61/34
After hearing pro/con (Favor/Oppose)	54/36	40/48	46/45

cent who weren't; on poor schools it was 59–35; to help the working poor, it was 38–53 against.

Insure the uninsured.   Next we described in simple terms the Two Percent proposals in each area. First we asked whether people favored or opposed the idea; then, using a common technique, we offered short "pro" and "con" arguments to see where support settled once people were exposed to the case against (see Table 12.1). For the uninsured, the proposal read: "Low-income workers who do not receive health insurance from their employers would receive a federal grant that allows them to purchase basic health coverage. The cost of the program would be about $80 billion a year." Sixty-nine percent favored this; 29 percent were opposed. Then people were told:

> "Supporters of this proposal say it is unacceptable that 40 million Americans lack health insurance, and that the right way to solve the problem is for government to give people some help in buying private insurance, not to have a government-run health system. Opponents of this proposal say that we cannot afford a new $80 billion federal program, and that its cost will rise as employers stop providing health coverage and make their employees rely on the federal subsidy. This will increase pressure for a government health system."

After this, 54 percent were still supporters, with 36 percent opposed. This support was consistent across most groups, including men (51–43), who, as we'll see, weren't big fans of the rest of the agenda. It was interesting to observe that Republican women favored the health care proposal by 52–32, whereas GOP men opposed it, 38–52. Maybe those ladies need to have a word with their husbands!

Low-income wage subsidy. For brevity and simplicity, we described the wage subsidy as analogous to the earned income tax credit, with which many people are familiar. "The federal tax credit for low-wage workers would be greatly increased so that a full-time worker receiving the minimum wage would have an income of about $9 per hour," we said. "This would raise the income of these workers above the poverty line. The cost of the proposal would be about $80 billion a year." Sixty-one percent favored this; 34 percent were opposed. Then came the arguments:

> "Supporters of the proposal say that people who work hard deserve to have an income above the poverty line, and that this will improve the lives of millions of children in working poor families. Opponents of this proposal say that people in low-paying jobs should improve their skills and seek better jobs, and that this will do more for their children than an $80 billion handout from taxpayers."

After this, the wage subsidy had 46–45 support (within the margin of error, and therefore statistically a tie). It won 51–39 among women; it fared poorly among men: 40–52. Independent voters supported the idea 48–43, after having been unwilling by a 35–51 margin to pay more taxes to help the working poor. Maybe they assumed someone else was paying.

What to make of this? "There's still a tendency of middle-class people to assume that people earning the minimum wage are very young," said Guy Molyneux, the senior vice president at Peter Hart Research who supervised the poll. "People get these jobs starting out in life, but the natural progression is to develop more skills and education and work your way up to better jobs. If someone isn't doing that, there's a presumption that there's something wrong with that person. A lot of middle-class people fail to appreciate the extent to which the modern American economy really does have millions and millions of these low-wage jobs that hard-working adults are still stuck in." In other words, a public education campaign will be needed before this wage subsidy can garner the sturdier support that action on health coverage seems to inspire. Still, the notion that an expensive-sounding new wage subsidy for the working poor appeals to big subsets of the population, and ties with voters overall, is hopeful, given that nothing like this proposal has been part of public debate since Bill Clinton succeeded in enacting a far more modest boost in the EITC in 1993.

Given voters' ambiguity, packaging the proposal so it is clear that the vast majority of people are not being asked to pay for it might help the sale. For example, the savings from canceling Bush tax cuts for upper-income Americans could be redirected to this wage subsidy. Packaging it this way, as a straight redistribution from the best-off to the working poor, also fits nicely with our discussion of luck. After all, if you think (with William Bennett, please recall) that luck, more than anything else, determines where people end up, then perhaps it's rough justice if poor workers hammered by forces beyond their control get a lift thanks to a cancelled tax cut that won't affect the lifestyles of the lucky few.

Better teachers for poor schools.   Here, too, we had to simplify the proposal from Chapter 6 to fit our short survey, while trying to capture its gist. "Federal funds would be provided to increase salaries in low-income communities so that these schools could attract good teachers," we said. "Teacher salaries would be increased 50 percent on average, with larger increases going to the best teachers. In addition, the rules would be changed to make it a lot easier to dismiss poorly performing teachers. The cost of the program would be about $30 billion a year." Fifty-nine percent favored this; 36 percent were opposed. The arguments followed:

"Supporters of this proposal say it is wrong that the neediest children often have inexperienced or unqualified teachers. We need to make teaching in poor schools the career of choice for talented young Americans who want to make a difference. At the same time, we need to make sure excellence in teaching is rewarded, and that poorly performing teachers can be dismissed. Opponents of this proposal say that the biggest problem in poorly performing schools is poor management and a lack of accountability, not a lack of money, and that this is why so many good teachers will not work in these schools. We should encourage excellent teaching by raising standards or by giving parents more choice of schools, instead of just pouring more taxpayer money into these schools."

After the pro/con, 40 percent supported the idea, and 48 percent did not. Women still supported it 46–40, but men opposed it 35–56 (down from 51–44 support before the arguments). People aged 18 to 34 were the strongest supporters, at 54–41. Support from independent men went down dramatically, from 50–44 in favor to 28–64 against after hearing the arguments; independent women still ended up supporting it 44–40, but this was down from 57–35 initially.

Plainly there's work to be done here. It would have to begin with a focused public education campaign (by candidates and others) to make people aware of the crazy situation today—in which schools in poor neighborhoods offer lower pay, terrible working conditions, and tougher kids compared to nearby suburbs, and then we wonder why their teacher corps is a mess. Without this context, the idea of big pay hikes to lure new talent to our toughest schools is obviously a tough sell. But in my experience most people get this picture quickly once you lay out the facts. In addition, our short survey question couldn't begin to capture the new things we would demand from teachers in exchange for higher pay—like a longer school year, the loss of traditional tenure, and increases in student achievement that determine a chunk of their compensation. These elements make the deal more tough-minded than it can initially sound without the fuller picture.

"There's a general sense that we've spent money on schools and it doesn't get better," said Molyneux, who has also done research for the American Federation of Teachers. "So how do we know this is going to really result in improved teaching? For $30 billion, what kind of as-

surance do we get that this is going to result in better schools?"
Molyneux felt the teacher proposal should be part of a broader education agenda that included standards, professional development, and
other such measures—so that the proposal is clearly seen as an effort
to address the problem of teaching quality (the end), and not the
problem of low salaries for teachers (a means to the end). Also, rural
voters didn't support the idea, which suggested the need to routinely
make clear that the initiative also applied to poor schools in rural areas, so these voters would know they have a stake.

My focus groups lent some perspective here as well. Women were
surprisingly harder on the idea of higher teacher pay than men; several felt teaching should be a "labor of love," and the idea that teachers might be paid so much more struck some of them as a corruption
of something chaste. By contrast, the men in my focus group were fa-
vorably inclined toward the idea. They mostly felt that "you get what
you pay for," that salaries of $100,000 or even $150,000 weren't crazy
for the nation's best teachers, and that society needed to offer "combat pay" in order for good people to take on these challenges.

Again, packaging might help. Consider the trade-off this way: The
nation can use $30 billion a year to eliminate the estate tax for heirs
in 3000 of America's wealthiest families—or use that same $30 billion
to bring a new generation of talent to America's neediest classrooms,
and make equal opportunity for 10 million poor children more than a
hollow ideal. Yes, some of the most powerful people in America say
"it's their money" (referring to the beneficiaries of an estate tax repeal)—but isn't it clear which use of these resources is in the national
interest?

The "crosstabs."   Much of the value in market research comes from an-
alyzing the subgroups into which larger samples can be divided. In the
trade, they're called "the crosstabs"—binders that show the results
sliced and diced by various permutations of sex, race, income, gender,
region, religion, political party, or whatever other groups the mind
can conjure for the politician (or detergent maker) to target. Our
crosstabs revealed that the strongest supporters of the Two Percent
agenda are women, people aged 18–34, blacks, and those earning less

than $30,000 a year (these groups also tended to feel that poverty is caused mostly by bad luck). A particularly encouraging sign is that suburban women, coveted by both parties, supported the three proposals after the pros and cons were aired. On the uninsured, suburban women approved by 53–32; on the wage subsidy, it's 49–38; on the teacher initiative, it was 44–41.

As Table 12.2 shows, men were less receptive to the Two Percent Solution. Independent voters (see Table 12.3) were encouraging, given that our poll couldn't stress the market-friendly approaches that each proposal entails. Indeed, Molyneux felt the overall results suggested that people viewed these ideas much as they would a traditional progressive agenda, with white men and Republicans generally disinclined. But while the Two Percent goals are progressive, the policies feature conservative means and would need to be marketed in ways that stressed this commonsense mix. "The question is, does emphasizing the market-based solution help you bring in Independents?" Molyneux asked. "I think it probably does. In the end what would matter about that (for both men and Independents) is, do you have voices from the right and center who stand up and say, 'This is a good idea.' If you've got John McCain behind one of these ideas that makes a difference. You need to have some credible voices who aren't already on the Left saying, 'Yeah, this makes sense.'" One promising note in this regard is that after two hours of talk, the men in our focus group tended to identify the agenda as "moderate," not "liberal."

Finally, the "age gap" on the Two Percent agenda (see Table 12.4) is striking, with 18–34s supporting all three proposals, seniors supporting only expanded health coverage, and a consistent 16 to 25 percent gap in the way youngsters and oldsters viewed these ideas. Lots of people have talked about how to engage younger Americans in the political process again, and this agenda seems to begin to strike the right chord. Seniors plainly require more to persuade them; maybe they're not accustomed to proposals that devote so much cash and energy to needs besides their own.

The arguments.   We tested several overarching arguments for the Two Percent package to see which resonated with voters. Two seemed par-

Table 12.2 The Gender Gap

Percent

Reaction to Two Percent proposal after hearing pro/con . . .
(Favor/Oppose)

	Women	Men
Universal coverage	57/29	51/43
Teacher initiative	46/40	35/56
Wage subsidy	51/39	40/52

Table 12.3 Independent Voters — The Two Percent Agenda

Percent

	Uninsured/ Universal Coverage	Poor Schools/ Teacher Plan	Working Poor/ Wage Subsidy
Should feds do more?	75	68	65
Are you willing to pay more taxes to address? (Yes/No)	58/36	57/36	35/51
Initial reaction to Two Percent proposal (Favor/Oppose)	69/27	54/39	60/33
After hearing pro/con (Favor/Oppose)	53/35	37/51*	48/43

*Independent women support 44/40; men oppose 28/64.

Table 12.4 The Age Gap

Percent

Reaction to Two Percent proposal after hearing pro/con . . .
(Favor/Oppose)

Universal coverage	63/31	45/40
Teacher initiative	54/41	29/54
Wage subsidy	50/48	34/48

ticularly promising. "This agenda is a smart investment in our nation's future," the survey said. "We will all pay a price if we do not provide a good education and real opportunity to the workers of tomorrow." Sixty-three percent of independent voters found this statement convincing versus 33 percent who found it unconvincing. Suburban women found it convincing by a margin of 69 to 29. The other promising argument got at the notion that this agenda wasn't "big spending," as critics would likely charge, but rather a shift in priorities. After all, how "liberal" can a program be if it leaves government smaller than it was when Ronald Reagan was president? "If you can gauge it as a candidacy based on national priorities," said McCain adviser Rick Davis, "then your response to these attacks would be, 'Look at how we waste money already. Sure, two percent of the GDP is a lot of money, but we're spending two percent of the GDP on bullshit right now.'" In our poll, this two-cents-on-the-dollar-smaller-than-Reagan-so-we-can-afford-it argument was convincing to 60 percent of suburban women, and unconvincing to 33 percent, suggesting that key constituencies valuing fiscal responsibility can be sold on the facts here.

———

What's the bottom line? Obviously there are limits to what a short survey at this stage can tell us. The public has not experienced the education campaign that would accompany this agenda. Nor has it heard the attacks it would doubtless inspire. Still, the findings were more promising than I expected. "This isn't going to be sold quickly and easily," Molyneux concluded, "but there is definitely an opening here."

Yet Rick Davis was right. This won't be an issue like civil rights or Vietnam, where an agenda bubbled up urgently from the grassroots. We'll need leadership to inspire followership here. My polling suggests that the public is ready for such appeals—more ready than one might expect, given the narrow bounds of public ambition in the last decade. That means that leaders in the public and private sectors have key roles to play in moving the country toward consensus on a Two Percent direction.

But a critical first step is for the press—our primary shaper of public opinion—to better fulfill its informational role. One of the strongest and nearly universal views expressed in my focus groups was the feeling that the press doesn't help citizens focus on issues that matter, but is instead preoccupied by trivia and scandals. "The press has to spend more time being informative about these issues," one woman said, to a table of nodding heads. "People are uninformed and they're intimidated because they don't know. And that's why they don't vote. They don't know."

Such hand-wringing often elicits weary sighs from top news editors and producers. It's easy to blame the messenger, they say, and if people didn't like to focus on scandals, reporting on them wouldn't boost circulation and ratings. Some skepticism toward the public's complaints is surely justified. But, as we're about to explore, the media's role in public life could be transformed in ways that answer these citizen concerns, and make our Two Percent Solution more likely, by a single little innovation from our most influential newspapers.

13

WILL THE PRESS
STEP UP?

Leonard Downie Jr.'s office on the fifth floor of the *Washington Post* building has walls of glass, from which the paper's executive editor can see the newsroom, and the newsroom can see him. On a hot summer afternoon I went to see Downie, who has had a distinguished career at the *Post,* dating from his days helping guide the paper's Watergate coverage. Downie served as the *Post*'s metropolitan editor, London correspondent, national editor, and managing editor before taking the helm as executive editor in 1991. An easygoing man whose appearance has been compared to Clark Kent, Downie has a reputation as a journalistic purist; on principle, for example, he does not vote, because he believes the act of voting would suggest he has an undue stake in public policy outcomes. I had already interviewed Downie's deputy, as well as several top editors at *The New York Times*—though not Howell Raines, the *Times*' executive editor until June 2003, who said he preferred not to engage on my themes. Downie himself hadn't been inclined to talk at first either. When I emailed a request for an interview, he wrote back that because my book had a policy agenda, it wasn't something that the news side of the *Post,* as opposed to the editorial side, should comment on. When I explained, however, that it was the *Post*'s *news* decisions I was interested in, especially decisions about what went on page one and why, Downie agreed to meet with me.

I went to see these editors because page one of *The Washington Post* and *The New York Times* play a unique role in our political culture. They set the agenda for the rest of the nation's print and electronic media, and put subjects instantly on the lips of every opinion leader in the country. Yet as we've seen in Chapter 2, the "stenographic" norms of journalism mean that these influential outlets largely cede this agenda-setting role to public officials, a practice that leaves debate impoverished at times when neither political party finds it convenient to address major problems. Is there a way to change this dynamic, so that the press can help create a Two Percent society more attuned to our biggest challenges? And can such efforts be squared with traditional values that govern the responsible exercise of the press's power? I had an idea for these editors that seemed to meet both of these standards, and that would be welcomed by the consumers of news in my focus groups who felt that the press fails to give them basic information.

After giving Downie an overview of the Two Percent concept, I began by asking him what the *Post*'s role was in situations when neither political party wants to address an issue that is obviously a big deal—a situation that had characterized the savings and loan crisis in the 1980s, I suggested by way of example, and that included the issues at the heart of the Two Percent agenda today.

"Our role is to continue to cover important situations like the S&L crisis, the health care crisis, et cetera," he said. "[But] it is not our role to tell the politicians what it is they're supposed to discuss during a campaign."

Why? I asked. This notion—whose agenda is it, anyway?—seemed to me central.

"Because that's not our role. Our role is to provide all the information we can to the American body politic and let them do with it what they wish. It's not our role to set the agenda. . . . It would be a very dangerous thing for us to be making our news decisions based on what we think government and the people ought to be doing."

I asked Downie how that works when it comes to page one decisions—those seven stories each day that the *Post* is telling the country

are the most important things in the world. As other top editors at
the *Post* and *New York Times* had explained to me, page one is usually a
hybrid. There are big "hard news" events that are no-brainers for page
one—an airplane crashes, a suicide bomb goes off in Tel Aviv, the
president gives the State of the Union address. On the softer side are
stories that help enliven the page as part of the overall "mix"—an in-
depth look at the offbeat, an exclusive that other papers won't have, a
fabulously told yarn that editors say "writes itself onto page one." But
after that, editors agreed, on most days there are stories that are entirely discretionary, where editors are choosing what belongs on the
most visible and powerful bulletin boards in our political culture.
These stories often involve sending teams of reporters off for months
of reporting. They immediately ricochet through the media and become top-of-mind for the nation's elites. How do you decide, I asked
Downie, what issues get that treatment?

"We think it's important *informationally*. We are not allowing ourselves to think politically."

Then if an impact on the public agenda is a by-product of this
work—?

"It definitely is."

OK, I thought. "If reluctant or accidental agenda setters are destined to be agenda setters nonetheless," I asked, "what is the framework through which you think about how to exercise that power
responsibly? Is that a fair question?"

"Yes, that is a fair question," Downie said. "What I don't want to
do is what Louis Seltzer at the *Cleveland Press* did." Downie said when
he was growing up in Cleveland, Seltzer, a famous local editor, decided that a man was guilty of murdering his wife and set about using
his newspaper to convince the entire community.

"I don't want to do that," Downie said. "He turned out to be
wrong. You can see easily that's an abuse of his power. But I would argue it would be a similar abuse of my power to say, this guy Miller's
got a great idea. This Two Percent thing, this really makes sense to
me. We are now going to make certain we focus on those aspects of
the public debate. We're going to ask politicians, why aren't you talk-

ing about the Two Percent Solution? We're going to run series on the Two Percent Solution. That would be equally distorting. What Kate Boo's series was about"—the *Post*'s Pulitzer-winning investigation of homes for the mentally ill that Downie had hailed as an example of the paper's finest work—"is intrinsically important—lives were at stake, lives were lost, governments were not carrying out their responsibilities. That is information people should have. What the people then do with that information is for them to decide. We should not be thinking in terms of setting a public policy agenda, we should be thinking in terms of setting an informational agenda."

"But the size of the box of things that are 'informationally important' is quite large," I said. "You—like anybody who has to budget resources and time and talent and energy and space—have to decide what subset of that box you're going to pursue. How do you set that agenda within the world of things your readers ought to know about from page one? How do you decide?"

"It is very difficult to talk about that—to give you a good conclusionary speech about that—because it is so organic," Downie said. "I don't sit here and set the agenda for *The Washington Post*." To be sure, Downie said, he and Steve Coll, his managing editor, make final decisions with their colleagues about what goes on the front page, or how reporting resources get deployed. 9/11 obviously called forth a massive effort. The *Post* covers AOL closely because it is a large, locally headquartered company. "It's an organic process of responding to the information we're finding," Downie explained, "and responding to events in society."

Downie's counterparts described a similar if also mysterious process of "news judgment." "You've got to make some judgment about when an issue has reached critical mass," said Gerald Boyd, *The New York Times*' managing editor from 2001 to mid-2003. Bill Keller, the *Times*' top editor, agreed. "It's sort of like the process a candidate has to go through to get on a ballot," he said, recalling his years in page one meetings. "You have to go out on a street corner and gather signatures. An issue has to go out on the street corner and gather some signatures before it becomes a front page news story."

I asked Downie, "Should the news side of an organization like yours have a perspective on what the most important challenges are facing the country?"

"No," Downie said instantly. This was interesting. Gerald Boyd had said yes. So had Allan Siegel, one of the *Times'* assistant managing editors. So had Bill Keller.

"No," Downie said, "we should have a perspective on what the important *informational* needs of the country are, and fill those needs."

How is that different? I asked.

"It's different because 'challenges' is subjective," Downie said. "You can disagree over what the most important challenges are. You can also disagree about the nature of meeting those challenges. That is to say, you can disagree over whether or not health care or something else is the most important challenge facing the country, and you can then disagree over how the health care needs should be met. Those are not things we should be thinking about in deciding how to cover the health care story."

I asked Downie if he would agree that—outside the "hard news" that makes page one—the decision about what else got front page play was an exercise of power.

"Yes, it is. . . . So we are creating an agenda," Downie added, "but not one that we're seeking to create for a particular reason," because the *Post* isn't looking to shape any particular outcome. "So yes, we've written about the uninsured, and if we don't have new information to write about the uninsured, we're probably not going to write about it. But that doesn't mean we shouldn't look to see if there isn't more information about the uninsured because it's an important situation, it's not going away, it's continuing. *So we do have a responsibility to keep trying to find ways to present people information about it, whether or not the politicians take it up in public debate*" (emphasis added).

A perfect segue, it seemed. I had an idea I wanted Downie to consider, a way to deal with the systemic problem he had just raised: the fact that what's *new* isn't the same as what's *important*. We obviously need our top news outlets to give us the latest, but it would transform public life if they could also keep us focused on the big things that matter. Wasn't this what people in my focus groups were asking for—

the part of them that wanted to be good citizens and knew how central the press was to this desire? I knew the feeling as a news consumer myself. In my business life and then while serving in the White House, I often felt like screaming, "Why wasn't the press doing more on x or y?" After I'd been a working journalist for a time, however, I came to see that as a practical matter, this wasn't a reasonable expectation *on issues where public officials weren't saying or doing anything*—that is, when there wasn't "news." Every good outlet could point to the long feature they'd done last spring on the uninsured, or the two-part series on the working poor the year before. But if nothing else was happening—no candidate calling for action, no governor trying something new, no million man march on the Washington Mall—you couldn't expect them to do a fresh three-part series on page one every few months. To be sure, the top editors at the *Times* and *Post* told me they should be doing more on big issues that were being ignored—but they also admitted that "triage" is a fact of newspaper life, and when there's not "news" on something, it is easily overlooked.

Still, I'd always thought, wasn't there some way that the most important daily bulletin boards in our public life—page one of the *Post* and the *Times*—could institutionalize regular attention for things that are important even though there's not "news" on them? Some device that would be consistent with these editors' sense that they should not be directing an agenda, but that would nonetheless perform a public service by mitigating the gap left when officials prefer not to address important issues.

"Can I throw out a crazy idea?" I said, laying on the table a mock-up of the front page of the *Post* I had prepared (it's reproduced on page 239). "Why not have a feature called 'Still True Today'?" I explained that this would be a small but visible line or two across the bottom of the front page; a kind of ticker tape, nothing that would interfere with 98 percent of the usual front page, where the big news of the day would always appear. But, in addition, in this small daily feature, you'd highlight facts that were, well, still true today. My own list would include things like "42 million Americans uninsured—80% in family with full-time worker," "2 million teachers need to be recruited in the next decade, while average teacher salary is $40,000," and so on, in the Two Percent spirit. You might go with a different subject each day, I suggested—say, health on Monday, education on Tuesday, the working poor on Wednesdays—but repeat the same facts each time. Obviously there are countless permutations. The exercise would require our top papers to put forward what they think are the most important things citizens need to remain aware of even as the news changes each day. It might help set the agenda for the papers' in-depth reporting projects. The art department could make sure this recurring feature was fun and lively. Who knows? If the *Times* or the *Post* started such a feature, the ripple effect might be huge. After all, the *Times* invented the op-ed page thirty years ago; today it's a national staple.

Downie's first reaction was that the Post did such stuff all the time, at least inside the paper. The foreign staff, for example, at one time did a weekly feature on countries of the world, with facts on everything from consumption of sugar to infant mortality to percentage of GDP devoted to health care.

"Whether we would do this on the front page strikes me as odd," Downie said. "I'm not saying I would rule it out on some sort of ideological or professional grounds, but it strikes me as just an odd use of front page space because we don't usually just put isolated facts on the front page. Usually it's part of a story, part of a purpose. The notion of 'Still True Today,' to me, verges on the editorial. It says, we want you to pay attention to this in particular even though there's no 'news' reason, there's no way in which journalistically we have redone this information, but we just want you to pay attention to the fact there are, say, unwed mothers in this country, and we're going to tell you often there are unwed mothers in this country whether you like it or not. That to me then becomes an editorial purpose, something that shouldn't happen in the news pages."

"How does it feel editorial," I asked, "as compared to the Kate Boo series, or things like that where it's a discretionary choice to—"

"Yeah, but that's original reporting of new information that people haven't had before," Downie said. "By definition, this is information people already know but you want to keep repeating until they do something about it, right? Isn't that your motivation?"

Still True Today: How It Might Look

The Washington Post

Women Say Harassment Persists in Va. Capitol

Lawmakers, Others Cite Kisses, Remarks

NSA Intercepts On Eve of 9/11 Sent a Warning

Messages Translated After Attacks

Jerusalem Hit Again by Blast

In Response, Israel Expands Seizures of Palestinian

'Combatants' Lack Rights, U.S. Argues

Brief Defends Detainees' Treatment

Bush Undeterred by Bombings

SEC Readies Reform Plan For Auditors

Oversight System Would Be Similar to Old Setup

Mexican Workers Pay for Success

With Labor Costs Rising, Factories Depart for Asia

U.S. Breaks Into Soccer's Inner Circle

It Took 4 Years to Transform Americans into a Contender

INSIDE

Bush to Seek Doubling of Africa School Aid

A layer of atmospheric pressure acted like a lid over the region, sending smoke from more than 250 mountain blazes cascading into the heart of the valley. Pollution readings for fine particles—the stuff that smoke is made of—soared to five times higher than normal in Sacramento."

Afghan Leader Appoints Rivals

A layer of atmospheric pressure acted like a lid over the region, sending smoke from more than 250

BWI Is No. 1

A layer of atmospheric pressure acted like a lid over the region, sending smoke from more than 250 mountain blazes cascading into the heart of the valley. Pollution readings

The Post on the Internet: www.washingtonpost.com

STILL TRUE TODAY **Health** • 40 million Americans lack health insurance: 80% are in families with full time worker • U.S. spends 14 % of GDP on health care, other wealthy nations spend an average of 9% • Medicare does not cover prescription drugs —For more on the "Still True Today issues" go to www.washingtonpost.com/stilltrue

STILL TRUE TODAY

Health • 42 million Americans lack health insurance; 80% are in families with full time worker • U.S. spends 14% of GDP on health care, other wealthy nations spend an average of 9% and cover everyone — For more on the "Still True Today" issues go to www.washingtonpost.com/stilltrue

I nodded, though I didn't agree with his "people already know it" point; polls regularly show Americans have a poor understanding of many basic facts of public life. In any event, Downie added, the *Post* has probably had the fact that there are roughly 40 million uninsured Americans in the paper fifty times in the last year.

"How many times on the front page?" I asked. I later learned that between January 20, 2001, the day President Bush took office, and September 10, 2001—my cutoff for obvious reasons—this fact never appeared on page one. It appeared eleven times during that period on inside pages. By contrast, during the same period in 2001, the Gary Condit–Chandra Levy story was discussed in 187 pieces in the *Post,* including twelve front page pieces. From July 1999 to March 2000, the period when Bill Bradley made the uninsured the centerpiece of his primary campaign, the number of uninsured appeared twenty-three times in the *Post,* including twice on the front page. This sample—as well as coverage in mid-2003 of early proposals on health care from Democratic presidential hopefuls—tends to confirm the view that press attention is driven mostly by what officials or candidates do.

"I don't know," Downie replied. "But the front page is a news decision. So I'm not going to arbitrarily put it on the front page because we think that people ought to do something about it. . . . If I'm going to repeat it on the front page for no good reason without context everyday, I'm doing it for a public policy reason and I'm not in business to do that." It's the kind of thing that could only go on the editorial page, he said.

I told Downie that when I shopped the idea to some other media leaders, they made the fair point that if I were merely pushing for my facts in this feature, I was just another lobbyist. So, I said to Downie, what if I frame my request not as, "put my issues in there," but simply urge the *Post* and the *Times* to have such a feature? *You* decide what ought to be highlighted as "still true today."

Imagine what might happen were this feature adopted and you'll see why I'm convinced it's so powerful. Say the *Post* and *Times* started running Still True Today or its equivalent at the bottom of page one every day, with facts about the uninsured, poor schools, and more. Conservative outlets, like *The New York Post* and *The Washington Times,* would instantly note it and slam the effort in their pages. Rush Limbaugh and other right-wing radio hosts would attack it as proof of the media's liberal "bias." The *Post* and *Times* would reply that they had merely decided to keep readers regularly informed about some basic facts on our biggest problems—and would these critics please explain why repetition of the fact that, say, 42 million Americans are uninsured bothers them? Or do they not agree it is a problem? The cable news networks, ever hungry to fill their 24-hour appetite for material, would find the controversy and the new practice wonderful grist, and before you know it the political culture would be filled with two debates. The first would be over the "legitimacy" of what the *Post* and *Times* were doing. The second debate would be about what are, in fact, the nation's biggest problems. *The Washington Times, New York Post,* and like-minded papers around the country might start running their own similar features, but stressing facts on marginal tax rates, government spending increases, or the number of annual abortions, much in the way *The Wall Street Journal*'s conservative editorial page does today. The *Journal*'s editorial page itself would slam the innovation as being highly revelatory about "the liberal mind."

But when the dust settled from this initial wave of controversy, the notion that our top news outlets would regularly and prominently hammer home facts about the big problems they saw would take hold—especially if reader surveys showed the feature to be popular. Network news divisions would then find it easy to do something similar on their broadcasts. Once the morning shows and evening newscasts started billboarding (say, in a brief Still True Today graphic while cutting to a commercial break) how many full-time workers live in poverty and how many poor children are taught by people who don't know the subjects they're teaching, these facts would become topics for kitchen table conversation. Before long they would become emblazoned on public consciousness. And once public attention to these facts becomes routine, the battle is half won. Remember what my pollsters said in the last chapter—using the fact "40 million" uninsured was verboten in a survey question, because *people will want to do something.* In polling, when people know the dimensions of a problem, it produces unacceptable bias; in real life, it inspires good citizenship.

And note that this is good citizenship promoted without any "spin." Just the repetition of important facts.

In calling for this innovation, of course, I run the risk that the facts that editors would stress would not be the ones I do—and so the public might come to think that high tax rates, for example, are our biggest problem, not the Two Percent concerns. That's a risk I'm willing to take. A Two Percent society requires an elite press willing to define what it thinks is important, and ready to regularize attention to those matters even when they're not in the news. My wager is that we've been sleepwalking on the Two Percent problems, and that if top editors were asked via this innovation to define the nation's chief challenges explicitly, the kinds of issues I've raised would emerge. This is not a call for a return to the partisan newspaper wars of the early nineteenth century, when each political party had outlets that purely parroted its party line. Indeed, the whole Still True Today idea is inspired by the fact that neither party is addressing these issues seriously, so the task has to fall to someone independent with the power to bring them up.

Downie, for his part, felt that no matter what facts were included in such a feature, it represented advocacy, even if only in two lines at the bottom of the page. "That's not our business," he said, "not on the front page." But was it really not advocacy, I thought, when *The New York Times* ran on its front page a series by David Cay Johnston on how the IRS spends more time and energy auditing poor people than it does auditing the well-to-do? Was it not advocacy when the *Post* ran on its front page the series by Kate Boo on abuse of the mentally ill? Implicit in the way they assign reporters to stories, I thought, Downie and his colleagues were already *advocating* a certain cast of mind and angle of vision for their readers. Yes, news organizations should strive to cover issues fairly, and reserve opinions on public questions for the editorial page, but this standard incantation obscures the reality that decisions about *what to cover* by their very nature reflect an opinion about what's important in the world. A feature like Still True Today, I thought, would just be a different way of exercising this same power. How could that be unacceptable?

"*It doesn't come organically out of the coverage of the news,*" Downie said. Now there's a line, I thought, that journalism seminars could chew on for years—it all depends, as the Clintonesque cliché now runs, on what you mean by "organically," "coverage," and "news."

"I love chocolate," Downie continued, tongue in cheek. "This could be devoted every day to the latest news about chocolate."

This is where many of the news executives ended up. Walter Isaacson, then president of CNN, said, "Why not, 'Still True Today: cats are more popular than dogs.'" "I can give you 500 things that are still true today," said Jeff Greenfield. Others objected because bare facts struck them as stripped down and therefore unjournalistic. "I think we can be more creative," Gerald Boyd, formerly of the *Times*, told me, meaning such facts should be integrated into real page one stories that engaged readers.

But how often, as a practical matter, would that happen on these subjects? Without officials or candidates doing something, it would be the once-a-year piece the *Post* and *Times* did on the uninsured, say, in the year before 9/11—nothing close to the daily ticker tape I was suggesting. What I was up against, I realized, was a sensibility gap. Michael McCurry, the former press secretary to Bill Clinton, explained it well. "Political communication," he said, "depends on repetition and driving your message home. That's why your politicians, when they're running for office, put their advertisements on night after night after night."

> Journalism is the exact opposite of that. Once we've told you something it's no longer "news" and so we're not going to revisit the subject. Once we've done our five-part series on the nature of the federal budget deficit, we've told you what you need to know and you should go out and act on it. There's no sense at all in the media that we have to keep reminding our viewers or readers over and over again what the basic facts are. There's not this sustained conversation that draws people back to the things they need to know in order to make decisions.

The different outlook McCurry describes is undeniably real. And yet it doesn't do full justice to the situation, because newspapers "crusade" often enough for "the crusading editor" to be a cliché. Maybe, in more precise terms, I was up against editors' reluctance to make the ways they exercise power more transparent. Maybe I was touching a nerve by questioning the "organic" view of how news priorities should be defined, asking why the random or "natural" array of even the most talented staff's interests was sufficient to assure that a top paper met its duty to inform readers on major issues without also laying out some kind of issue matrix against which to measure its coverage. Maybe editors were uncomfortable choosing these items more explicitly—and therefore more accountably—without the cloak of "news judgment."

Still, all I could ask for was a hearing. And Downie and other top editors at both papers had been more than generous in engaging on the idea. I still believe they should test Still True Today, or something like it, with their readers. Public officials, media critics, average citizens, and others with a stake in public life could use the notion to start an overdue conversation in the profession. The press has a crucial role to play in fostering a Two Percent Society. The question of that role's legitimacy, as framed by a leader like Leonard Downie, comes down to this: Is the press's exercise of discretionary agenda-setting power via original reporting *different in any meaningful way* from the press's exercise of discretionary agenda-setting power via the prominent repetition of selected facts? Is it even supportable to make such a distinction in the face of the massive information gaps that citizens face in understanding the nation's biggest problems? I'm convinced that if the *Times* or *Post* adopted such a feature, it would shoot through our political culture and quickly transform public debate in ways that no other tiny innovation could. It's worth remembering that the alternative to our top press outlets devoting, say, 2 percent of the front page to an idea like this is to allow America's political agenda to be defined almost solely by those aiming to win elections. As we've seen, this is usually a very different exercise from trying to solve public problems.

A combination of Still True Today, plus user-friendly injections by the press of the basic public finance literacy we've covered throughout the book, can begin to make America safe for the more adult political conversations that a Two Percent Society requires. Nurturing this climate should be one of the press's overriding goals. After all, suppose we reach the year 2015 or 2020 and have 60 million uninsured, the worst teachers still serving the neediest children, and growing ranks of full-time workers in poverty? If we don't address these problems, it stands to reason that every institution that has power in our society should feel complicit in the failure. Any definition of "powerful institutions" has to include our most influential media. And those with power have a responsibility to help shape public discourse in ways that give serious problem-solving a fighting chance.

14

BUILDING A
TWO PERCENT AMERICA

The question is how you change the whole national debate so that you force the different constituencies to change. Is that what it comes down to in your view?"

So said a Silicon Valley business leader after we'd spent an hour on the Two Percent ideas. In his view, businesspeople would jump at the "two cents on the dollar" notion if they thought it would actually buy the reforms we've discussed, and thus produce real progress, not more of the usual charades. Put that way, of course—*change the national debate so that the constituencies change*—the task sounds daunting. But John Maynard Keynes made the enduring case for optimism in the darker days of the 1930s, another moment when capitalism's weaknesses demanded reform in order to preserve capitalism's strengths. "I am sure that the power of vested interests," Keynes wrote, "is vastly exaggerated compared with the gradual encroachment of ideas."

As we've seen, the Two Percent Solution builds into modern capitalism fierce commitments to equal opportunity and a minimally decent life within a high-growth economy. In the end, however, the creation of a Two Percent Society turns on something more elusive and essential than resources and reform. It requires a change in the habits of mind now prevalent in America's public culture—a perspective characterized by cynicism (and even self-dealing) among elites, and apathy and resignation among ordinary citizens.

Today the problems of health care, schooling, and wages are viewed as intractable; efforts to address them seriously are cast as quixotic and doomed. After all, we're told, the political process has been hijacked by ideologues and special interests on both sides. Bold ideas make easy targets. The best our political leaders can do is signal that they "care."

So runs the world-weary wisdom.

By contrast, the Two Percent mind-set knows these problems have answers, and draws strength from the knowledge that getting serious doesn't require a "revolution," but modest—literally, marginal—changes in the allocation of national resources and attention.

The conventional wisdom holds that public life forces us to chose sides—Democrat or Republican, liberal or conservative. With a Two Percent mind-set, citizens of all stripes would instead choose real answers over today's bipartisan make-believe, building a critical mass across left, right, and center that drags both parties to the table to cut a deal.

The conventional wisdom says that "getting ready for the baby boomers' retirement" means making sure Social Security and Medicare are solvent, implicitly warning that there is no cash left over to solve the problems of nonelderly Americans who are left behind. The Two Percent mind-set turns this premise on its head—arguing that if we don't get serious now about the uninsured, poor schools, and a living wage, we'll not only violate American ideals of justice, but undermine the growth needed to pay for our aging population.

Add it up, and the Two Percent mind-set shifts the burden of proof in public life. The question about a Two Percent Solution is no longer, "How can we do this?" The question becomes, "How can we not do it," when so small a set of changes can vanquish so large a set of problems.

Leadership, Followership, and Luck

Since today's tyranny of charades is manmade, we can unmake it. But whose responsibility is that? It's an old debate. Walter Lippman said the problems of modern society were too complex for average citizens to play any role in governance; a cadre of elites was needed to manage affairs on behalf of the ignorant masses. John Dewey said faith in democracy meant exactly the opposite: Public education held the promise that Americans could truly choose for themselves.

The truth is that a Two Percent Society demands better leaders and better followers. The dialogue between them that lies at the heart of democracy has broken down. Citizens, fed up with today's dysfunctional debate, essentially tell elected officials, "We don't trust you because you don't tell the truth." Officials, in essence, reply: "We don't trust that if we tell you the truth, you won't throw us out." This mutual distrust between leaders and citizens may define the ultimate American gridlock—a stasis more crippling and fundamental than that produced by party differences or electoral parity.

To repair public life in the Two Percent spirit, our leaders have to risk being more candid about our challenges. Part of the blame for their reticence lies with us. We and the press have trained our politicians to be enormously risk-averse. You would be, too, if one misstep could flush twenty years of hard work down the drain and end your career. The pressures of survival in today's political–media culture have warped our leaders into cardboard versions of humanity. That kind of discipline, a mix of safe "red meat" for the faithful and bland platitudes for the rest of us, is seen as a prerequisite for survival. Yet behind the mask we force them to wear, our leaders are almost all fully equipped, psychologically complex, three-dimensional *Homo sapiens*. What's more, I'm convinced that at this moment in history they'll discover that candor is less risky than they suspect—if they take the chance.

John McCain's presidential campaign in 2000 proved that the crisis of trust in public life has reached a point where there's now an enormous market for straighter talk. People respected McCain even when they disagreed with him. So just imagine the reaction the first time a prominent Democrat starts telling his liberal base the truth: that Republicans who want to control soaring costs in Medicare are right! That liberals need to stop demagoguing them on the issue and realize that once the boomers retire, the enemy of the social programs they cherish will not be the heirs of Newt Gingrich, but spiraling health costs—and that every unnecessary dollar devoted to Medicare is a dollar that can't help a poor child.

Or imagine the first time a Republican tells her constituents that the Democrats are right in saying we need to put off further tax cuts until we've gotten serious about equal opportunity and a decent minimum in America, and until we've taken care of Social Security and Medicare for the long haul. And that conservatives need to stop demagoguing liberals on taxes, and start a grown-up conversation about what we want from government as the boomers age, and how we're going to pay for it.

If I haven't yet exhausted your capacity for fantasy, imagine this, too: What if both sides came together and said, "I'll get serious about teachers if you get serious about vouchers?" and vice versa.

Sounds unthinkable, perhaps, by today's standards, but the Two Percent mind-set offers the language we need to move past the hackneyed political "logic" and false choices that can never solve our problems. Only a vision ambitious enough to seem impractical can inspire Americans to reengage with politics, and lift interest groups out of today's unproductive trench warfare in pursuit of a common good.

Our leaders need to recall that in previous eras, when the time was ripe, such strategies brought historic progress. In his classic work *The American Political Tradition,* the historian Richard Hofstadter brilliantly analyzed the different but equally vital roles of Agitator and Politician in a democracy. The function of the agitator, who appealed to conscience and common sense, "was not to make laws or determine policy, but to influence the public mind in the interest of some large social transformation." By contrast, he wrote, the politician's object "is not absolute right, but . . . as much right as the people will sanction. His office is not to instruct public opinion, but to represent it." Yet at rare moments in history, when a social crisis matures, Hofstadter saw that these roles might powerfully blend. Then "the sharp distinctions that govern the logical and doctrinaire mind of the agitator become at one with the realities, and he appears overnight to the people as a plausible and forceful thinker."

Hofstadter was writing about the anti-slavery movement. But what if the next decade—with the inevitable rethinking that will be forced upon public policy by the boomers' looming retirement—is another of those moments when the agitator's urge to fundamentally shift the debate has the chance to blend with the politician's drive to "ride the tiger" and consolidate existing social forces? What if this means we're entering a rare season in which more honest talk has a chance to "break through" and succeed politically, making forms of leadership possible that would seem too risky in normal times?

In my mind there's little question that we are on the threshold of such a moment. But ultimately there's only one way to get the Two Percent leaders we need: by becoming the Two Percent citizens that produce them.

The citizen's job in a democracy is to make the world safe for leaders to do the right thing. That can happen only when citizens are engaged in the questions of the day. The good news here, as my polls and focus groups suggested, is that people are ready. As I've given talks around the country on the Two Percent Solution as a work in progress, I have had this sense reinforced. People of all political persuasions are hungry to be brought into the problem-solving process by their leaders, rather than condescended to as passive recipients of the same old symbolic appeals.

Twenty-five hundred years ago, the Greek statesman Pericles described the culture that produced Greece's golden age. The secret of Athens' success?

> Here each individual is interested not only in his own affairs but in the affairs of the state as well: even those who are mostly occupied with their own business are extremely well informed on general politics—this is a peculiarity of ours: we do not say that a man who takes no interest in politics minds his own business; we say that he has no business here at all.

To be sure, this is not a call for overworked moms and dads to start studying up on domestic policy each night after tucking the kids into bed. But it is a reminder that without a threshold level of engagement in public questions, citizens can't form the constituency for sanity that makes elected officials decide it is safe to be sane. The fascinating thing about democracy is that good leaders are produced by good followers, and good followers are produced by good leaders. Of course, this dynamic works in reverse to produce bad versions of both as well. It's a virtuous or corrosive cycle. The press, as we've seen, has a central role in making engaged citizenship possible, making it likelier that virtue prevails.

So, Two Percent citizens need to be engaged—that's straightforward. But what attitude, what sympathies and biases, should Two Percent citizens bring to the public square? It is here that we come back to the question of luck—and to the profound role that citizens' values play in the political process.

Daniel Yankelovich, the social scientist and student of public opinion, argues that we suffer from a basic misunderstanding of the public's role in making democracy work. Under the prevailing wisdom, the experts and elites who govern us extrapolate from their own approach to public affairs in thinking that information is the key to sound policy. They therefore look with horror at surveys that show most Americans are ignorant of everything from the names of Supreme Court justices to the location of other countries on the map. This revulsion at public ignorance leads experts to feel they have little to gain from seriously consulting the public on major policy questions. Rather, they view public opinion as something to be understood or manipulated only insofar as it may present a barrier to well-informed solutions, or as a factor to be dealt with after the fact to sell a fix arrived at from on high.

While not downplaying the virtues of a better-informed public, Yankelovich insists that this focus on how much *information* the public has mastered misconstrues the public's role in the ongoing symbiosis between those who lead and those who follow. Instead, he argues, the indispensable prism the public brings to such questions is to see them in terms of *values*.

On the issues at the heart of the Two Percent agenda, after all, the facts are not mysterious or difficult. If most Americans don't follow the details of health policy or school reform closely, it's probably because they feel they've hired politicians to handle this job for them. Yet the questions these facts ultimately yield when framed as policy

choices involve values. Should we increase the burden on affluent senior citizens, for example, in order to pay for school improvements
for poor kids? Or does that unacceptably punish successful seniors
who were promised certain benefits and who paid into a system for
decades expecting to receive them? Experts can't resolve such questions because they don't have "right" answers. Only the public, by ex-
pressing its values, can tell political leaders how to handle such
trade-offs.

As we've seen, the value that can underpin consensus on the Two
Percent Solution is sensitivity to the pervasive role of luck in human
affairs. Heightened appreciation of this truth—that a large part of
where we end up in life is shaped by the pre-birth lottery, and other
factors outside our control—can reinvigorate America's public commitments to equal opportunity and a minimally decent life.

When it comes to the role of luck versus hard work and personal
initiative, my Two Percent poll suggests that Americans are curiously
torn. We tend to believe that rich people are rich mostly due to their
own efforts, but that poverty is due mostly to bad luck and circumstances outside a person's control. It is interesting that this view of
poverty and luck tracks closely with party identification: Democrats
think poverty is mostly a matter of bad luck by a margin of 59 percent
to 31 percent; Republicans say it's lack of effort by 53–31. Today's increasingly pivotal Independent voters think more like Democrats on
this question, saying poverty is mostly due to bad luck by a 51–33 margin. My poll also found that the richer people are, the more likely they
are to feel that their wealth is a function of effort as opposed to luck.

But there is a counterintuitive phenomenon within this upper-income group that is instructive. Wealthy Americans view public life in
large part through the prism of taxes, because they are asked to pay a
lot of them. Yet Hollywood stars don't gripe about higher taxes the
way most other wealthy Americans do—and they overwhelmingly
support Democrats who seem likelier to raise them. Why? My theory
is that these supertalents are more sensitive than the average rich person to the portion of their wealth that's attributable to luck. Yes,
there's hard work and persistence and making your own breaks, but
the voice, the presence, the body (well, minus certain modern en-

hancements) clearly come from God. The idea that beneficiaries of such income-enhancing blessings might be asked to bear more of the burden of government seems fair to them, not cause for resentment. Even though similar accidents of birth (that is, brains) account for the lofty incomes of, say, corporate lawyers, they're much more likely to credit their toil, presumably because what they do all day is less pleasant. (If I'm right, maybe the platonic ideal for tax reform would combine a flat tax on income that's due to one's own efforts and character, with sharply higher rates on income derived from an excess of gifts from God. Over to you, IRS.)

I know, I know: arguing that Barbara Streisand exemplifies a Rawlsian sensibility on luck that other Americans should adopt will leave many conservatives chuckling, if not racing for the exits. But it turns out that some of today's most prominent conservatives embrace the centrality of luck in different terms. Consider that scourge of liberals, Charles Murray, the libertarian author of *Losing Ground,* which discredited the welfare system, and *The Bell Curve,* which set off an uproar by arguing that IQ was mostly inherited. Murray plainly acknowledges the power and relevance of luck:

> As one wise man put it, "He is certainly not a good citizen who does not wish to promote, by every means in his power, the welfare of the whole society of his fellow citizens." That is Adam Smith talking, the apostle of laissez faire. This injunction applies not merely to poverty but to all the human predicaments that arise from the randomness of life and lead us to say, "There but for the grace of God go I." To some extent life is indeed a lottery, as the social democrats insist. . . . We all need a little help from our friends, and some of us need a great deal. What becomes of those who are helpless, or luckless or perhaps simply feckless must deeply concern any human being worthy of the name. So say all of the world's great religious traditions.

Humility and awe in the face of luck's dominion, then, are the values that engaged Two Percent citizens should bring to bear on choices about our public responsibilities. People who identify themselves as "Christian conservatives" have come up to me after speeches on these ideas and said, "I support what you're saying," quoting the Bible on how we are judged by how we treat the least among us. If Hollywood stars, famous libertarians, and these good folks can find a common language here, surely the rest of us can join the Republic of Luck.

Imagine

Imagine the America we will have created if the Two Percent Solution becomes a reality in the years ahead.

In this America, millions of Americans no longer consider the emergency room their "doctor." No one fears bankruptcy if illness strikes their family. The health care debate is focused where it should be—on controlling costs while improving quality—instead of on how to plug perpetual gaps in a system where 15 percent of the population lacks basic coverage.

For the first time, many of the best teachers in America gravitate toward the kids who need them most. Many of the best college graduates choose teaching as a career. This new respect for teaching percolates through the culture—so that award-winning teachers seem as glamorous as sports heros. Schools in poor neighborhoods are clean and renovated. Poor children show up in kindergarten having had the preschool experiences that more affluent families take for granted, and that set the stage for real learning. A million poor families have a choice among schools, freeing many from schools that are still failing, and putting pressure on the system to improve faster.

Life still isn't easy for tens of millions of workers at the low end of the income scale—but these citizens feel buoyed by the sense that their country truly values work. Indeed, when work means health coverage, good schools for the kids, and more of a living wage, it's a little easier to pay the bills, and the American dream of upward mobility seems less out of reach.

When it comes to public life, no one mistakes America for Athens, but there's undeniably a more grown-up and less demagogic debate taking place about national priorities. A critical mass of leaders in both parties have risked being candid, and they've found that candor sells. There are still ideological differences about policy, of course, but politicians increasingly find themselves pushed, partly by logic, and partly by the fiscal pressure of the boomers' retirement, toward "ideologically androgynous" answers, and a greater sense of unity in the face of common challenges. The business community welcomes the more economically rational approach to progressive goals now central to political life—an approach that doesn't see the answer to every social problem as a new burden on business. Business leaders have subsequently become a stronger constituency for the public interest, not merely their own firm's or industry's parochial financial interest. Average citizens have become a constituency for sanity themselves. It's not a nation of political junkies, to be sure, but ordinary people talk more about public questions—not least because they have Patriot dollars to spend in each election on the candidates and causes they believe in, and so feel a greater stake in the debate.

Our leaders and the press fill public life with conversations about how to face the aging of our population while meeting other public goals. And the progress we've made on long-festering problems like the uninsured breeds new pride and patriotism among Americans. The Two Percent Society has enhanced America's standing on the world stage, since America's deepest social blemishes—which other nations cited as proof that the giant had feet of clay—have been removed. Indeed, our progress inspires fresh talk globally about the American model of civilized freedom, which is producing more growth and now also more justice in mutually reinforcing ways. This is especially impressive when America's tax rates are still substantially lower, and its rates of job creation substantially higher, than those of every other advanced nation.

Even if you don't agree with every detail of the solutions we've discussed, it should be clear that America can choose something like this path. Which makes it only fair to ask those who reject this agenda: What's *your* vision for America? Is it a country in which 40 million to 50 million of your neighbors are uninsured as far as the eye can see? An America where poor children are taught by unqualified teachers in broken-down schools forever? A nation that pays lip service to the value of work by leaving tens of millions of people who work full-time in poverty in perpetuity? And where elections are endlessly dominated by special interest cash in ways that mock the very idea of democratic self-government?

We shouldn't be content with this pinched vision when a vastly better America is just two cents on the dollar away. Forget the cynics and naysayers who say such things can't happen, because what happens in America is up to *us*. In a democracy, after all, we get the government we deserve, and with a little imagination we can deserve better. The comforting reality is that the iron law of politics still holds: Politicians will scramble to lead any parade that forms, even if it means stepping up to the truth.

POSTSCRIPT

Getting to Two

If You're an Interested Citizen

If you're interested in the Two Percent ideas and want to help build a movement to make them a reality, check in at www.twopercentsolution.com. It's the virtual headquarters for the nationwide grassroots community that can inject the Two Percent agenda into the 2004 presidential campaign and make it a lasting feature of public life. A critical mass of "Two Percenters" among Democrats, Republicans, and Independents can embolden officials to step out of their ideological and interest group straitjackets and push toward the "grand bargains" and real fixes we need. The web site is a place where Two Percenters can exchange ideas, get information on how and where to make a difference, and build momentum. After all, if we don't make the world safe for our leaders to do the right thing, who will?

Those registering at the site will receive my syndicated column by email, plus regular policy analyses, fresh details on what's "Still True Today," and updates on how to move the cause forward.

In addition, for readers whose work touches directly on public life, here are some other concrete ways to begin moving America from here to Two:

If You're a Foundation Executive

On virtually every issue we've discussed there's a central role for creative foundation leadership. The most urgent task is to legitimize and popularize the ends and means we've been exploring. This will require foundations to emphasize macro questions of taxation and spending in ways that haven't been their focus. It means supporting or creating institutions that can package and market ideas in ways that bring goals like health coverage for all or great teachers for poor children back to the mainstream, where they belong. In most cases it's not new research that is required; the problem is that good research doesn't get packaged into a form that can move public debate. What's needed is the strategic, politically minded marketing of ideas that progressive-minded foundations have generally neglected.

In addition, the country needs a vehicle that can galvanize establishment thinking and leadership on the Two Percent issues. My candidate is a National Commission On Everything Else We Need To Do (Besides Social Security and Medicare) Before The Boomers Retire. That's a bit wordy, so maybe a National Commission on Nonelderly Priorities will do. It could be convened by a coalition of foundations from across the political spectrum (and might ideally have bipartisan government sponsorship as well). Its mandate would be to identify and prioritize what resource-sensitive needs the nation should address in the next decade, apart from the elderly health and pension issues that are already front and center. The commission would be asked to produce a blueprint that squared the funding of these needs with the funding required to finance the boomers' retirement. And it would be asked to provide intensive public education on our coming fiscal collision and the challenges it poses.

Obviously a bold call for a commission doesn't in itself solve anything. But if conducted and publicized properly, it could be the vehicle that helps reorient national debate in ways that both political parties would welcome, because both must shortly figure out how to integrate the needs of graying boomers with the needs of the rest of America. The idea is to create a safe space for establishment figures from all sectors to move beyond normal constituency concerns and think broadly in the national interest.

Foundations, and university presidents, should also take the lead in shaping the Manhattan Project-style effort we need on health costs, aimed at slowing their growth in ways that actually improve quality—

so that government will have money available for other purposes once the boomers retire. Many foundation leaders don't yet appreciate it, but finding and marketing the ideas needed to slow the growth of health costs as the boomers age will do more to make social justice affordable than any other activity the nonprofit sector could undertake.

If You're in the Press

The "Still True Today" feature discussed in Chapter 13 obviously isn't all the press can do to help us get from here to Two. To help raise awareness of the Two Percent issues, and make it less easy for officials to bamboozle the rest of us, here are three other ideas:

New "beats." Apart from what they place on page one, top news organizations direct attention through the way they define reporters' "beats." Why not add beats on the uninsured; or the working poor more broadly; or the teacher quality challenge specifically (including the teacher unions) as a sub-beat within "education"? Shouldn't it regularly be "news" in the richest country in the world that someone dies because they can't afford to go to a doctor? Or goes broke trying to get well?

New "policy truthtelling." News outlets often feature "Ad-watches" that assess whether specific claims or charges made in political campaigns are true. But, as political professionals in both parties know (and count on), they don't routinely assess the substantive pros and cons of major policy proposals. With rare exceptions, the press offers "he-said, she-said" reports. "The Democrats say the GOP is out to gut Social Security," we're told, "while the Republicans say they're the only ones with a plan to save it." Which is it? Or is neither claim particularly useful in sizing up reality? "Democrats say most of the Bush tax cut goes to the wealthiest Americans," we're told. "Republicans say it's aimed at all incomes." Who's right? You decide.

It's possible to imagine a different approach. If the provision of fair-minded and accessible policy analysis were considered a central role of top press outlets, especially during presidential campaigns, there are countless variations one could imagine. A "Solutions Watch," for example, might assess particular proposals, and render a verdict as to whether they are "symbolic or substantive." A recurring "What Are They Really Calling For?" feature could tease out agendas in a similar spirit. This isn't tantamount to making people take their medicine—it could be done in ways that are punchy, fun, and interesting.

The argument against offering fair-minded policy analysis is that it's impossible to do—you'd end up "favoring" one side or the other. That's too easy an out. My own experience examining these issues with liberals and conservatives is that it's nearly always possible to explore the pros and cons in ways that fair-minded people on both sides respect. The bigger risk for the press (in terms of how such policy analysis is perceived by officials to whom they want to preserve "access") may be that both political parties will often seem unserious if their ideas were given such scrutiny—a different breed of scandal than those our "adversarial" press usually reports. But if our leaders aren't serious, or their policy claims are grossly misleading, who else is going to tell us?

New quantitative context.   Politicians rely on the power of big-sounding numbers to give token proposals the illusion of seriousness. If President Bush offers a proposal with $70 billion over ten years for the uninsured, and the headline the next day is "BUSH OFFERS $70 BILLION PLAN FOR UNINSURED," it's a victory from the White House's point of view, because it communicates that the president cares about a problem and is "doing something." A smarter, more accurate headline would read "BUSH OFFERS PLAN TO AID ONE OF EVERY SEVEN UNINSURED AMERICANS." After explaining what the president proposed, the piece would ask why Bush was choosing to address only this portion of the problem. The same need for context applies to Democrats, of course. When John Edwards says he wants to spend a fresh $3 billion a year to help poorer districts hire better teachers, the press should ask how many teaching positions can expect what kind of impact from such a plan, compared to how many would need to be affected to seriously address the problem. By our analysis in Chapter 6, for example, it takes $30 billion, not $3 billion, to get serious.

The point is that the press needs to insert high in the story a sense of how a proposal compares to a reasonable definition of the problem. Few journalists do this routinely today. It requires reporters, editors, and producers to practice a disciplined line of questioning. How do you define the magnitude of the problem your proposal is aimed at? How far does your proposal go versus that magnitude? Why does it go this far, and not to the full extent of the problem you define? This simple rubric can be applied to just about everything—schools, prescription drugs, economic growth plans, Social Security reforms, etc.

If You're a Big Campaign Donor

Everyone acts as if today's big political donors are evil. I say they're an underutilized resource. These folks tend to be highly successful businesspeople who got where they are by knowing how to make things happen. And one thing is sure: If the wealthiest few thousand donor-activists in America became convinced the Two Percent agenda was desirable, it could happen.

The fact that these donors have the ear of our leaders presents an enormous unexploited opportunity. Big donors I've spoken with say politicians tend to respect them for two things—their wealth and their insights into the industry from which they made their money. When they venture beyond this, even very wealthy and successful men and women tend to feel (with reason) that they're being humored. But imagine if a critical mass of big donors from both parties came together to study and develop an agenda for the national interest like the one we've been exploring, and then vowed to push it with leaders on both sides? With their existing access, some fresh policy credibility, and a little PR savvy, the impact of such a bipartisan marquis donor network could be substantial. All it would take is a few big donors in each party to agree to work together, and they'd be off and running.

If You're in Business

Good CEOs would never run their businesses issue-by-issue in the anti-strategic way politicians tend to manage public policy. Yet business groups have largely accommodated themselves to this political reality. "We think of the uninsured over here, we think of the education reform process over here, we think of fiscal policy and retirement security over here," John Castellani, president of the Business Roundtable, told me. "We think of these all in different pods because that's the way the policymakers think of them, and also deal with them, in terms of both design of the programs and their funding. Our political structures are constituent-responsive, not strategic."

We can't afford another decade without strategic thinking in public life. CEOs, and the groups through which they engage in public questions, are uniquely positioned to become a constituency for a real strategy on national priorities in the Two Percent spirit.

If You're a Politician

Politicians might sit down quietly with thoughtful colleagues in the other party and explore the meaning of equal opportunity and a decent minimum in the Two Percent spirit. They might develop a bipartisan caucus that refines an agenda informed by the problem-solving Two Percent mind-set—and that proposes new budget processes that institutionalize attention to these questions. How low does annual "discretionary" spending as compared to "entitlement" spending (like Social Security and Medicare) need to go, for example, before a conversation about the balance is triggered? How much more has to be spent on the elderly than on children—or on near-term consumption versus long-term investment in research and development and infrastructure—before a debate must be forced? Such a caucus might promote a shared definition of the choices ahead as the boomers near retirement, become an invaluable resource for improving media coverage, and bring new urgency to the idea that inexorable fiscal pressures call for rethinking on all sides if we're not to put justice and growth at risk.

ACKNOWLEDGMENTS

This book would not have been written without the support of some rare friends. First among them is Barry Munitz, the indefatigable president and CEO of the J. Paul Getty Trust. Barry urged me to pursue the Two Percent idea when it was barely two percent of an idea, offered encouragement and wise counsel at every turn, organized sessions at which I previewed the book's themes with diverse leaders, and arranged the funding that made the work possible. Everyone should be so lucky to have a Barry Munitz in their life. Ted Mitchell, the dynamic president of Occidental College, embraced Barry's idea of creating the fellowships at both institutions that supported the book's writing. Barry and Ted have been sounding boards and advisors throughout the project. I'm deeply grateful for their friendship and support.

The Annie E. Casey Foundation stepped in at a critical moment (and with lightning speed) to provide funding for the Two Percent poll and focus groups. Special thanks to John Monahan, Senior Fellow at Annie E. Casey, and to Ralph Smith, the foundation's Senior Vice President. Some of the ideas brought to critical mass in this book were initially developed during my 1999–2001 fellowship at the Annenberg Public Policy Center of the University of Pennsylvania, funded by The Pew Charitable Trusts. My enduring thanks go to Rebecca Rimel and Don Kimelman at Pew, and to Kathleen Hall Jamieson at Annenberg.

PublicAffairs has been a great place to get into the book business. My gifted editor, Paul Golob, made this book much better than he found it. What more can one say? Peter Osnos, PA's driving force, was an enthusiast throughout. Thanks also to the rest of the PublicAffairs team, including Lisa Kaufman, Gene Taft, David Patterson, Nina D'Amario, Kasey Pfaff, and Melanie Peirson Johnstone, for tolerating a first-time author's endless queries, insecurities, and noodging.

Early versions of some of these ideas appeared in my syndicated column for Tribune Media Services, and in articles for *The New York Times Magazine, Time, The Washington Post, The Wall Street Journal, The Washington Monthly, The New Republic,* and *U.S. News & World Report.* My thanks to the editors of these publications. Special thanks go to the late Michael Kelly, Cullen Murphy, and Jack Beatty of *The Atlantic Monthly,* where the ideas in Chapters 5 and 7 were originally developed at length. Other ideas were previewed in commentaries for National Public Radio's "Morning Edition," where my editor, Susan Feeney, made sure they were easy on the ear.

A number of busy people took the time to read chapters or sections of the draft and offered helpful comments. I'm grateful in this regard to Bruce Ackerman, Charles Blahous, Stuart Butler, Michael Casserly, William Gale, Dan Katzir, Wendy Kopp, Lawrence Korb, Robert Litan, Michael O'Hanlon, Robert Reischauer, James Shelton, and Tom Vander Ark. Bruce Ackerman and Edmund Phelps patiently endured rounds of email questions over many months on their ideas. Edward Lazarus offered ongoing advice and encouragement beyond the call of duty. David Frum, my radio colleague, took the time to help me better understand the conservative view of the case I was making, and to coach me on some subtleties of the book world. Mitch Daniels was generous with his time, and in his willingness to engage on the Two Percent ideas, something for which I'm especially grateful given that I've been a frequent Bush administration critic. Countless radio listeners and readers of my column who've taken the time to email their ideas have forced me to consider myriad points of view and continually refine my thinking.

Guy Molyneux at Peter Hart Research was the official pollster for the Two Percent Solution, and offered helpful advice on framing some arguments. My agent, Philippa Brophy, believed in the book and helped me navigate the business side of publishing with grace.

Policy analysts at a number of institutions were generous with their time and thoughts as sounding boards, and also helped me nail down some facts. Thanks to Larry Mishel and Jared Bernstein at the Economic Policy Institute; Robert Greenstein, Michelle Bazie, and the rest of the talented staff at the Center for Budget and Policy Priorities; and Robert McIntyre of Citizens for Tax Justice. Several education researchers at RAND offered thoughtful reactions to my teacher plan and a once-over on its costs; thanks to Dominic Brewer, RAND's education director, for arranging this. Barry Anderson, my former colleague at the Office of Management and Budget, helped coordinate some fact-gathering from the smart staff at the Congressional Budget Office. Conversations and email dialogues with a number of busy people were also helpful at various points; my thanks here to Arlene Ackerman, Drew Altman, Byron Auguste, Lee Bollinger, Paul Brest, Steven Brill, Albert Carnesale, James Carville, John Cogan, Jon Cowan, Bob Denham, Ed Feulner, Joel Fleishman, Bill Galston, Alan Garber, Les Gelb, Vartan Gregorian, Reed Hastings, John Hennessy, Antonia Hernandez, Rick Hess, Chris Jennings, Steve Kirsch, Will Marshall, Peter Peterson, Trevor Potter, Uwe Reinhardt, Michelle Rhee, Richard Riley, John Roos, Jay Rosen, John Rother, Andrew Rotherham, Al Sikes, James Smith, Debra Stipek, Douglas Varley, Daniel Yankelovich, Barry White and Chris Whittle. Many others who contributed critical ideas are mentioned in the text; I'm grateful also to certain other officials who prefer to remain anonymous.

Melora Krebs-Carter, a former strategic planner for Barbie (now *that's* a great title) now at Stanford Business School, provided crack research assistance. Sheila Pannitti ably transcribed dozens of interviews. Roberta Shanman and Barbara Neff at the RAND library retrieved many hard-to-find articles. Michael Rich at RAND arranged for their help. Bill Grieb helped me survive a feared hard-drive crisis. Thanks also to the creators and managers of the web search engine Google, which is a peerless resource for anyone who does this kind of work. It's crazy they don't charge for it.

I owe three special intellectual debts. Charles Peters, the founder and longtime editor of *The Washington Monthly,* gave me my start moonlighting as a public policy writer in 1989 when I was a management consultant. He also set me on the path toward this book by instructing me early on that "you can't just tell people what you're against—you've got to tell them what you're for." Thanks also to the late economist Herbert Stein, whose slim 1989 volume *Governing the Five Trillion Dollar Economy* introduced me to the notion of "budgeting GDP" as a way of thinking about national policy. Alice Rivlin asked me to join her in the Clinton White House, and thereby afforded me the best real-world policy and political education one could ever imagine. Alice represents a blend of integrity, intellectual rigor, and a commitment to public service that's inspiring, and that those who've worked for her can only hope to partially emulate in their own careers.

My mother, Marianne Miller, and my father and stepmother, Tim and Simone Miller, were always there to lend an ear or offer advice; I'm truly grateful for all they've done and do. My in-laws, Lynn and Emil Hubschman, and Albert and Judy Greenstone, tossed in great ideas, and were unflaggingly supportive, despite the burdens "the book" often put on their daughter. My uncle, Bernard Petrie, offered frequent encouragement, and helped arrange a visit to the Hoover Institution to test early versions of these ideas. Our daughter's nanny, Zoila Benitez, helped keep our family on track and made any number of "crunch" periods far more sane.

My biggest debt of gratitude is owed to my immediate family. Amelia, my wonderful six-year-old, lost far too many nights and weekends with Daddy for the cause. Amelia's insightful questions and advice, even at her tender age, made the book something we really shared—and her excitement when the galleys arrived with the big "2" on the cover is an indelible memory. Amelia thinks the next book should be a kids' book that she gets to illustrate. Sounds like a plan.

Finally, and above all, comes my wife, Jody. It's hard to know how one woman could manage to be so wondrous an editor, muse, policy advisor, chef, businesswoman, mother, co-conspirator, and temptress. It's even harder to fathom how I got lucky enough to spend my life with her. Jody put up with my endless narcissistic book-related demands with more good cheer than they merited. She's made this book, and my life, better than they probably deserve to be. Here's to you, Zelda.

INDEX

PublicAffairs is a publishing house founded in 1997. It is a tribute to the standards, values, and flair of three persons who have served as mentors to countless reporters, writers, editors, and book people of all kinds, including me.

I. F. Stone, proprietor of *I. F. Stone's Weekly,* combined a commitment to the First Amendment with entrepreneurial zeal and reporting skill and became one of the great independent journalists in American history. At the age of eighty, Izzy published *The Trial of Socrates,* which was a national bestseller. He wrote the book after he taught himself ancient Greek.

Benjamin C. Bradlee was for nearly thirty years the charismatic editorial leader of *The Washington Post.* It was Ben who gave the *Post* the range and courage to pursue such historic issues as Watergate. He supported his reporters with a tenacity that made them fearless, and it is no accident that so many became authors of influential, best-selling books.

Robert L. Bernstein, the chief executive of Random House for more than a quarter century, guided one of the nation's premier publishing houses. Bob was personally responsible for many books of political dissent and argument that challenged tyranny around the globe. He is also the founder and was the longtime chair of Human Rights Watch, one of the most respected human rights organizations in the world.

———

For fifty years, the banner of Public Affairs Press was carried by its owner, Morris B. Schnapper, who published Gandhi, Nasser, Toynbee, Truman, and about 1,500 other authors. In 1983 Schnapper was described by *The Washington Post* as "a redoubtable gadfly." His legacy will endure in the books to come.

Peter Osnos, *Publisher*